Telling the Truth to Troubled People

Books by Dr. Backus

Finding the Freedom of Self-Control
The Good News About Worry
The Healing Power of a Christian Mind
The Hidden Rift With God
Learning to Tell Myself the Truth
Telling Each Other the Truth
Telling the Truth to Troubled People
Telling Yourself the Truth (with Marie Chapian)
What Your Counselor Never Told You

Telling the Truth to Troubled People

William Backus, Ph.D.

BETHANY HOUSE PUBLISHERS
MINNEAPOLIS, MINNESOTA 55438
A Division of Bethany Fellowship, Inc.

Published by Bethany House Publishers
11400 Hampshire Avenue South
Bloomington, Minnesota 55438
www.bethanyhouse.com

Bethany House Publishers is a Division of
Baker Book House Company, Grand Rapids, Michigan.

Printed in the United States of America

Library of Congress Cataloging-in-Publication Data

Backus, William D.
    Telling the truth to troubled people

    Includes index.
    1. Pastoral counseling. 2. Counseling. I. Title.
BV4012.2.B26   1985   253.5   84–28413
ISBN 0–87123–811–X

WILLIAM BACKUS is founder of the Center for Christian Psychological Services, and an ordained clergyman in the Lutheran church. He is also a licensed Consulting Psychologist. He has a master's degree in theology from Concordia Seminary in St. Louis and a Ph.D. in clinical psychology from the University of Minnesota. Dr. Backus has conducted follow-up studies of his clients, which show a 95 percent improvement rate, compared to a 67 percent success rate for other methods of therapy. The difference, Dr. Backus says, is "the truth of God as revealed in the Word."

Dr. Backus practices at the Center for Christian Psychological Services, Suite #104, 2780 Snelling Avenue North, St. Paul, Minnesota, 55113. Telephone 651–633–5290. E-mail: bbackus@juno.com.

Contents

Introduction

"What do you plan to offer readers that they can't find in the excellent books on Christian counseling already available?" Carol Johnson, Managing Editor of Bethany House, asked me when I proposed doing this book. Carol, concerned about good stewardship—of time, finances, creativity and marketing skills which go into a successful publishing venture—was suggesting, gently, that there are already books, good books, now on the market for Christian counselors. So why should another one be published?

The recent renewal in the Church has been accompanied by a great interest in reaching out to people who have problems. A veritable geyser of counselors, Bible study and prayer group leaders, and spiritual ministers, all willing and eager, have found themselves in a unique position to offer spiritual counsel to the "walking wounded" who fill the pews of our churches. As my editor pointed out, a torrent of books pertinent to counseling has poured out of Christian publishing houses. And many of these works do have lasting value.

Particularly worthwhile are writings by Dr. Gary Collins, Dr. James Dobson, and Dr. Larry Crabb. Dr. Crabb's work has recently attracted my attention anew, especially for its success at formulating a specifically Christian psychology based on a Christian view of man, man's fundamental problem, and the transcendent Source of resolution for that problem in God's revelation. In my view, Crabb has done remarkably well at avoiding the pitfall of offering psychological theories and garnishing them with Christian-sounding phrases.

So why do I think there is room for one more book on counseling? The present volume has several features not commonly found in the existing literature. They are, I believe, becoming important for Christian counselor training.

1. *Integration*. It is becoming increasingly obligatory for Christians offering counseling to troubled people to acquaint themselves with what is known of clinical conditions, their diagnoses, courses,

and treatments. Many Christian counselors have rejected this knowledge, assuming that clinical psychology is nothing but worldly values surreptitiously palmed off on unsuspecting patients. Although values form an important part of psychotherapy, and the values of secular clinicians are at odds with those of Christians, there is nevertheless an increasingly large body of empirical knowledge which makes a difference in treatment. Specific treatments exist for specific conditions, and it is incumbent upon workers in this field to know which is which.

The time is past when the church can tolerate pious but opinionated counselors who insist on exorcizing demons out of people who actually need lithium. This book is a beginning. It attempts to teach counselors something of diagnosis and specific treatments, although it cannot possibly exhaust the subject. All this is integrated with and governed by Christian understanding and values.

2. *Specific instructions.* Many of the volumes now available for Christian counselor training concentrate on developing an understanding of how the human condition gives rise to problems, the relationship between past and present in human emotional disorders, and the power of God to heal and alleviate misery. I have tried to offer the reader understanding too, but in a context of very specific instruction in methods. Formats for sessions, how-to-do-it dialogue samples (as well as how-*not*-to-do-it samples), and concrete directions for performing certain counseling operations are presented. It is possible for those who sense God's calling to a counseling ministry to learn from this book a definitive set of procedures as to what they are going to do in the counseling session.

3. *An eclectic counseling method which is based on "truth therapy" is offered.* Although the current popularity of cognitive psychology attests its effectiveness as an explanatory device as well as a powerful change method, Christian authors have been slow to see that it offers a unique opportunity for integration with scriptural reality. The basic tenet of cognitive psychology is that what people believe and tell themselves determines their behavior and their feelings about life.

This very point happens to be the axis on which Christianity turns: belief, faith, is the key to everything! An earlier book authored by Marie Chapian and myself has offered self-training in changing one's own harmful misbeliefs (see *Telling Yourself the Truth*, Bethany House Publishers, 1980). Our second book was released in the spring of 1984, also from Bethany. Entitled *Why Do I Do What I Don't Want to Do?*, it teaches the reader to apply "truth therapy" to the work of overcoming sin. Since the present volume is meant to train counselors in the use of truth therapy, I suggest readers acquaint themselves with both earlier books. They are in no sense prerequisites for the use of this manual, but they will be helpful in showing how "misbelief therapy" works in a self-help setting. The present volume offers training in methods for applying this misbelief therapy in Christian counseling.

4. *Questions for review.* The reader will find review exercises at the end of each chapter. Although it has been clearly demonstrated that effective learning is aided by practice in recall, many training resources have been published offering no opportunity for the reader to recall what has been read.

Conscientious review at the end of each chapter using the materials and questions provided will increase the value of this book to the reader who wishes to be a student of Christian counseling and is essential for the reader who wishes to actually apply the skills offered in this book for helping others. The formation of groups and classes for the study of counseling methods is strongly encouraged, and for these groups the discussion questions offer a ready resource.

CHURCH COUNSELING CENTERS

The current spiritual renewal of the Christian Church has seen many innovations. One of the most exciting is the interest in lay Christian counseling which has emerged. The New Testament pictures the Body of Christ as a ministering fellowship, meeting human need with the wisdom of God. What more is necessary to mandate the establishment of lay counseling centers in churches?

Many have done it. One of the first such centers was established at North Heights Lutheran Church, Roseville, Minnesota, under my direction and supervision. Currently, approximately forty lay counselors, trained and closely supervised, see close to sixty counselees each week at the church. These lay counselors are presently augmented by a physician, Dr. Keith Oelschlaeger, who treats patients referred to him for possible psychotropic medication (medication which affects mental functions). This program has proved itself effective over the six years of its existence. The present book has grown out of training sessions which I conducted for the preparation of new counselors.

It is anticipated that, within the next ten years, many more churches will establish counseling centers staffed by trained and supervised lay counselors. To equip these counselors is one of the purposes of this manual. I believe instructors will find it a most valuable resource in the work of restoring primacy in counseling to the Christian Church where, in my opinion, it has always belonged.

Recent media publicity concerning the nation's first clergy malpractice suit has caused some concern among the nearly two million clergymen in the United States. Parents of a young man who committed suicide while under pastoral counseling have charged a California church with responsibility for his death. As this book goes to press, the courts have not yet made a final determination. Though national media attention has given the case far greater significance than is actually warranted, church groups who plan to set up a counseling program may wish to investigate the possibility of malpractice insurance.

CASES DESCRIBED IN THIS BOOK

The individual stories and dialogues presented in this book are composites, not those of particular individuals. Changes in detail are therefore extensive. No case example is that of an actual person. I regret the loss of veracity this approach necessitates. Nevertheless, confidentiality of all counselees *must* be respected, and for this it is not sufficient to merely change names.

The created composites are, however, true in basic thrust and an important teaching tool for this work. The events described are those which actually do occur in the consulting room of the practicing Christian psychotherapist.

ACKNOWLEDGMENTS

This book would not have been written except for the constant and unremitting encouragement of my wife, Candy. Her prior conviction that what would come out of my word processor would be worth publishing kept me going, even when I couldn't, of myself, believe it. Morris Vaagenes, Senior Pastor of North Heights Lutheran Church, made the counseling center there initially possible. The numerous brothers and sisters who have so faithfully served on the staff of the center are responsible, under God, for its success in turning lives around. My editor, Carol Johnson, has patiently explained publishing and contracts. Lance Wubbels and others on the staff of Bethany Fellowship, Minneapolis, have made valuable editorial suggestions for improving the manuscript. My daughter, Christa Templeton, devoted her considerable skill to the arduous task of creating the index.

William Backus
Forest Lake, Minnesota
Pentecost, 1984

Part One

COUNSELING AND THE CHRISTIAN CHURCH

CHAPTER ONE

So You Want to Be a Counselor!

"Doctor Backus, could I talk to you for a few minutes?" The middle-aged gentleman was breathless and obviously excited about something. I had just presented a lecture on stress, so I assumed he wanted some help with the tensions in his life.

"Certainly. Let's just step into this office, out of the crowd. Now, what's on your mind?" I disposed myself to listen to another recital of psychopathological woe.

"Well, Doctor," he replied, "I just wanted to ask you how I can become a Christian counselor and do what you're doing. I'm an executive at _____ Corporation, and I've done well there. But I feel God has told me to get into something where I can serve Him more directly."

So it wasn't a matter of life stresses. He wanted to become a counselor. I frequently run into Christians who believe that they are not fully serving God in their daily calling as a manager, a mother, or a plumber. Although I couldn't agree with his notion that there was something superior about the ministries of preachers, counselors, and missionaries, he hadn't asked me to expound on the Christian calling. He wanted to know how to become a counselor.

I tried to supply the information he requested, describing the various academic programs leading to degrees in counseling-related fields.

"Oh, but all that would take years. I'm too old for those programs. I want to get started right away."

I suggested that he might join a class I was going to offer to train counselors for the free clinic sponsored by our church. He agreed to think about enrolling. I concluded our session by informing him that we select counselors from among those who have completed the training. So he could not count on being one of those selected. I would be attending to the students' performance in class as well as seeking the direction of the Holy Spirit to determine who seemed qualified to serve.

WHO CAN BE A COUNSELOR IN THE CHURCH?

This was not an unusual conversation. I recently lectured at a conference on Christianity and psychology attended by over three hundred people. Many of those attending had come to learn how to become counselors in the service of God. The question I was asked most frequently in the halls and at the lunch table was the question of the corporation executive: How can I become a Christian counselor and where can I get training?

Who can counsel? Doubtless, every human being who has any kind of warm relationships will find himself counseling occasionally, since people naturally help one another, listen to one another, ask and give advice.

But not everyone is qualified to counsel in the church, under the church's Spirit-given license to minister to spiritual and emotional need. How can you tell if the Holy Spirit has called you to be a counselor?

MOTIVES

Motives are an important consideration. Be aware of your own motives. And don't kid yourself. The flesh will want in on the program! If the following symptoms are true of you, beware of your motives.

Perhaps you feel your fleshly muscles bulge with the sense of power as you use another person's extremity to dominate and control. Being sought after as a helper gives your pride a not-too-subtle anointing. When some helpless sufferer hangs on your every word you feel wiser and more important than you know you actually are. And in addition you feel indispensable. All this for simply sitting in a chair and listening to another person talk! For many, it appears to be a deal that's hard to turn down.

I suppose it's almost superfluous to say that God doesn't need flesh-motivated ministries. There are already plenty of those around. If you are interested in learning what this book has to teach you, and you are willing to work at equipping yourself, your motives may be right. You may truly have a call from God.

Look for motives like this: You deeply want to obey God, not just exercise your curiosity about other people's troubles. You have wisdom, or the Spirit-given ability to make solid practical decisions. This wisdom bears such fruits as a healthy, outgoing life pattern. Evident in it are the signs of love to your family and neighbors. You are submitted to the Word of God, and you seek God's Word and study the Bible not just to understand but primarily to obey His will as it is revealed to you. You are a functioning member of a Christian fellowship, in peaceful submission to those in authority in the Body of Christ.

You see, you need more than just the conviction that you are a "good listener."

Another potent qualification is the gift of knowledge or spiritual intuition. This work of the Holy Spirit will supernaturally enable you to sense untold truth about another person. The gift of knowledge may operate seldom or frequently. I wouldn't make it a requirement for becoming a counselor, because it is apt to appear for the first time while you are doing the work. If you have already experienced it, it may be a sign of qualification.

You must be willing to study and learn psychological truths. A small group of willfully ignorant Christians excuse their disdain for learning by insisting, "I don't need all that; I have the Holy Spirit and there's no need to learn anything from man." These people are characterized by the great damage some of them do.

One exceptionally good qualification, I have discovered, is to have an intercessory ministry. Much of the counselor's actual work is accomplished outside the session through intercessory prayer. If you don't pray much for others, there is little reason to expect that you will see much success with counselees.

Since you will, if you become a counselor, hear things that are shocking and evil, you must have extraordinary love for people. Living a self-centered life while you try to counsel others will not work. You will quickly become sour and pessimistic and this will become evident in your miserably low improvement rate. You will, of course, blame this on the counselees. Unless you have been filled with the love of Jesus for human beings when they are at their worst, you won't be able to cope with all the garbage dumped on your desk.

SO WHAT DO I NEED TO GET STARTED?

Let's assume God *has* called you to be a counselor and that you have the basic equipment and motivations we have discussed. Now what?

Now you ought to acquire or make sure that you have acquired the following:

1. *Knowledge of fundamental Christian teaching.* If you don't know that in God's kingdom it is considered higher and better to serve than to be served, you're likely going to teach worldly values to others without even knowing the difference. If you haven't discovered that chastening has a primary place in the Christian life, you won't be able to help others who are experiencing such dealings of God. Being well-versed in biblical truth is the most basic requirement.

2. *Training in descriptive psychopathology (abnormal psychology, it's sometimes called).* You *do* need to grasp what is known by psychologists about the various diagnostic syndromes you're likely to come across. Learn what their causes are (so far as is known), what

can be done to help those suffering from them, and what their connection might be with sin, grace, spirit, and perhaps, deliverance.

3. *Know about various clinical treatments.* Medication, electroshock treatments, conditioning, response prevention, exposure, stress inoculation, desensitization, reinforcement, and punishment training will for the most part be done, not by you, but by a professional psychologist. Nevertheless, you need to know what they are and what they involve.

4. *Know all you can about the place of belief and self-talk in generating human behavior.*

5. *Know from experience the place of belief in the Christian life, its transforming power when its object is truth, and the methods for helping others to share this power.*

SUPERVISED PRACTICE

Start humbly. Get training and supervision. Initially your counseling efforts will be rudimentary and you will need supervised practice to learn well. Surgeons don't operate skillfully just by reading a book, listening to a lecture, or even experiencing an operation done on themselves. They practice under supervision. Golf and driving skills are acquired the same way. Find a counselor with skill and experience who is willing and able to supervise your work. This can be done by the supervisor's commenting and making suggestions on the basis of your ongoing reports on the sessions. It can be done by reviewing audio or video tapes of your counseling. And a good deal can be done by some supervisors if they are willing to show tapes of their own work in action to the trainee. You can learn much from a model.

The supervisor can be a psychologist or psychiatrist, a social worker, a pastoral counselor, or a practicing lay counselor. It would seem essential to work with a supervisor who is skilled in applying the truth of Jesus Christ to daily living.

If possible, take a course. This book can help you. It is a manual you can use to discover diagnosis and treatment techniques for some of the most common problems brought to a Christian counselor. You may want to refer to it for help later, after you begin trying your wings. Often it will give you suggestions. Some of them may afford insight into the case you're working with. Also, you will find principles you can apply to most of the work you do in thinking about and dealing with human emotional and mental disorders.

SUMMARY

Many people today want to become Christian counselors. Since so many are seeking to fill this role, it is important to be certain you have a genuine call from God to counsel in the church. Research your own motives and take note. There is much in counseling to appeal to the flesh. Wisdom, knowledge, willingness to learn, a previous intercessory ministry, and love for people are important qualifications. You should learn scriptural and spiritual truth, a good deal about psychopathology, and how these are related.

Acquaintance with various clinical treatments used by professionals will be useful. Know the vital place of belief in the psychological and spiritual life. Start with humility and willingness to learn. It is important to find a supervisor to help you.

FOR REVIEW AND DISCUSSION

If you are in a training class or just using this book to train yourself, you will find that working through the questions at the end of each chapter will help you to master the material. For example, try these:

1. What's wrong with the notion that only pastors and counselors truly serve God?
2. Why do you think so many people want to be counselors?
3. Can you name some of the appeals of counseling to the flesh? Have they been a problem in your life?
4. Name some qualifications one should have before beginning to prepare for counseling others.
5. What should you learn from this book and other sources?
6. Why is supervised practice important and how can it be obtained?

CHAPTER TWO

Counseling Belongs in the Church

It may surprise you to learn that counseling and even psychological diagnosis belong in church. Since the earliest times, people have brought their behavior disorders to the pastor or priest for healing.

There was even a very ancient system of diagnosis. We have copies of it from as early as the fourth century. The diagnostic system of those early times was a list called *The Seven Deadly Sins*. We will discuss this interesting diagnostic scheme in a later chapter.

In a sense, the treatment of people who are suffering from behavior disorder has been preempted by the Johnny-come-latelies of medicine, psychiatry, psychology, and social work. And very recently a long string of other counselors has been added to the list: chemical dependency counselors, school counselors, vocational counselors, family counselors, marital counselors, and many, many others.

In view of the history just sketched, there is every reason why it is legitimate for pastors to do this work. Unfortunately, seminaries have frequently taught pastors an inferiority complex in this regard. As if pastors do counseling by the sufferance of psychiatrists. As if counseling belongs in a medical office. In my own training for the pastorate, we were taught to defer to the psychiatrist. He was considered the expert on human behavioral order and disorder, the professional who would know what was *really* wrong with people.

I now believe that it is proper for pastors to do counseling, and that they need not obtain permission from any other group of professionals. In fact, I believe counseling *belongs* in the church and that psychologists and psychiatrists should play the role of assistants to the Body of Christ in healing emotional disorder.

Lay Christians too may have counseling ministries in the church. Good order and the welfare of counselees require that they perform their ministries under the direction of the pastor and as his assistants and yokefellows. But both pastors and lay counselors ought to avail themselves of the knowledge and skills gained by psychological scientists and practitioners, as well as the skills of the physician who may often make a distinct contribution to the treatment of disordered feelings or behavior.

CHRISTIAN COUNSELING IS DIFFERENT

Christian counseling is not just ordinary talk therapy done by someone who goes to church on Sunday. It trains in different values and grows out of different premises.

Without exception, secular counseling systems assume that God is irrelevant to human well-being, emotional or physical. Problems confronted in psychotherapy or counseling have to be solved using the resources of human beings themselves. There is no help from the transcendent God. Such systems must lack ultimate values and deny fixed truths. What is good for you and what is true are treated as relative, rather than fixed and absolute.

The major premise of Christian counseling is that truth makes people free when they believe it and obey it (John 8:31, 32). Here, the task in counseling is to replace misbeliefs with truth. Truth is firm and fixed because it is grounded in God who does not lie. The person who, through counseling, becomes better able to know, think, and do the truth will attain real and lasting freedom from the results of misbelief, from neurosis and uncontrolled harmful behavior.

The Christian counseling method developed in this book therefore represents the joining of two streams. One is from the science of psychology, the other from the Holy Scriptures.

The Scriptures teach that we don't have to be content with relative notions about truth. We can actually know ultimate truth about reality. In fact, we can even have a personal relationship with God himself through the life, death, and resurrection of Jesus Christ. When we believe this, the Spirit of truth literally teaches us the truth through the Word of God. When a person comes to believe the truth and actively cognizes it (uses it to live by), that person will experience emotional and behavioral consequences which are truly positive and healthful.

From the stream of psychology we have selected two traditions out of the dozens of theories and systems of psychotherapy which have been published. These two traditions or branches are:

Branch 1. The old "talk therapy" or "talk cure" of Sigmund Freud. Though this method was all the rage through the 1950s, very little research has supported the validity of psychoanalytic theory or the therapeutic effectiveness of psychoanalytic counseling tactics. Yet many of the observations made by analysts are undeniable. They have seen and described the human soul, saturated with sin. They have, for example, produced dramatic demonstrations of the infinite capacity of man for self-deception. The psychological defenses are often shown to be man's lies to himself about himself. The analysts have likewise forced us to recognize transference, the tendency to import past reactions into present relationships; resistance, the human desire to make the most of illness and to remain sick rather than change; incestuous and other sexual phenomena previously unrecognized as causes of sin and illness; and the way experience shapes human sexual development.

Some notions bequeathed by psychoanalysis are illegitimate. For example, the belief that human wholeness results from making the unconscious conscious, that it is crucial to dwell on early memories, and that it is somehow the past that needs to be fixed. This last idea is not really taught by psychoanalysts, but is a distortion of their views commonly found among Christians.

Branch 2. Cognitive behavior modification. In the 1920s, psychology was self-consciously trying its best to develop a science rather than remain merely a branch of philosophy. Psychologists were becoming frustrated in the attempt to make a science out of mental events. These events, taking place only in the mind, were not subject to observation and measurement, the usual tools of science. In 1929, a psychologist named John B. Watson broke radically with the past and began to deal with observable behaviors rather than inner mental events.

Behaviorism, made most famous by Pavlov's celebrated dogs and B. F. Skinner's astounding pigeons, got rid of the mind altogether. The behaviorists determined to conceive of man as a sort of black box. Nothing in the secular view of man prevented this mechanistic hypothesis. "We cannot know what is going on inside the box," said the behaviorists, "but what is to prevent us from observing relationships between inputs and outputs?" Thus they analyzed behavior into stimuli and responses and developed a science. This science would study relationships between stimuli (inputs into the black box) and responses (behaviors emitted by the black box).

Nevertheless, it became increasingly apparent to most psychologists that what was inside the box was so crucial that you couldn't dispense with it, at least in man. In spite of the secularist psychologists' passionate desire for a simple machine with which to work, they discovered that man thinks. And man interprets, believes, intends, repents, evaluates. Man *cognizes*.

In the 1960s, Albert Ellis published his Rational Emotive Psychotherapy. He worked at the task of changing damaging thoughts and beliefs in his patients. Ellis thought that neurotic people made themselves sick by their irrational beliefs. The criterion of truth he selected was human reason.

In the next decade, Beck, Mahoney, Meichenbaum and others began to publish research demonstrating that therapy which brought change in cognitions did indeed make people better. With these pioneers, cognitive behavioral therapists today believe people are sick because they hang onto false and harmful beliefs. For the most part, these scientists have ignored a glaring problem: how to establish criteria for what is true and what is false; how to find a definition of "right" thinking. Without a firm anchor for truth in God's Word, man is hard pressed to defend any statements whatever as "true."

But Christian teaching has long pointed out that unaided human reason is an unreliable guide to truth. While reason informed by God's revelation can be most helpful, human reason quickly goes awry when it attempts to determine truth without God's revealed Word. This becomes clear to any Christian reading Albert Ellis' notions about right and wrong in human behavior.

The counseling method taught in this book brings talk therapy and cognitive behavior change methods together. The counselor attempts to help the counselee discover his harmful cognitions, grasp their false character, and replace them with the truth.

THE CHRISTIAN CRITERION

Let's suppose you are going to try to change the thoughts in some "black box" by rooting out a person's misbeliefs and replacing them with the truth. What can you use as a guide or criterion to determine what is true and what isn't? The Christian criterion for the contents of the black box is the truth of God. This is, of course, the criterion Jesus himself recommended. And in the Christian view of things, the ultimate source of the distortions and irrationalities which disorder human lives is the devil. Thus, the Scriptures offer their own criteria for behavior and their own use of "cognitive therapy."

Paul, in Philippians 4:11–13 (RSV) is telling us that he had acquired a method for handling stressful circumstances. I believe Paul had learned the same method set forth in this book: truth therapy. "Not that I complain of want; for I have learned, in whatever state I am, to be content. I know how to be abased, and I know how to abound; in any and all circumstances I have learned the secret of facing plenty and hunger, abundance and want. I can do all things in him who strengthens me." How? I believe he did it by telling himself the truth, by cognizing and believing interpretations and attributions which made hardship acceptable to him.

SUMMARY

Counseling is only one of many ways to become whole. Prayer, deliverance, study of the Scriptures, changing one's circumstances, medication, and wisdom gained through experience can bring healing too. Counseling is *dialogue intended to heal*. The Christian community has done counseling for many more centuries than the behavioral and medical professions, and does not need to defer to them. But it can and should learn from them. From the "talk cure" of Sigmund Freud, the behaviorism of Watson, and the current burgeoning research into the place of cognition in human behavior, a therapeutic method has developed in psychology which provides a fitting and agreeable framework for the practice of counseling based on the Christian belief that truth can make you free. This agreeable framework is currently known as *cognitive psychology*.

FOR REVIEW AND DISCUSSION

1. Name three kinds of intervention for behavior problems other than counseling.
2. Define counseling.
3. Why is it historically the province of the Christian Church to do counseling?
4. What insight does Jesus' word in John 8:31, 32 give us about counseling?
5. Describe two branches of psychology flowing into the stream of Christian counseling as presented in this book.
6. Why is psychoanalytic counseling inadequate for Christians?
7. Do you think, since the truth will free man, it is usually sufficient to just read Bible passages to suffering people? Why?

Part Two

DISCERNMENT, DIAGNOSIS, AND CHANGE

CHAPTER THREE

Looking Under the Skin

(Discernment, Assessment, and Diagnosis)

"How on earth did you know that?" The dark eyes showed amazement and the petite face wore a quizzical expression. I had just told her that she appeared to me to be having problems with the management of angry feelings and impulses, especially toward her husband. It was all true, but she had not told me anything about her anger.

Nevertheless, the well-dressed 38-year-old woman admitted that she had come to find help for her anger. "I've tried everything, but I can't control or rid myself of angry feelings toward my husband. I honestly don't know whether the problem is him or me," she explained.

In spite of her wonderment, I had not done anything miraculous. I had merely made reasonable inferences from her test materials and her habit of always smiling, even when what we discussed was anything but pleasant or funny.

People often think that psychologists can read their minds. Sometimes, in social situations, they steer clear of us because, as one man explained, "I feel like you can see right through me." Counselors can't "see through" others. Only God is able to know us through and through and to see everything we are. But it *is* important for all counselors to learn to "look under the skin"!

Discernment, assessment, and diagnosis all have to do with determining what's wrong. Too many counselors, even professionals who have had inadequate training or experience, accept whatever the counselee says as "the problem," instead of making their own observations and formulating their own conclusions. The counselee says, "I'm depressed." The counselor writes in her notebook, "Counselee is depressed." The counselee cries and the counselor writes, "Counselee is weeping, clearly due to depression." But crying can be expressive or manipulative. If it is manipulative, that means the counselee is crying to cause you to think what he wants you to think. Learn not to take what the counselee offers at face value.

KNOWLEDGE AND DISCERNMENT

A brand new lay counselor in the church was ministering to a 56-year-old married woman when, suddenly, the counselor "saw" in the Spirit a picture of the woman falling or jumping into the huge, evil-looking jaws of a whale. Quickly, another scene followed: telephone wires being cut. The young counselor knew instantly in her spirit that the woman was planning to kill herself, and that she had already cut the phone wires of communication. The counselor was terrified and perplexed, but finally decided to share her insights.

The astonished counselee admitted that she was suicidal and that she had told no one. During the ensuing conversation, the counselor tried to get through to this poor woman and help her construct a plan to break her discouragement. Despite this intervention by God himself, the counselee was not receptive. She took her own life by hanging herself. Sadly, the vision had been prophetic.

During counseling, the person who seeks the Lord's revelation may from time to time be given a thought, an impression, a vision, or possibly even a word from God which will impart information not available otherwise. Frequently these gifts of knowledge come at crucial moments in the course of treatment and may create a turning point.

Discernment is the spiritual gift of differentiating between causes. With it, the counselor can distinguish the flesh from the Spirit, and even know the presence of evil spirits as causes of behavior. Often discernment of the counselee's positive spiritual qualities and relationships may be given. I am often quite aware of the fact that the person before me is a deeply committed Christian who walks closely with Jesus Christ long before a word of this has been mentioned between us.

DIAGNOSIS AND ASSESSMENT

The word *diagnosis* comes from two Greek words which literally mean "knowing through." The Greek word means "make a decision." The counselor must learn as much about the counselee as possible. This is nearly always more than the counselee can tell about himself. Diagnosis is knowing what is the matter. To do adequate diagnosis, you must do more than just listen.

Assessment means sizing up the situation and determining the difficulty. Fitting together causes, determinants, and consequences, selecting probable successful interventions, are all involved. Assessment is quite similar to diagnosis.

All these processes will occur together in the Christian counselor who is allowing the gifts of the Holy Spirit to operate in his work. He will sense the Spirit's prompting as well as attend to the empirical evidence. He will combine all available information. His conclusion may be critical for the life of the counselee.

MORE THAN MERE WORDS

In the clinic waiting room, there are usually a number of counselees who pass their time reading while they wait to see their therapists. Diagnosis begins by observing counselees in that setting. Once, after walking through the waiting area, I entered the office of my associate, pastoral counselor Erwin Prange, and said, "You have a new counselee waiting for you. And he will be diagnosed schizophrenic." Prange later confirmed the diagnosis for the 26-year-old man whose disease I had sensed just by walking through the waiting room.

The sense I had relied on for my conjecture was smell. Sometimes you can smell schizophrenia's peculiar, sour odor. On this occasion, it pervaded the waiting room, especially in the vicinity of this counselee.

I am recounting the story to illustrate a lesson new counselors often have trouble learning: Don't just listen to the counselee's words— or mental content. Observe, touch, and smell. Listen to music as well as words, to the tones and volumes of voices, to the speech difficulties and errors, to the qualities of voices.

Sometimes you have to deliberately break the habit of listening only to content. Think and pray. Turn off the inflow of the counselee's speech content and ask, "Lord, please tell me what is going on here. Please give me your own discernment and understanding." Then pay attention to the Spirit speaking within you. Notice your own spirit's reaction to things. Tune in on your feelings, too.

RECIPATHY

The counselee was eager to explain why he had consulted me. When he had described his difficulties with his father he said, "So I came to talk to you. I wanted to discuss this with someone objective."

Now that's the last thing I am—objective! At the moment, I was full of feeling for the young man. I felt love, trust, and the strong desire to go fight his battles for him. I wanted in the worst way to put in their places those employees in his father's business who were going out of their way to give him difficulties.

It may be news to you, but it's true: psychologists have feelings!

Often they have strong feelings for their counselees. When you are a counselor, you will marvel at the power of the feelings counselees elicit in you. They are not all positive either. Feelings elicited by the counselee in the counselor are sometimes called "recipathy." You must learn to pay attention to them for diagnostic purposes. If this counselee makes you mad, she probably has exercised that talent widely and may have difficulties in her relationships on account of it. If she makes you want to hold her and tell her, like a mother or father to a little child, "Everything's going to be all right," she probably pulls tender feelings from others too.

Above all, get rid of the notion that you are to be objective, and to have no feelings toward counselees. A judge should be objective. A counselor can and should have feelings and pay attention to them.

Notice that I am not saying you should act on your feelings, just be aware of them and make inferences from them. Counselors must be in control of their own emotional expression because untrammeled expression of feelings can create enormous difficulties for the counselee and result in backlash for the counselor.

INFER AND DEDUCE

Although you are not a judge, you are a detective of sorts. Agatha Christie's famous detective hero, M. Poirot, does little to solve crimes except sit in his chair and process evidence until he deduces a solution. When you read one of the Poirot stories, you sense that you, too, are invited to engage in the process of deduction and reasoning. So the counselor must practice the making of inferences from evidence.

What does it mean that the counselee denied being upset about that? Anyone would naturally feel quite angry about such an event. And why did he deny it so vehemently? Why does he refuse to confirm any of my interpretations? Even the ones that are certainly correct? Why does what I say seem to displease him so? As you seek answers to questions like these, you formulate or sketch out in your mind a theory about what's wrong.

ACTIVELY FORMULATE

Actively formulate what's going on. Don't be content to just try to get everything and remember it or write it all down. Try to sum up what causes what, and how the person comes to be hurting as he is. How does the history you have obtained relate to the present problem? Come up with a clear and unambiguous definition of the problem as it really is. Generally this involves describing in terms of concrete behavior rather than foggy abstractions, and focusing on examples of the behavior you are talking about. Create a clear analysis of what supports the counselee's maladaptive behavior today (not merely what may have begun it in the dim, distant past). Finally, formulate a diagnosis.

WHY A FORMAL DIAGNOSIS?

Formal diagnosis involves classifying the counselee into a category. Schizophrenia, depressive disorder, hysteria, psychophysiological muskuoskeletal disorder—these are examples of the classifications or categories involved in psychological diagnosis.

"Oh, but such labeling is dreadful. It pigeonholes people instead of treating them as unique individuals." A classic objection. And it's not totally without merit.

But the arguments *for* diagnosis outweigh the arguments against it, in my opinion. For one thing, you don't *have* to dehumanize and pigeonhole people in an unloving fashion if you are relating to them in the love imparted by the Spirit of God. Moreover, when you determine a formal diagnosis, you immediately know a good deal about the counselee that he hasn't told you. That is because you know what the syndrome involves. Also, the formal diagnostic system used by physicians, psychiatrists and psychologists brings some order into the otherwise chaotic jumble of counselee complaints and problems. Thus it facilitates a sensible approach to treatment.

Here are some more reasons for making a diagnosis:

1. (I want to make this point emphatically because it is so new to Christian counseling.) *Diagnosis is now related to treatment.* Some instances: Agoraphobia may be helped by the counselor taking the counselee out to a shopping center or to some other frightening place. Compulsive problems may require referral for response prevention and exposure. Obsessions may be treated with a procedure called *thought-stopping*. Depression may make it mandatory to medicate. The older psychotherapists rarely had such discriminations to make, since there were so few specific treatments in the past.

2. *Diagnosis yields additional knowledge.* Once you have a diagnosis for a counselee, you know more about him than he has told you. That is why it would seem mandatory for counselors to know descriptive psychopathology. We know that anxiety patients are terribly concerned about the opinions of others. Knowing the syndromes opens a file drawer of probabilities about the counselee you have classified.

3. *Diagnosis may lead to an understanding of causation.* Although knowledge of causes in psychological disturbances is very rudimentary and primitive, there are instances in which causes become knowable and significant.

One example of such a situation is the counselee whose disturbed behavior is due to a brain syndrome, that is, to some organic illness or insult to the central nervous system. The counselor who tries to treat such behavior by uncovering facts about the counselee's relationships is barking up the wrong tree in a situation where *it makes a difference*! The counselee could die from the cause the counselor is missing!

In today's clinical practice it is not uncommon for therapists to misdiagnose the depressive phase of a bipolar disorder as a depressive neurosis. The syndromes may appear identical, and unless a good history is taken, the proper diagnosis is missed. This leads to missing the cause (which in bipolar disorder is internal and biochemical) and failing to suggest proper treatment (which is likewise, at least in part, biochemical).

I have seen examples of spiritual diagnosis given during ministry with no attempt to relate the insight to current causes. These fragmentary insights are sometimes delivered in isolation from other relevant variables. Neither counselor nor counselee tries to work them into a more comprehensive diagnostic picture. So counselees are told that the sole cause of the difficulty is that they "have a spirit of fear" and "it needs to come out." Since the counselee's fear is related to his misbeliefs about other people, and change must take place in the counselee's self-talk or internal monologue, little or nothing is achieved by the subsequent efforts to "cast out" the diagnosed entity. No doubt all maladaptive human fear has a demonic origin, but skilled diagnosticians are careful to deal with the mechanisms by which the enemy has been eliciting fear in each particular case.

So, while the interview proceeds, the counselor will be considering diagnosis with part of his mind while he listens with another part. You will learn to rely on a number of cues, including but not restricted to what the counselee tells you. You will also pay close attention to posture, actions, facial expression, modulation of voice and expression, grooming, dress, attitude, style, and—occasionally—what the counselee doesn't say.

In addition, diagnosis is an important element in case planning. In the next chapter, we will learn how to plan the counseling of a person.

SUMMARY

The Christian counselor, like other counselors, needs to determine what is wrong in the counselee's life. Discernment, assessment, and diagnosis are involved. Discernment and the spiritual gift of knowledge are supernatural, God-given insights into the meaning of behavior. Diagnosis and assessment involve putting together information from observation and listening to formulate a conclusion. All this is necessary for understanding what the counselor is doing and for selection of a plan of treatment.

FOR REVIEW AND DISCUSSION

1. What is wrong with simply taking everything the counselee says at face value to arrive at your diagnosis?
2. Name some things you can learn about a person's problems from looking; from listening to voice rather than content; from smell; from touch.
3. In what sense is the counselor a detective?
4. Would it be best for a counselor to be objective? Reasons?
5. How do you feel about the issue of formal diagnosis?
6. Explain *recipathy* and think of some things you could know about someone by means of it.

CHAPTER FOUR

Planning Treatment in Advance

"Before you build a tower, count the cost!" said Jesus (Luke 14:28). He seems to approve of advance planning for projects (not necessarily for self-protection and self-provision).

Counseling goes better when both counselee and counselor have agreed on a plan. Yet untold numbers of Christian counselors haven't even heard of planning. Even professional therapists occasionally stumble along with neither the doctor nor the counselee having the slightest idea what they are trying to do together.

Most readers of this book wouldn't build a snow fort without a plan, let alone a tower! And you certainly wouldn't want the captain of your 747 jet to amble aimlessly around the heavens with you aboard! Counselors, too, need to plan. This chapter will provide directions.

In the not-too-distant past there was no case planning for a counselee beginning psychotherapy. All were treated in a similar fashion anyway. Most therapists did the same thing with all patients: some version of psychoanalytic depth psychological probing, or whatever the therapist called his standard approach to patients. And if there was any difference in the therapist's maneuvers, it was a difference between him and other therapists rather than in the way the therapist treated his various counselees.

Similarly, Christian counselors were not taught to plan. Indeed, for some Christians, the notion of planning is anathema. They believe that planning in advance prevents relying on God and walking by the Spirit. It never occurs to them that the Holy Spirit can give guidance during advance planning as well as "in the clinch."

No longer is this the situation. It is now appropriate to plan treatment in advance.

MULTIPLE TREATMENTS AVAILABLE

Multiple treatments are available to the Christian counselor. For instance: I am beginning work with a young male graduate student who is suffering from persistent negative thoughts called *obsessions*. I must consider when and whether to use many options available to him. A few procedures available for this neurotic problem: cognitive restructuring (called "truth therapy" or "misbelief therapy" in this book), thought-stopping, medication, stress inoculation, relaxation training. My initial plan calling for medication and cognitive restructuring is having little effect, so I am planning further with the counselee. In this process I will suggest we train him in thought-stopping, a procedure for eliminating persistent unwanted thoughts. (Note: As explained previously, this case and others to be described are composites, created to protect the confidentiality of actual counselees.)

Here is a partial list of procedures now available for treatment of various behavior and emotional disorders. Not all of them will be practical for the Christian lay counselor to actually *do*, but with training he can do many of them. And he should know they exist for purposes of referral when they seem indicated. They will be more fully discussed later; no need to define them here:

truth therapy or misbelief therapy (our mainstay)
medication (by referral to a psychiatrist or physician)
systematic desensitization
contingency management
stress inoculation
modeling
role play
behavioral rehearsal
covert rehearsal
covert sensitization
conditioning
response deprivation with exposure
deliverance ministry
confession and repentance
forgiveness

and more. The purpose of this partial list is to impress the fact that there are options, and since there are options, advance planning is necessary today as it never was before such options were known.

CHRISTIAN COUNSELEES COLLABORATE

As we depart from the medical model, and the notion that emotional problems are illnesses needing treatment by a physician, it has become more common to consider the counselee a collaborator with the therapist. He is called a "counselee" rather than a patient. His ideas are solicited in planning treatment. The counselor who involves counselees as active collaborators rather than passive patients will produce better outcome and foster less dependency. This approach recognizes that God has made the counselee responsible for his own life and behavior, and that the counselor cannot take over for him.

PLANNING SAVES TIME

Planning ordinarily leads to faster results than simply letting the hours run on. Even though Christian counseling is often offered free, or at low rates, it is nonetheless important to economize to make as many people beneficiaries as possible. Planning saves time.

COUNSELEES SHOULD HAVE A SAY

Loving respect for your counselees requires that you allow them to participate in determining what activities the two of you will engage in. It is not loving to impose procedures on them. Collaborative planning allows counselees to give informed consent to and even help create procedures to be used in their treatment.

PSYCHOLOGICAL TESTS

One of the most powerful aids to diagnosis available to the contemporary counselor is psychological testing. Good tests in current use have been scientifically constructed. They will yield valid information to the counselor. Properly used, in conjunction with other information, test results can increase insight and consequent effectiveness manyfold. In the next chapter (5), we will learn more about psychological tests and what they can contribute.

Recently, computerized psychological test interpretation has become a reality. Any counselor can, at a reasonably low cost, obtain superb and precise test interpretations based on the computer's unique ability to store research information and generate accurate and pertinent narrative reports. *You don't have to be a psychologist to use test results.* Computerized interpretations now available spell out the implications of test scores in a form you can use.

Although you don't have to be a psychologist to use test results, you should obtain them through a psychologist. Many psychologists use computerized test interpretations and can help you to obtain access to these services for your counselees. The psychologist can oversee the process to make sure you understand the test results you are given as well as to provide a responsible professional check on the selection, use, and final adequacy of the testing process.

There are numerous tests. Obviously, the test or test battery should be chosen to contribute to diagnosis. At the Center for Christian Psychological Services, we always administer a battery of tests to new counselees. The printout will be in my hands before the first interview. There are several tests and inventories in our battery. They were carefully selected to give some information on each counselee's social history and background, an estimate of his current intelligence level, a rapid index of his present depression level, and some idea of the counselee's physical complaints and illnesses.

The mainstay of the battery is the MMPI (The Minnesota Multiphasic Personality Inventory). You can, if you wish, obtain personal experience with the MMPI by finding a source of computerized interpretations of this test to use with some of your counselees. You will soon become aware of the diagnostic power of this much-researched instrument.[1]

A PLANNING FORM FOR COUNSELING

On pages 38 and 39 is a form you may copy and use if you choose. It is to be completed by the counselor during or after the initial interview. On it you will have recorded diagnostic and treatment decisions arrived at by the counselee and you.

HOW TO USE THE PLANNING SHEET

Chief complaint: The chief complaint is the counselee's presenting problem—the difficulty he announces as primary and (usually) first in the order of difficulties he describes. This is the admission ticket to counseling. You may ask the new counselee to tell you about this first. "What brings you in to see me today?"

You will discover that counselees with similar problems see the chief complaint differently. A counselee having panic attacks may complain first about pressure on the job or marital difficulties, and only later reveal the terror she experiences in her panic attacks. Or she may announce that her reason for coming in is the panic attacks themselves, and only later reveal the stressors in her work situation and in her marriage.

Problems and goals in treatment: To open up the first interview, tell the counselee that your object is to come out with a plan. To make a counseling plan we need to formulate goals. "You have some goals in coming here. We need to find out what those are, and to discuss them together. They may be the goals we will finally agree to work on, or we may hammer out some additional goals. It could happen that I won't think one or the other of your goals is realistic for us to work at; if so, I'll tell you. Or I may think your goals can be better achieved at some other place or with some other kind of counselor."

Prayer for revelation of the goals God desires this counselee to

---

[1] Readers who wish to obtain computerized test interpretations can learn how to do so by writing to Minnesota Psychtests, Inc., 2233 Hamline Ave., Suite 435, St. Paul, MN 55113.

achieve can be offered in this interview.

During the problem and goal development process, both counselor and counselee are focusing on certain ground rules for the work they will do together. It is as if the counselor is alerting the counselee to the work ahead in terms like these:

1. We are aiming at something, not just passing time or "talking it out."
2. *Change* is the name of the game; change in the counselee's thoughts, feelings, attitudes, and/or behavior.
3. The kinds of changes we will aim at are determined by the revelation of God's will for you.
4. We are positively oriented, and are interested in wholeness, not pathology. You may tell me what's *wrong* with you, but I'd like that to be subordinate to what's going to be *right* with you. Think of this not as just a "gripe session," but as a time to move ahead and accomplish some wonderful new things.

Particularly in marital counseling I try to establish this goal orientation. It is most difficult there because counselees often believe they are expected to complain about one another. Each spouse tries to persuade the therapist that he is mostly righteous while his spouse is mostly fault-ridden. Some couples simply can't be persuaded to work toward goals. They insist, over the counselor's objections, that they *must* tell their long tales of injustice and abuse. That is a very bad prognostic sign.

Even counselees presenting themselves for individual counseling may have to be urged and motivated to do more than just complain. Not everyone really wants to set change goals and work hard to achieve them.

Goal orientation helps the counselor get away from dwelling solely upon the negative, and spending endless hours just digging for "the root of the problem" rather than moving the counselee toward a new life in Christ Jesus.

In addition to goals, we must think in terms of malady or problem. What is presently preventing your counselee from arriving at the goals he has stated he wishes to achieve? What things are now wrong which are preventing the achievement of those goals? This is another form of diagnosis, i.e., of noting what's wrong. In this form, we do not classify the counselee, as we do in formal diagnosis. Here we describe the specific pathological behaviors the counselee is currently engaging in. Counselees often tell us that their problem is someone else's behavior. But the counselor must translate this into the counselee's problem if he is going to achieve change.

For example, when the counselee tells you, "My problem is that my father is trying to seduce me" (as a 26-year-old woman recently said to me), you must be coming to some tentative conclusions in your mind: "She is probably telling herself she won't be able to say 'no'

COUNSELING PLAN

Date _____

Counselee's name _____

Address _____ Date of birth _____

Phone _____ Age _____ Marital Status _____

Chief complaint: _____

_____

Problems to be resolved:

1. _____

2. _____

3. _____

4. _____

(Use reverse side or additional sheet if needed)

Goals to be attained:

1. _____

2. _____

3. _____

4. _____

(Use reverse side or additional sheet if needed)

Formal diagnosis: _____

Additional diagnoses (if applicable): _____

Physical problems and illnesses: _____

Current stressors in counselee's life situation: _____

Spiritual status: _____

Counseling plan (frequency, methods, length of time projected): _____

_____

and will then hate herself and feel awful. Or, it could be that she is upsetting herself by telling herself how her father shouldn't be this way, how terrible it all is, and how upset she should be." You have thus recast the problem in terms the counselee can deal with because it is her behavior, not her father's, with which you and she will have to work.

If you begin by formulating specific problems, you will work effectively with concrete difficulties rather than vague generalities like, "He has a poor self-image," or "She has a negative attitude." Problem orientation helps the counselee look for the concrete behaviors now causing pain and anxiety. He will see more clearly that specific behaviors must change.

About goals and problems:

1. They should be concrete and behaviorally defined, not vague and abstract.

Here are some concrete goals you can use as examples:

- Counselee will practice telling herself the truth about her self-worth at least once daily.
- Counselee will arrive at work on time at least 4 days out of 5.
- Counselee will report no suicidal thoughts for at least two weeks hand running.
- Counselee will meet at least twelve people he has not met before.
- Counselee will read Scripture daily.

Here are some concrete problem formulations:

- Counselee avoids situations in which others watch him perform.
- Counselee believes that what others say about his performance is so critical he cannot risk being judged.
- Counselee fantasizes adulterous sexual behavior three or four times each day.

2. They should be relevant to the *counselee's* aims in seeking counseling. Sometimes you want a counselee to change something the counselee doesn't want to change. Even if you feel strongly about the trait or behavior, you are not likely to succeed in modifying it unless the counselee himself can see clearly how it relates to his reason for seeking help.

3. They should be stated in such a way as to make evaluations possible. That is, you should be able to make quantitative and qualitative judgments about the extent to which they have been achieved at the end of your work.

Not, for example, "He needs better feelings about himself," but, "His score on the Beck Depression Test should be down to normal by the end of treatment." Or, "His self-talk log should reflect no unchallenged negative and false self-statements." Or, "Counselee should report spending less time thinking about his shortcomings."

Diagnostic insights: The planning sheet contains space to record a formal diagnosis. Later on, you will learn to derive some diagnoses from symptoms and characteristics of the problems counselees present to you. You should study a good text in abnormal psychology as an aid in gaining this type of insight. Sometimes more than one formal diagnosis will apply to a single counselee, so space is provided for additional diagnoses.

Physical problems and current illnesses may have bearing on the counselee's difficulties and should be asked about and noted.

Current situational pressures and stressors must be considered and noted.

Counseling plan (frequency, methods, length of time projected): The planning form has a space for writing the goals and procedures you and the counselee have agreed on.

Here is how we summarize for the counselee: "It looks as though your goal of being comfortable when you are answering questions in your discussion group can be achieved. I can teach you some of the skills involved and then let you practice with videotape so you can observe and improve your own performance. Does that sound agreeable?"

If the counselee agrees, we will write, "modeling, role play, rehearsal, and video feedback" under methods and procedures. Examples of other procedures included in planning are: "prayer and private study to seek God's will," or, "work with therapist to develop understanding of God's painful dealings in life of counselee." Many times we decide to record "truth therapy to restructure counselee's beliefs about relationships," or "training for parents in skills to control child's behavior."

CONTRACT

A contract has now been entered into by counselee and counselor. The counselor will do his best to assure that the counselee understands the goals and methods to be used. This is especially important when things are likely to go differently than the counselee anticipated from watching therapy done by actors on TV.

When the counselee understands the contract, both counselee and counselor participate in formulating it in writing on the contract form. They spell out what they will do, what goals they will strive to achieve, and any additional agreed activities (e.g., relaxation training).

It is important to estimate how long they will work together before terminating, or at least how many sessions they will work before they reevaluate in the light of the counselee's progress (or lack of it). In addition, the counselee is informed and agrees in writing to the foreseen costs, if any, of the treatment.

Such agreements insure that there will be a collaborative team, counselor and counselee, working together to achieve the counselee's goals by changing the counselee's behavior.

Some of the mystique of counseling may disappear with the use of such joint planning, but what is gained is the dignity and worth of the counselee. Another result of such collaborative planning is to alter the counselee's expectation that he will be a passive patient while he is spiritually and mentally operated upon. He now gains the far more healing notion that he is a human being, and that he has an important role in the process of change God is working in his life.

SUMMARY

Planning before you begin something has a scriptural basis, and it is an excellent practice for counselors. Counselee and counselor begin by working out a plan together based on diagnosis, testing, counselor's and counselee's insights, and the special understandings imparted by the Holy Spirit. They specify problems and goals concretely and agree that they will aim at achieving those goals they have noted. They will agree also on any methods or special techniques to be employed, and will discuss the likely duration of the counseling and costs, if any. A contract is arrived at which both agree to try to fulfill. In this way, the aims and methods for achieving them are shared and the counselee is made aware from the beginning of the responsibility God has given him to help himself and not just present himself passively to be helped.

FOR REVIEW AND DISCUSSION

1. Give reasons why planning counseling is a good idea.
2. What arguments might some counselors offer for *not* planning? Can you counter those arguments?
3. What is the medical model of counseling?
4. Why is it inappropriate for most Christian counselors to use?
5. Why is diagnosis important?
6. How can you begin the first interview so as to elicit the counselee's *chief complaint?*
7. Give some reasons for discussing and specifying goals.
8. Why should you try to reformulate problems in terms of the counselee's own behaviors?
9. Look at the examples of concrete problems and goals and then create some examples of each yourself.

CHAPTER FIVE

What You Should Know About Tests

Christian counselors, even pastors who have been trained for counseling, frequently do *not* use psychological tests. I have heard very few of them give reasons for this neglect.

"I'm not trained to use tests."

"Tests are dehumanizing."

"I don't need them."

None of those reasons will hold water. If the Lord has given us tools with which we can work more effectively, it seems dumb not to use them. Why pound nails with a rock when you can use a hammer? Why should a physician take your blood pressure by feeling your arteries when he can use a sphygmomanometer and a stethoscope? And why should a Christian counselor bypass the information about his counselee which a good test will give him?

True, there was a time when you had to know a good deal to use most tests. And only thoroughly trained psychologists are qualified to judge and interpret test results. But it is not true that no one else can obtain test interpretations and reports. Psychologists will furnish them if you refer your counselee to them for testing. And now that computers have begun administering, scoring, and interpreting tests in plain English, it is easy and inexpensive to obtain high quality and informative test results on your counselees.

There are hundreds of psychological tests available. Each one was constructed to serve a particular purpose. There are tests for:

Intelligence. These can be used by the counselor to determine within what intellectual ballpark his counselee is currently functioning. Is the counselee's problem related to a big gulf between his intelligence and the demands of his situation? A test in the hands of someone who knows how to use it can help answer this question.

Vocational interests. There are numerous tests on the market which measure interests related to job satisfaction. When the counselee's difficulties appear to stem from job unhappiness, the counselor might want to use a vocational interest inventory. Many excellent interest tests are available. The results are often printed out by computers scoring them. A consultation with a vocational counseling expert can help you to understand and explain the test results effectively.

Personality. Such a wide range of personality tests exist that it is very confusing to the counselor who would like to obtain the information these tests offer, but does not know how to select an instrument for accomplishing what he wishes. Some of these tests are of the type called *projective* tests. *Projective* tests ordinarily must be given by an expert specifically trained in their use. They present an ambiguous stimulus, such as an inkblot, and ask the counselee to describe what he sees. The assumption is that the counselee's responses will be determined by his personality traits rather than by the character of the stimulus if the stimulus is sufficiently ambiguous. Other personality tests are called *objective. Objective* tests present unambiguous items in the form of questions or true-false statements. Results are numerical and scores must be interpreted by an expert.

If you are preparing to become a lay counselor in your church, you will not, I assume, have acquired the expertise and training necessary to administer or interpret psychological tests—either objective or projective. This does not mean a closed door to test information. Counselees can be asked to obtain testing at the office of a psychologist with the understanding that the psychologist will report results to the referring counselor. These arrangements should be made with the psychologist by the counselor in advance of referral.

Another option which is becoming increasingly available for the use of lay counselors is computerized psychological testing. The counselee is asked to complete the answer sheet which is then forwarded to the psychologist offering computerized test interpretation. The computer is fed the counselee's answers and renders a very complete interpretation in plain English which can be understood and utilized by counselors untrained in the specifics of test interpretation. The computer must be used under the supervision of a psychologist, but its printed interpretations are frequently far more complete and detailed than those produced by the psychologist without the use of the computer. And they are often less expensive. Information on how you can find such facilities was given in the last chapter.

THE MINNESOTA MULTIPHASIC PERSONALITY INVENTORY

Only objective (rather than projective) tests are amenable to use at low cost by the untrained person, so we will confine the remainder of our discussion to the most widely known and best-researched of all the objective personality tests, the Minnesota Multiphasic Personality Inventory (The MMPI).

The MMPI consists of 566 statements to which the counselee is asked to respond true or false. These items are scored in batches called "scales," each of which measures a particular trait. The ordinary clinical profile will provide scoring on thirteen scales: three scales measure various kinds of invalidity (such as painting a too favorable picture of oneself), while the other ten scales measure clinically significant attributes (for example, depression). In addition, optional scoring may be obtained on literally hundreds of so-called "research" scales to measure numerous additional traits.

It is the opinion of the author that the MMPI is the best available personality test for counseling use. It was developed in a manner which, for its time, was revolutionary and which will be explained later. Furthermore, this particular test has been the most researched of all the objective personality tests. Much more factual information is available for interpretation. It would take many years of psychological research to accumulate the knowledge for any newer test which has been stored up in the annals of psychology on the MMPI. For example, we know that one particular profile is associated with a higher rate of hunting accidents than any other type of MMPI profile. Many such useful bits of information exist for use in detailed MMPI interpretation.

Most people do not understand how the MMPI and other modern psychological tests are derived. They imagine that such tests are simply "cooked up" by an expert who makes up a long list of questions which the expert thinks will measure the trait in question. For example, it is assumed that for a test of anxiety you would get an anxiety expert to write a batch of items which he has reason to believe anxious people will endorse. Then you administer them and make what you can of them.

This is not the method of construction of the MMPI. Before MMPI authors Starke Hathaway and J. Charnley McKinley tried the empirical method of test construction, tests were put together in much the manner of the above popular theory. But the MMPI was constructed empirically. And that's a different story.

These authors had a revolutionary idea for their time (1931, the era of the WPA, funds from which financed the work). They asked, "Why not find out from experience which items might measure which traits? Instead of arbitrarily determining in advance that a certain batch of questions will likely measure a certain characteristic, why not see first how test items actually work?"

So they constructed and collected a large number of items which could be answered true or false. They were not at all particular about what each item might or might not measure. They had no preconceptions.

They collected a huge potful of items. They then asked a large number of people to answer their items. These first respondents were to furnish a more or less normal baseline, so the authors made sure none of them was currently under the care of a physician or a psychiatrist. These people constituted the group they called "normals."

Then the test builders invited a number of people who were diagnosed as suffering from depression to respond to their items. When this step was completed, they did some calculations.

Were there any items out of the potful which depressives answered in a different way than the normals? Yes, there were. And those items became the scale for measuring depression. This scale, with the items on it selected because for some reason depressed people responded to them in their own special way, represented a great step forward in personality testing. The items were chosen because they *actually worked*.

More steps of a technical nature were involved in the scale development process, but this description is sufficient for the purpose. I want to make the point clear that most of the scales for the MMPI were developed, not by an expert writing items which he *assumed* would work, but by the empirical process of determining first which items *do* work.

BUT, PEOPLE CAN CHEAT!

You have doubtless already thought of the other problem which had to be tackled by the test builders. People like to look good—usually. So what's to keep them from answering questions in the way they think will make them look best? What about cheaters?

For that matter, what about cheaters taking the test to try to look bad? Who would do that? People who want to prove they have a very bad psychological illness so they can collect disability insurance, obtain sympathy, or just get some time to rest in the hospital might have reasons for wanting to look bad.

So the MMPI constructors introduced another revolutionary (for their time) feature into their inventory: validity scales. These scales, of which there are three on the MMPI, are able to help a trained clinician determine when persons taking the test are stretching the truth one way or another.

WHAT YOU CAN LEARN FROM THE COUNSELEE'S MMPI

When you read your counselee's MMPI profile interpretation, you will not only learn about the pathology he or she has claimed. You will also learn something about the way the counselee approached taking the test. This in turn may help you to know in advance how willing that counselee will be to work on self-change. And it will certainly help you to know how seriously to take the things this counselee has told you about himself on the test.

What you as a counselor can get from an MMPI will vary, depending on the counselee and the profile generated. Some profiles are more informative than others. Normally, you can expect to get a diagnostic picture which will help you to confirm or disconfirm your own impressions. It will likely give you some ideas you hadn't even thought of.

For example, the MMPI should tell you with some precision how depressed your counselee was when he took the test. You can learn whether your counselee is suffering from a neurosis, a psychosis, a personality disorder, or a situational crisis. It will help you to learn whether the elements of the disorder are chronic, long embedded in the counselee's personality structure, or acute, arising recently in reaction to some disturbing crisis situation. The profile may help you to learn whether your counselee feels bad though he tends to live circumspectly, or whether he does things contrary to law and morality to get himself into tight spots. You should learn something about how efficient or disturbed the counselee's thinking is, as well as a good deal about the kinds of psychological and interpersonal tactics he is likely to engage in to protect himself from psychological pain. Occasionally you will be given some probable diagnostic labels with the MMPI interpretation. Diagnosis should be made with the entire picture in mind, and not just from the test. Nevertheless, the test may be helpful in suggesting to you what diagnostic terms you ought to consider.

We have concentrated on the MMPI, not because there aren't any other good tests, but because space forbids discussing them all. The one best test for diagnostic purposes is, in my opinion, the MMPI. Therefore it has been discussed at some length so the counselor who uses it may be familiar with the test, its functioning, and its background.

SUMMARY

In this chapter, you learned that psychological testing can be most helpful to you in arriving at an understanding of your counselee and his problems. It is difficult to grant validity to objections some counselors offer to the use of such tests, since they do contribute to diagnosis. The differences between projective and objective tests was discussed, and the MMPI was described so that counselors will have some background on the construction of this test. It is, in my opinion, the best available personality test for diagnostic purposes, partly because so much is known through research about the meaning of MMPI results.

FOR REVIEW AND DISCUSSION

1. Give some objections offered by Christian counselors to the use of tests.

2. What are the arguments for using tests?
3. Describe the differences between projective and objective tests of personality.
4. How does the average person assume that tests are constructed?
5. Describe the construction of the MMPI.
6. Tell something about each of the validity scales on the MMPI.
7. List some things you might learn from an MMPI interpretation.
8. What kinds of tests are available other than personality measures?

CHAPTER SIX

The Limits of Counseling

The course of lectures on Christian counseling was drawing to a close. At the end of the evening a woman who had attended faithfully and taken notes furiously came forward to talk.

"I don't know about all this," she said. "There seems to be so much to learn! And I'm trying my best. But I just don't feel like a counselor. In fact, all this information has just made me feel that I'll never be able to do it! Maybe I should quit now."

My courses in Christian counseling are demanding. They involve exhaustive coverage of the abnormal symptoms and syndromes church counselors are liable to see. Often the students taking the class say that, though they acquire a huge amount of knowledge, they are disappointed by the feeling that they could never learn to apply it all.

"I don't know how to counsel," they tell me.

And I agree. You are not a counselor because you have read a book, nor are you a counselor because God has called you. You need *experience. And not just any experience. You need supervised experience.*

Please don't be disappointed if, upon finishing this book, you come to the realization that reading a book doesn't make you a Christian counselor. That realization is nothing but healthy self-knowledge.

IT'S BETTER TO BE AWARE OF YOUR LIMITS!

The readers who cause me concern are those who too readily overestimate their ability, those who believe they really need no training.

"I have the Holy Spirit, so why should I go to all this trouble? Knowledge of things like psychology is worldly and just gets in your way. I'd rather rely on the Lord." But the Lord never urges us to refuse an opportunity to know more about what we are doing in His service!

"Now that I've read Backus' book, just let me at 'em" is another mindset I am concerned with forestalling. Doubtless there will be any number of readers who will try practicing their insights on unwilling and unsuspecting friends and family.

We will now discuss the activity of counseling itself. But don't be disappointed if the feeling persists that you still aren't trained. You won't be, not completely, even after you read and digest all this book has to offer you.

RESPECT FOR THE LIMITS OF COUNSELING

I want you to know and respect the limits of counseling from the very beginning. After you have become an excellent counselor with years of experience, you will still need to face the limits of the counseling method. This is a good time to learn your limits as a counselor.

Pastoral counselors sometimes expect themselves to perform without limits. They often become victims of their own feeling that they should solve other people's problems for them. Thus they feel guilty about drawing a line and saying, "I can't do more than that for you. The rest you must do yourself." Christian lay counselors too often think they must be omnicompetent to help others. "Whatever the problem, just call on me" is the message they project.

Occasionally, in this book, dialogues will be presented to illustrate a point. Most of them are actually reproduced from sessions with counselees. The details are changed, but the dialogues are for the most part true to life. They are meant to serve as models for Christian counselors in training. Sometimes they are negative models. That is, you will want to avoid acting like the person portrayed in the dialogue. Of course, some dialogues will offer positive models for you to emulate.

A NEGATIVE MODEL

Here is a negative model. This very poor performance by an experienced psychologist (the author of this book, as a matter of fact) will serve to illustrate how easy it is to get trapped by our own conflicting personal feelings elicited by people demanding help we cannot give.

Notice how the doctor creates an impossible situation which simply infuriates the patient and probably destroys the relationship. Let's call the psychologist Dr. John.

The telephone rings at Dr. John's home. It is 7:30 a.m. The doctor is trying to get through his morning prayer and Scripture reading time and get to work. He answers the phone:

Patient: Dr. John? I just don't know what to do. I'm all tied in knots this morning.

Dr. J.: Don't you have an appointment with my associate, Pastor Manning?

Patient: Yes, I've already seen him a couple of times. I've seen hundreds of people and they don't help. I'm about to give up.

Dr. J.: We really haven't started working with you yet. I chose Pastor Manning for you because he has been helpful to people with problems like yours.

Patient: What do *you* think it means to be a Christian?

Dr. J.: I'm not going to get into that with you now. You can discuss it with your therapist.

Patient: I just can't go on. I'm hardly doing anything. I'm not going to work much. I don't even feel like trying anymore.

Dr. J.: (sounding edgy and irritated) We can help you only if you are willing to help yourself, you know.

Patient: Well, I just don't feel like trying to help myself anymore. I've had it. I don't think I can try.

Dr. J.: (more irritated—after all, it's not *his* counselee, and why can't all this wait for Manning?) There's no way anyone can help you unless you are willing to put some of your effort into it. You'll have to work this out with Manning.

Patient: (feeling, accurately, that he's been dismissed) You're an irresponsible idiot!

Dr. J.: (by now, furious) I'm not interested in hearing *that*! (Doctor hangs up in frustration)

AN EXERCISE OF SKILL DEVELOPMENT

For your own skill development, refer to the dialogue above and
1. Analyze the counselee's feelings. Do you think the counselee is intentionally playing games? Genuinely desperate? Trying to see how far he can draw the doctor into his net?
2. Can you grasp the doctor's feelings? Why did he become irritated? How do you evaluate the doctor's handling of the counselee's situation?

A BETTER MODEL FOR YOU

Now consider the following dialogue sample. This is a plausible alternative to the foregoing. Pick it up where the counselee has just said, "I don't even feel like trying anymore."

Dr. J.: You've come to the end of your rope.

Patient: Yes, I don't even want to try.

Dr. J.: You feel you've done everything, tried everything, and nothing has helped.

Patient: That's how I feel.

Dr. J.: And you probably don't have much hope that a new counselor can help you any more than the others have.

Patient: How can he help? What's he gonna do different?

Dr. J.: It must be hard to try to work to get better when you feel so hopeless.

Patient: Yes, it is. (Pause) I guess I don't give a counselor a whole lot of help when I feel this way. (Pause)

Dr. J.: (says nothing, just waits for counselee)

Patient: Well, maybe I should give this guy a chance—give it one more try.

Dr. J.: What time is your appointment with Pastor Manning?

Patient: Two o'clock tomorrow. I'll be there. Thanks, Doc.

AN EXERCISE TO TRY

For an exercise, analyze what happened that was different from the first dialogue. Do you think the doctor has different objectives in this revised dialogue than he had in the first sample? In what way?

The dialogues you have just read were included to teach you that the counselor can become threatened and behave badly because of his own belief that it is imperative to be able to help, no matter what you are asked to do or when you are asked to do it. Given that deep belief, the counselor finds himself in conflict and becomes irritated and aggressive in the dialogue above. Like others, pastors and Christian counselors may believe that God requires them to help *no matter what*.

TRYING TO DO EVERYTHING ACCOMPLISHES NOTHING

A clergyman attending a seminar for counselors was called to the telephone by one of his counselees. Although the receptionist explained that the pastor was in a session and that the message to return the call would be given to him, the counselee insisted on immediate service, demanding that the receptionist leave her desk, find the clergyman, and put him on the telephone *now*. Later, the pastor explained. She called him six times that day. And on each call, he felt forced to listen to a repetition of her painful feelings.

Why did this pastor agree to be at the beck and call of the counselee, though his ministry and marriage were clearly being hurt by her demands? Conversation with him revealed that he carried around and endlessly regaled himself with a number of misbeliefs. Some of them were the following:

COMMON COUNSELOR MISBELIEFS

- I must be available at any and all times for whatever demands anyone wants to make on me, because I am a Christian.
- I must literally *be* the solution for my counselee's problem, rather than help her to solve her own difficulties.

- Anything else I am doing does not matter compared with the emotional needs of a counselee.
- Of course I am not God—but I have to come close to being God—omnicompetent, omni-everything, for everybody who needs me.
- I must never say no.
- Loving people means doing exactly what they want.

Not only did the counselor have a head full of such nonsense as the above, but he had taught the same nonsense to his counselee. By his behavior, he had trained her to behave as badly as she did on the day of the conference. Counselees learn rapidly, often without being told, what the rules are, and if the rules are determined by the counselor's erroneous perceptions of his own function, the counselee will generally acquire similar erroneous beliefs.

COMMON COUNSELEE MISBELIEFS

This counselor's counselee, along with many other counselees, believed that:

- My pain, if it is sufficiently intense, entitles me to demand and receive total attention from my counselor at any time I wish it and no matter what else he may be doing.
- If my counselor ascribes such power to my painful feelings that they can command his behavior, I can reasonably expect others to conform to my wishes in the same way.
- I can and should expect any Christian, because he is a Christian, to go out of his way to do as I wish.
- I need not solve my problems. That is up to my counselor.
- I need not take the trouble to control myself. It is easier and more gratifying to control others.

What ultimately suffers under such circumstances is the counseling. It doesn't only suffer, it fails. Counselors must give up the misbelief that they absolutely have to deliver all kinds of help, whether they can or not, whenever and wherever the counselee demands it.

"CALL ME ANY TIME!"

I have heard counselors tell people, "Just call me any time—whenever you need me I'll be there." If the counselee takes this seriously, the counselor will face plenty of conflict and trouble. Too many calls at the wrong hours, repeating the same list of woes, and the would-be helper begins to sense deep irritation ("I'm tired of this. Besides, I've already told this guy what to do about that a dozen times. Why doesn't he think for himself just once?"). But now, the counselor feels another unpleasant emotion: guilt. "How can I possibly be a genuine Christian when I feel so angry and irritated at this poor counselee?" he asks himself. Castigating himself for his feelings, he feels even more miserable. And every thought connected with the counselee in question opens up this can of worms in his emotions. Unless things are put right with the truth, the relationship is doomed to rapid destruction because the counselor *is not God.*

This sort of thing means that you, as a counselor, can live only in the forgiveness of sins through the cross of Jesus Christ, not by virtue of your own marvelous and righteous performance as the best of all good Samaritans. And it also means that—unlike God—you have limits. As does counseling itself. Recognize and set those limits.

TIME LIMITS FOR YOU TO SET

For instance: Because you are not God and not infinite, your sessions cannot go on forever. Yet many Christian counselors fear setting limits on the length of the session. They expect the counselee to do it. The counselee, understandably, stays as long as he enjoys talking. A few three-hour sessions, prolonged by the fact that many counselees find talking to a willing listener one of life's most exhilarating experiences, and the counselor's enthusiasm has cooled. Again he feels guilty and conflicted about the negative feelings he can't seem to push down, and with his emotions in a tangle, the counselor proceeds to ruin the relationship.

Most therapists observe a standard length of time for sessions of psychotherapy. They spend fifty minutes with the counselee, and leave ten minutes of the hour to write notes on the session and prepare for their upcoming therapeutic encounter.

The counselor must take initiative in ending a session. This is not comfortable for most people at first, since in their experience, socially, the host never takes the initiative in ending a visit. "I just can't do it," one timid trainee told me. She learned how and became quite adept at terminating her sessions right on time.

Here is how it's done. When the time has come for the session to end, (1) the counselor talks rather than terminating right after the counselee has said something. Counselor might say, "Well, it does sound as though you will want to give some more time to working on your fear of meeting other people. Our time for this session is up—" (2) At this point, the counselor rises and begins walking toward the door, continuing to speak something like this: (3) "Let's make an appointment for the same time next week. Meantime, I'll be expecting you to work on the projects we agreed you'd do for homework." (4) The counselor now opens the door and ushers the counselee out, usually with a warm, "See you next week."

SOME OTHER LIMITS FOR YOU TO SET

In the same way, you must learn to set limits on phone calls between sessions. Learn to say, "I don't want you to call me between sessions unless there is a most unusual emergency because counseling works better if we save material for the sessions we are scheduling each week."

Be careful about fulfilling requests to do things other than counseling for your counselee. For example, counselees should probably be refused when they ask you to:

1. Serve as a reference when they apply for work or school. Prospective employers become curious about the counselee's pathology when they know they are talking to his counselor. Questions may be asked which you can answer only to the detriment of the counselee. It is relatively easy to explain to counselees who want to give your name as a reference, "The information your counselor has about you is rarely the kind of information you would like your prospective employer to have, at least initially. You would be better off not to use me as a reference."

2. Tell things to others on behalf of the counselee. If only the counselor would call her husband and let him know what her real needs are! The counselee may ask you to do such tasks on the grounds that she herself cannot be effective. "He won't listen to me. But he'll listen to you, I know." Or, "You can say it so much better than I can." Resist, even if this praise flatters you!

3. Straighten the counselee out for someone else. Frequently, relatives, spouses, roommates, parents, friends send someone in to be "fixed" by the counselor. These people may have urged the counselee to come in for help, and feel a proprietary interest in the process. They telephone wanting a report from the counselor or desiring to impart information they are sure the counselor needs but will not be told by the counselee. They may request that the counselor attempt to change the counselee in some respect, presenting their arguments for the desirability of the change. Remember, you are working for God and the counselee, not for the other interested party. If you try to fulfill such requests, you will find yourself in the middle of conflict and in trouble with your counseling relationship!

4. Furnish transportation or other services to facilitate the counselee's performing some of the goals of treatment. If the counselor broadens his activities to include those of chauffeur, laundry person, maid, baby-sitter, money lender, cook, and whatnot, the counseling relationship will suffer a nearly fatal case of emotional conflict in both counselee and counselor.

People become counselors out of a deep desire to help others. And that's great. But the desire to prove yourself helpful and useful may also lead you to become involved in activities which take you far beyond counseling. A good deal of experience has shown that these ventures often (not invariably) result in nearly unresolvable conflict for counselor and counselee. For this reason, I am strongly recommending that (especially beginning) Christian counselors avoid them like the plague. Remember, this advice is given, not to protect the counselor, but to protect the counselee, whose interests are the primary concern of the counseling ministry in the Christian community.

The purpose of this chapter has been to call to your attention the fact that counseling has limits. The counselor who knows those limits and his own personal limitations will likely be more effective than the counselor who tries to imitate God, being omni-everything, meeting all needs, fulfilling all requests. The counselor who tries to be God will likely terminate a confused relationship, by now rued by both himself and the counselee.

SUMMARY

Supervised practice is needed for you to become an effective Christian counselor. The material in this book, though necessary, is not sufficient for the development of counseling skills. Find a supervisor.

Counseling has limits. It will not help everyone with every problem. And if you are to function well in the role of a counselor, it is important to set limits on what you will attempt to do and how available you can attempt to be. Failure to recognize limits is like trying to be God. And it frequently results in failure of an attempt to counsel.

FOR REVIEW AND DISCUSSION

1. What do students of counseling need in order to develop requisite skills?
2. Why isn't it usually sufficient to receive the Holy Spirit and read a book of instructions?
3. What are some kinds of activity on behalf of counselees which counselors should ordinarily avoid?
4. Why isn't it selfish to say no in some of the situations discussed?
5. Why is it loving to set limits on sessions and terminate them when the time has come to end them?
6. What harmful emotions are generated in a counselor who tries to respond to anything and everything the counselee requests because he feels he should?
7. What is the standard length of time for most counseling sessions and why is that length of time sensible?
8. Do you think it is wise at the outset of counseling to promise the counselee that you will get all the problems solved? Why or why not?

CHAPTER SEVEN

What Do We Mean by "Abnormal"?

"Well, that's normal, isn't it?" I can't tell you how many counselees have uttered those words following some interpretive therapeutic observation about their feelings or behavior. And it is obvious to me that the counselee is hoping that I will confirm that the behavior is, indeed, normal.

We are all eager to believe that we are basically normal, even if we are seeing a psychologist for treatment. And, curiously, we want to be told that the very behavior we are working to change is, well, *normal*.

Yet the notion of counseling implies that something is *abnormal*. Why else would we treat it? Diagnosis is based on a discipline called *abnormal psychology*. The making of a diagnosis implies the ability to distinguish the normal from the abnormal. And the entire enterprise of counseling and therapy depends on the assumption that there is a way of discriminating normal from abnormal behavior.

What do we mean by *abnormal* behavior? How can we determine what is *abnormal*? In order to declare something abnormal, we need to have a clear picture of what is normal. The words "normal" and "abnormal" come from the Latin root of the word "norm." Where are norms for human behavior to be found?

If you read the first chapter or so of any textbook on abnormal psychology, you will find that the author has trouble coping with this notion. The reason is that there are no scientifically valid criteria for human behavior. No norms. So the writers of these texts must rely on some very unsatisfactory invented norms. They are unsatisfactory because no single set of norms holds up across the varieties of bahaviors which the textbook will go on to label *abnormal*. Here are some of the criteria which are used in the practice of psychology to classify behaviors as *abnormal*:

SOME TEXTBOOK CRITERIA FOR ABNORMALITY

1. *The statistical criterion.* According to this criterion, a behavior is abnormal if its incidence in the population is infrequent. Thus, an IQ of 60, a catatonic stupor, and the delusional belief that one is God are all abnormal because they are extremely unusual among human beings.

But other behaviors which are also called *abnormal* are not at all rare. What about alcohol abuse, marital maladjustment, and the unrealistic management of anger? These behaviors are all too common in the population, yet they are among the syndromes commonly diagnosed and treated as *abnormal*.

2. *The personal discomfort criterion.* According to this criterion, a behavior is abnormal because it creates or involves a good deal of personal pain and psychological distress. Hence, obsessions such as the intractable worry that one has committed the sin against the Holy Spirit and cannot be forgiven are abnormal. Depression is also abnormal by the criterion of personal discomfort.

But manic psychotics are frequently high and euphoric, denying that they are the least bit uncomfortable; sociopathic personalities are likely to be comfortable even when causing great harm to others as they further their own shortsighted ends. Many of the sexual disorders are quite pleasurable and, of themselves, involve no personal discomfort.

3. *The social noncomformity criterion.* According to this criterion, some behaviors are abnormal because they violate recognized social norms. And this criterion does work for some syndromes described in the diagnostic manual. Child molesting, exhibitionism, and voyeurism are in violation of social norms and are therefore treated as syndromes. But the Supreme Court in the United States has declared that prayer in public school classrooms violates social norms and is unconstitutional—yet there is no such syndrome in the diagnostic nomenclature (terms and categories). Meanwhile, both smoking and abortion are legal and socially approved in the United States. Yet both are abnormal according to the most reasonable criteria.

Perhaps the reader can now see that science cannot provide suitable criteria for normality in human behavior. This pursuit becomes an embarrassment to the psychologist-authors of textbooks. If the reader has an abnormal psychology text available, reading through the chapter on criteria will demonstrate the point again. The truth is, there is no clear definition of abnormality apart from the revealed will of God.

SIN AND PSYCHOPATHOLOGY

There is an absolute criterion available, but it is not available through scientific research or observation of behavior. We find it only through the revealed will of God given in the Scriptures. That is where abnormal behavior is defined. And it is called "sin." Although the word "sin" has become a neglected term among those who desire to learn about behavior, they will have to resurrect it or maintain the present uncertainty about what is abnormal.

The call for a new look at the idea of sin has been issued by Dr. Karl Menninger in a book called *Whatever Became of Sin?*[1] Dr. O. Hobart Mowrer wrote an article for a professional psychological journal entitled *"Sin": The Lesser of Two Evils.*[2] Both writers call attention to the fact that moral concepts must be related to the notion of psychopathology or deviance in behavior.

The idea that there is only one true and reliable set of rules for what is pathological, or bad for man to do, is an old idea which has been rejected by many psychologists. They are thus left with no choice but to declare that human beings must develop their own criteria. These criteria are not fixed nor objective. They are not anchored in anything other than subjective values. Thus, they have never proved satisfactory. So we take the point of view in this book that absolute moral criteria exist and can be grasped and understood through study of the Bible. These absolutes are teachings about God's will for human behavior.

CHRISTIAN COUNSELING, THE ORIGINAL THERAPY

Long before there was a branch of medicine called *psychiatry*, and before the branch of philosophy called *psychology* ever began to deal with human soul pain, the Christian Church ministered to emotional and mental disturbances. For centuries, priests and monks in the confessional heard the difficulties of their brothers and sisters and applied the Word of God to help them. This counseling predates psychiatry by 15 centuries!

The best confessors were sought out, just as the best psychotherapists are sought out today, and people traveled from all over Europe to counsel with them. Just as psychotherapists do today, these counselors attempted to diagnose the difficulty and to provide advice and friendship to help the sufferer to health. They also had a theory about how emotional problems originated.

The historic Christian theory of emotional maladjustment held that emotional pain came from indulging in actions and beliefs which were not in accord with the revealed will of God. This behavior is called *sin* in the Christian view of man's troubles.

The entire Christian faith is a spelling out of the details of God's action in Jesus Christ to save human beings from sin. This action

---

[1]Karl Menninger, *Whatever Became of Sin?* (New York: Hawthorne, 1973).
[2]O.H. Mowrer, *The American Psychologist*, 1960.

was taken by God, not because He is full of hang-ups about certain behaviors, but because He knows that indulging in them will ruin human existence. Because God is a perfectly loving Father, He has done what any truly loving human father would do: He has made a way for His children to be saved from what destroys their well-being.

That Way, according to the Bible and the testimony of Jesus himself, is Jesus Christ. By His life of sinless obedience and His death and resurrection, He did all that is necessary to cure human sin with its attendant illnesses and hang-ups. Every maneuver of the Christian counselor amounts to an attempt to set this truth to work in the life of the counselee.

AN OLD DIAGNOSTIC MANUAL

The pastors of old even had a diagnostic manual. Of course it was revised from time to time over the centuries, but one of the earliest forms of this diagnostic scheme was written by a monk called Evagrius of Pontus (c. 346). Evagrius described a small number of behavioral traits which he had noted were related to human difficulty and suffering. Out of his list grew the descriptions known today as "The Seven Deadly Sins."

John Cassian brought the list to the West and incorporated the sins as diagnostic terms into two manuals[3] he wrote for monasteries founded by him at Marseille. Seven diagnostic categories called *The Seven Deadly Sins* thus found their way into popular usage. Many, many writers published discussions of the sins. Numerous subcategories were developed.

To help the reader understand how much Cassian's descriptions resembled current clinical diagnostic descriptions, I am going to include a paragraph from his discussion of the deadly sin of *sloth*. You will notice its resemblance to what we today call *depression*.

> Our sixth combat is with what the Greeks call *acedia* which we may term weariness or distress of heart. This is akin to dejection and is especially trying to solitaries, and a dangerous and frequent foe to dwellers in the desert; and especially disturbing to a monk about the sixth hour, like some fever which seizes him at stated times, bringing the burning heat of its attack on the sick man at several and regular hours. Lastly, there are some of the elders who declare that this is the midday demon spoken of in the ninetieth Psalm.[4]

THE SEVEN DEADLY SINS LISTED

Here is a list of the seven sins used as a scheme for diagnosis in an age when man's behavior disorders were universally considered transgressions against God's law:

---

[3]Cassian, *De institutis coenobiorum* (c. 420) and *Collationes Patrum* (c. 426–428).
[4]Cited in Wenzel, Siegried, *The Sin of Sloth*. "Acedia" in medieval thought and literature (Chapel Hill, N.C.: The University of North Carolina Press, 1967).

pride, envy, anger (wrath), greed (avarice), sloth, lust, gluttony

Be sure to notice that not one of these is "a sin" in the ordinary conversational usage of the term. Not one is a single act which anyone can "commit." They are traits. That's what made this list useful as the core of a diagnostic system for behavioral disorders.

To be sure, most of us are accustomed to using the word "sin" to mean single actions, individual chunks of behavior. If I tell a lie or steal a diamond or blaspheme God, I sin.

The Bible refers to another way to think about sin. At times, the writers of Scripture discuss sinful *traits* in a way that sounds as though they were talking of something inside, under the skin.

SINS AS TRAITS "UNDER THE SKIN"

For example, Peter urges his readers to "Put away all malice and all guile and insincerity and envy and all slander" (1 Pet. 2:1, RSV). Notice that the sins in this passage are not individual acts. Instead, they are described as qualities inside the readers. It is as if Peter was describing some things located in his readers' insides.

Malice, guile, insincerity, and envy were thought of as tendencies to behave in certain evil ways. And Peter talks as if those tendencies were within. This is precisely the way psychologists today think of hysteria, depression, or paranoia.

Psychologists look at such under-the-skin traits as dispositions to behave in certain ways. More precisely, they see them as tendencies to emit behaviors of certain definable classes. When they say that someone is *depressed*, for example, they mean that he has a disposition to engage in certain kinds of behaviors. That is, there is a high probability that he will talk about how bad he feels, look sad, lie around not doing much, say negative things about himself and his life, move more slowly than usual, and have difficulty falling asleep.

In exactly the same sense, when Peter writes that his readers have the trait *guile*, he means they have a high probability of engaging in behaviors of a certain kind: lying, putting up a front, pretending they're better than they are, making others think something that is not true, etc.

WHY WE NEED TO SPEAK OF TRAITS

When we describe people, we are practically forced to use trait terminology. We wouldn't consider it a very good description of Edna if her counselor merely listed some things Edna has done. For example, suppose the counselor told us, "Edna walked to a chair and sat down. Then she talked. Some of the things Edna has done today are: she ate breakfast, went sailing, shelled some peas, and darned a sock."

Of course some of that information could possibly be useful in understanding more about Edna. But no such list, however long, could be what we mean by description. It wouldn't be a description of Edna unless it included generalizations, terms which describe what Edna is habitually like.

For example, we would want the counselor to be able to tell us things like this: Edna is anxious, insecure, and abnormally disposed to think the worst of others' intentions. Those words tell us more than mere episodes out of Edna's stream of behaviors. They tell us about what Edna is likely to keep on doing unless something can be done to change her and to alter things we think of as "inside" Edna.

PSYCHOTHERAPISTS PROMOTE THEIR VALUES

Today, mental health workers usually label the traits they find troublesome as *problems* rather than *sins*. In this way they hope to avoid judging and condemning their counselees and to keep the discussion neutral in respect to values.

Some researchers have turned up evidence that the effort to avoid values and judging is extremely unsuccessful. Psychotherapists push their own values on counselees no matter how hard they say they try not to.

Meanwhile, they avoid the term *sin* and thus may omit responsibility and moral accountability. Often their counselees may get the impression that they are helpless victims of something called "mental illness" visited on them by mean parents or a heartless society. When someone is led to think he is a *victim*, he is encouraged to forget that he is a responsible human being who has been contributing to his own misery, and who must answer for his own behavior. And it is difficult to convince such a person that he must take steps to help himself.

CHRISTIAN COUNSELORS TALK OPENLY OF SIN

While it is certainly important not to engage in condemnation and callous judgments, the Christian counselor cannot take a morally neutral position, any more than the secular counselor does in actual practice. Unlike the secular counselor, the Christian counselor won't even pretend to be morally open. Instead, he lays his cards on the table. He will openly and deliberately help the counselee to determine what is sinful and contrary to the truth in his behavior and beliefs. Then he will find it natural to label deviant behavior and destructive misbeliefs for what they are: sin. But the Christian counselor will not get far if he engages in put-downs or self-righteous finger-pointing.

Instead, the counselor and the counselee will agree to collaborate in the task of determining what the counselee is doing, believing, and telling himself to make himself miserable or to cause his behavior to backfire. And always the norm which undergirds the whole endeavor will be the Bible with its revelation of God's will for man's beliefs and actions.

Several writers, besides Menninger and Mowrer, have called attention to the fact that emotional disorder is related to sin. Jay Adams (in all his books, *Competent to Counsel*, for example) has pointed to the need to reinstate Christian categories in our dealing with deviant behavior. Marie Chapian and I have published a book on the subject of sin and how to deal with it.[5]

As we proceed in learning to diagnose and counsel people with emotional problems, we will utilize the familiar psychiatric diagnostic nomenclature (terms and categories), but will try to remain aware of the fact that all of these represent the presence of dispositions to belief or action which are at variance with the will of God and thus with reality.

COUNSELING TO "SAVE FROM SIN"

It is imperative to emphasize that the Christian counselor works with God himself to accomplish in the counselee the very thing God came to do for him in Jesus Christ. Jesus came, according to the Bible, to "save people from their sins." To save them from the doing of their sins, not just the consequences of sin and misbelief. Christian counseling, shaped by the Spirit of God in the counselor, works together with God to bring about the separation of people from their sins (and thus, from their psychopathology as well).

A DIAGNOSIS OF ANXIETY

Let's look at an example of how to diagnose a counselee's difficulties with due attention to the *sin* percolating itself through and through his troubles. The diagnosis of the student before us is that of anxiety. What follows is a description of his complaints from a clinical point of view:

The counselee exhibits tension, apprehension, and vague, free-floating anxiety which might originate from a socialization process in which parents both demanded perfection and kept the child uncertain as to what the standards for the child's performance actually were. The consequences in this case would be: fear, low frustration tolerance, a view of the world as cruel, limiting of activities to avoid anxiety, and difficulty concentrating and thus learning. In addition, the counselee suffers from periodic intense

---

[5]William Backus and Marie Chapian, *Why Do I Do What I Don't Want to Do?* (Minneapolis: Bethany House Publishers, 1984).

anxiety attacks in which the heart pounds, sweating is profuse, counselee can't get enough air, dry mouth, light-headedness, diarrhea, shaking, and the need to urinate frequently. This might all be precipitated by behavior which is either unacceptable to the ego or fantasized unacceptable to the ego, or by fear of disapproval and rejection by others.

The foregoing is a typical description of a psychological illness from a psychological diagnostic source.

It all sounds so neutral and "medical." How can sin be involved in such a description? A counselor therapist might utilize such a description. Notice that there is nothing in the above analysis which a Christian therapist would need to reject. But he might want to add to it.

HOW CAN SIN BE INVOLVED?

For example, a person unclear about his standards of performance might not know or give due attention to what the Lord actually requires. Or lack of clarity might suggest that the person understands God's requirements of him, but is concerned and uncertain only about human requirements. In this case, he actually believes something like the following:

I am liable to make a mistake, to blow it. And if I do, that will be a dreadful disaster beyond which there is no hope. I probably won't make it through school, especially at this rate. And furthermore, there's this awful anxiety. People will notice and if they do they'll decide I'm not fit to graduate. It's so dreadful that I can't control it and to top it off, everyone is going to reject and disapprove of me. Nothing could be more horrible!

Notice that these beliefs which run through the counselee's head and cause his autonomic nervous system to shift into emergency mode are contrary to facts revealed in the Word of God. If we were to distill the truth of the Word and replace the student's harmful beliefs with that truth, it might go something like this:

Of course I can make a mistake. I'm far from perfect and can't expect that I will suddenly produce pure, unadulterated perfection. When I make a mistake, most people will understand, because they're not perfect either. It's usually not a major catastrophe. Actually, I know that God has sent Jesus to rescue me from my sins and mistakes and their consequences. I can trust Him to do the job right and quit telling myself how utterly horrible it will be if some human being decides not to like me. Furthermore, getting through school is *not* the most important thing in the world. If I should, for some reason, fail to make it through school, God is still in charge and He has a perfect plan for me.

The sensitive reader will be able to compare the two samples of inward verbal behavior and note that the first one contains symptoms of several sinful dispositions: pride, idolatry (loving career more than anything else, including God), self-rejection, man-pleasing, for example.

MISBELIEFS DON'T JUST HURT—THEY ARE SINFUL, TOO

Such things will be noted in the diagnostic formulation of the Christian counselor, too. Clearly, the misbeliefs themselves, harbored and repeated over and over, aren't merely painful and unpleasant. They are sinful. And the truth, by contrast, when it replaces them, does more than improve the counselee's emotional tone; it also pleases his heavenly Father.

SUMMARY

In this chapter we have seen that the entire discipline of Abnormal Psychology is at sea without a compass regarding the concept of deviant or abnormal behavior. Abnormality without a fixed norm is meaningless. And the attempt of secular psychotherapy to omit norms for morality in behavior has failed to work. Christian counselors have an ancient tradition which predates contemporary psychiatry by many centuries. In this tradition, the syndromes used for diagnosis were often *The Seven Deadly Sins*, and the task of counseling was to assist people in becoming free from their sins. This is the task of Christian counselors today. Finally, we demonstrated with the aid of a diagnostic description how sinful beliefs and values contributed to the misery of anxiety on one counselee's situation.

FOR REVIEW AND DISCUSSION

1. With what notion does the first chapter of nearly any text on Abnormal Psychology have to struggle, perhaps in vain?
2. Why are the norms in scientific psychology so unsatisfactory?
3. What are some of the criteria used to determine when behavior is normal or abnormal?
4. Show what is unsatisfactory about each of the criteria you listed in #3.
5. Where can you find an absolute criterion for human behavior? Give an example of such a rule or criterion.
6. Give a historical reason why the Christian Church should not take a backseat to psychiatry and psychology in counseling.
7. Tell what traits are.
8. What are the seven deadly sins?

9. Show how they are different from individual sinful actions.
10. Why do mental health workers label some traits as problems rather than sins?
11. Should the Christian counselor avoid using the term *sin*?
12. What did Jesus Christ come to earth to do for people?
13. How can the counselor view his work as cooperating with God?
14. Show what is sinful about some common misbeliefs. Show how the truth which replaces them can be pleasing to God.

CHAPTER EIGHT

Truth, the Fiery Core of Counseling

"I'm a hopeless person and there's no way out," Gene thought as he structured a plan to kill himself with carbon monoxide. He believed something devastating to human beings. Was it true?

"I can't stand anxiety!" Millie told me at the session when we were working out a program for her to begin leaving her protected cocoon of isolation to meet other people. She was convinced of the validity of her statement. Was it really true?

"Other people shouldn't treat me the way they do!" You will hear that statement from more than one counselee. Is it really so?

"I *have* to have someone to love me." "There's no way things are going to get better." "I desperately *need* drugs, alcohol, or banana splits." These notions are believed tenaciously by people seeking help. Are the statements true?

Jesus made the point that the question of truth is primary. It makes a great difference whether you know and believe the truth or tell yourself clusters of untruths. "If you continue in my word, you are truly my disciples, and you will know the truth, and the truth will make you free" (John 8:31–32, RSV). Every psychotherapist and counselor experiences the factual precision of that statement many times each day. People are riveted to their problems and sicknesses by believing notions which are untrue; and they begin to experience freedom the *very moment* they believe and tell themselves the truth instead.

The core of this book is here. We have come to the continental divide, the great watershed. What we have said up to now is peripheral. All treatment to succeed permanently must rest its validity on the power it has to inculcate truth. No matter what details and methods we learn in diagnosing and treating problems presented to us, the underlying event taking place in the counselee will be the substitution of truth for error and correct belief for wrong belief.

At this point, I fear the reader's reaction. Perhaps you are misunderstanding, as so many do when they are first exposed to the startling assertion that *truth heals*. You may be thinking, "Yeah, sure. But it doesn't work for me. I know all that Bible stuff. And I've already told myself to shape up and it hasn't helped."

It is critically important to recognize that most of us have been brought up in a culture where it is officially unsophisticated to believe in such a concept as *truth* in any but the most metaphorical sense. Someone tried to count and concluded that the average person in our world tells two hundred lies a day.

It is widely believed that there is no absolute truth since people have varied opinions about nearly everything. Truth, it is assumed, is whatever suits your purpose at the moment. Truth is whatever you choose to say to get what you want. The primary function of words is to manipulate behavior, not to communicate fact-based reality. Or, truth is words you tell yourself to make yourself feel better rather than to get yourself into sharp contact with reality as it is outside your skin.

Please look again at the statements quoted from actual counselee depositions given above. Think. Are they factually so? Clearly, the reader who has an anchor in the truth as it is revealed in Jesus Christ will see that none of them are literally correct. Unless your definition of truth is the same as your definition of a person's opinion, unless you are a casualty of a culture believing that there is no absolute truth, you will conclude that they are contrary to experience and revealed truth.

REMEMBER

The man or woman who would set others free must first experience freedom.

THE COUNSELOR MUST LEARN THE TRUTH

The counselor can well afford to take the time and make the effort necessary to do a good job. But beyond all the learning of technique, he needs to learn the truth—the truth that sets free. I myself do the things I am teaching you to do, not just in treating my patients who come to me for psychotherapy, but in my own life. And I teach my family to do them too. The truth is not just a medicine which the doctor administers to the patient, but it is a way of life which the counselor can follow to experience exactly how the doing of the truth will set him free from his own hang-ups and behavior problems.

You can be helped in applying the truth to your own situation through the book *Telling Yourself the Truth* by Marie Chapian and myself. There we offer practical teaching to the person who desires to begin walking in the truth for increased emotional and behavioral wholeness.

WHAT IS THE TRUTH?

Here at the outset it is important for your progress to grasp just what I mean (and I believe Jesus means in John 8) by *the truth*. The biblical notion of truth includes several dimensions, all of which offend the contemporary mind because they require agreement that the truth is absolute. This absolute truth is:

1. *A Person.* How can a Person be the truth? You can begin to grasp this notion only if you clear your mind of the Western idea that truth is a foggy abstraction and try to get in touch with the Hebrew way of thinking about truth. Here, truth is doing what you have said you'll do. God is true because His Word always comes true. In Jesus, God actually carries out the ransoming of mankind which He had promised to perform from the very day of man's fall into sin. Therefore Jesus is the "only-begotten God" being true to His promise. He is *the Truth* because He is God coming true or being true to His Word.

2. *The Word* which conveys information about that Person and His work of doing what He said He would do. This good news is the gospel, a message which in its very substance is the truth.

3. *The Bible* is the supreme resource for those who have a desire to come in contact with the truth. It is supreme for many reasons, but one which is pertinent here is that it has been composed under the direction of the Spirit of God so that in it the truth is especially protected from error. That same Spirit will meet the person seeking to obey God and will positively lead that person into the fullness of the truth.

4. *Any statement whose meaning fits the way things really are.* Truth of this kind resorts to empirical observation and to reasoning, as well as to revelation, for its basis. We can trust such sources because we can trust what God has revealed to us about them. The God who always says and does what is true made human senses and reason. It is therefore possible to consider them reliable and to take their conclusions as truth—with one important qualification. Truth conveyed by our senses and our reason is always subject to correction by further and more complete evidence, and it is always subordinate to God's revealed truth.

Personal bondages from which the truth has power to deliver include such ordinary human difficulties as habitual persistent behaviors we feel powerless to stop repeating. Smoking, overeating, blow-ing our tops, and drug-taking are examples.

A second group of truth-sensitive human difficulties are persist-ent, inappropriate, negative emotions like anxiety, resentment, ir-ritation, and depression. For purposes of clarifying the dynamics of truth therapy in this chapter, we will focus on persistent, painful emotions. The truth can set us free from this sort of misery.

WHAT IS AN EMOTION?

It will be useful to focus our attention at this point on an analysis of emotion. To see what an emotion is, we can try to remember what happened in ourselves the last time we experienced a powerful emo-tion. Please try to think back to such an event in your own life. Usu-ally, when I ask a class to do this, they have some difficulty telling me what an emotion is, even though all of them have experienced emotions many times. The dialogue often goes like this:

Backus: What is an emotion?
Class: A feeling.
Backus: Yes, that's a synonym for it. What can you tell me about emotion?
Class: It's a reaction.
Backus: Of what? What's reacting?
Class: Your mind?
Backus: Is that all? Is an emotion a purely mental event?
Class: No, your body reacts too.
Backus: What happens in your body when you're having a strong emotion or feeling—fear, for instance? Suppose I made one of you get up here and give a lecture without any chance to prepare. What would be going on in your body?
Class: I'd be shaking all over.
Backus: What else?
Class: My heart would pound so hard I'd think it would be about to slam right through my chest.

Your own recollection of physical events occurring when you felt strong emotion will probably include many of the following events: heart rate increases; blood pressure rises; face flushes or pales; palms, underarms, face, and forehead sweat; intestinal motility increases (or decreases); muscles tense; urination becomes frequent; muscles trem-ble; pupils dilate; respiration rate increases; mouth feels dry; head feels light . . .

The list may not be exhaustive, and no one person at any given time needs to be aware of all the events. In fact, people vary greatly in their awareness of bodily changes like these. But everyone has experienced some of them and can identify with them.

One more component must be mentioned, and it is really quite central to our discussion. The bodily events listed occur quite similarly in all sorts of emotions. The same bundle of responses with little discernible variation occurs whether we are afraid or angry, in love or sexually aroused. The purely physical syndrome we have described is known variously as the Arousal Syndrome, the Fight or Flight Response, the General Adaptation Syndrome (G.A.S.), because it is largely undifferentiated according to the particular emotion one is experiencing. Thus, whether you walk into your kitchen and find your one true love waiting for you or a venomous cobra coiled to strike in front of the refrigerator, your response will likely be very much the same set of reactions.

So what makes it possible to know whether we are, at the moment, feeling the room rock because we are madly in love or scared to death? Angry enough to be livid or all fired up with enthusiasm?

I once heard Dr. Val Arnold describe an interesting experiment which demonstrates that people don't always know precisely what emotion they are experiencing when they are in a state of arousal. It seems that the experiment was arranged for a weekend night at a nurses' dormitory. As men called at the desk for their dates, they were directed alternately to the first-floor waiting room or to one on the seventh floor. And the receptionist apologized, "We are sorry the elevator is not working so you will have to walk up."

Then each man was questioned by a researcher. The subject was asked to estimate with a number between 1 and 10 what his level of sexual arousal was at that moment. As you might have guessed, there was a difference between the men who waited on the first floor and those on the seventh. Those who had had to climb stairs had interpreted their high level of autonomic nervous system responding as "sexual arousal" and thus gave themselves higher numbers than those in the other group.

BELIEF, THE MISSING INGREDIENT

Evidently, the missing ingredient, the element in an emotional response which enables us to identify the emotion we are currently feeling, is a belief. What the men waiting for their dates believed about their current situation determined their conclusion that the rapid heartbeat they felt was due to sexual arousal.

If you believe that the object coiled in front of the refrigerator is a cobra, your belief will enable you to label your arousal as "fear." If you believe the object in your kitchen is your sweetheart, your belief will enable you to label your feelings as "love." It is evidently our interpretation of the situation which enables us to know what specific emotions we are feeling.

Now perhaps we can identify what an emotion is. It appears to be a state of physiological arousal together with belief or interpretation of the situation eliciting the arousal. In other words, an emotion is a response to a stimulus. And what is critical for our purposes is this: the stimulus to which our bodies are responding is a belief in our heads!

WHAT IS AN EMOTION?

An emotion is a response of a number of physical systems to something we believe.

You will apply this key insight in counseling by asking yourself, when a counselee wants help with persistent negative emotion, "To what belief or set of beliefs is this unwanted emotion a response?"

THE INTERNAL MONOLOGUE

In order to find out, you will need to investigate a domain in the counselee's psyche known as the "internal monologue." Some psychologists have referred to this function as the "self-talk."

The *internal monologue* can perhaps best be understood by imagining that your brain has a small cubicle in it. Perhaps you can picture a little booth like the cab of a truck right under the top of your skull. In this cubicle sits a verbose little person who does nothing but talk—to you. You can begin to appreciate why some psychologists have called him or her a "monologue" when you realize that the talk evidently proceeds through all your waking and sleeping hours. Yes, even while you're asleep the self-talk continues.

Investigators at university sleep centers hire students to occupy special beds in the laboratory. Wired to machines which measure brain waves, heart rate, blood pressure, and so forth, the subjects fall asleep while an investigator monitors and records their functioning.

It used to be thought that mental activity pretty well stopped during stage-four sleep. At that stage, the brain wave is a large, slow "delta" wave, and the person is in the deepest level of sleep. No dreaming occurs.

But when experimenters began waking subjects out of stage four and asking them to report, the scientists got a shock. The subjects frequently would rub their eyes and announce things like, "I was just thinking about that test I have to take tomorrow!" Imagine! That little person under your skull chatters nonstop, probably even while you sleep!

WHAT IS THE INTERNAL MONOLOGUE?

It is a function in every person's mind which talks, probably night and day.

EMOTION AND THE INTERNAL MONOLOGUE

Now we are ready to tie emotion to the internal monologue. You will remember that an emotion is a response to a stimulus, and that the stimulus must always be a belief or set of beliefs. But we are not constantly responding emotionally to every single belief we hold stored on the shelves of our minds. That would be impossible.

Just think of all the things we believe at any given time! Such facts as the annual rainfall in Berkeley, the name of the chairman of the annual church dinner, the precise wording of John 3:16, the eighth commandment, and the multiplication tables. We all have countless beliefs about politics, religion, interpersonal relations, and the values we assign to our various aims in life. Clearly, we are not at this moment responding to or even thinking of most of these millions of beliefs.

Our emotions at this given moment are responses to the beliefs we are, at this instant, repeating to ourselves in our internal monologues.

Thus, a feeling or an emotion is a result of what we are at the moment believing and telling ourselves from within. And a persistent, unwanted, negative emotion is our response to persistent repetition of certain beliefs in our internal monologue—repetition we may be only dimly aware is occurring.

RANDY'S "BAD DAYS"

Randy was having a bad day. He frequently had such "bad days," he told me, and he really didn't know what caused them. "Just got up on the wrong side of the bed, I guess, Doc," was his explanation. We spent an hour trying to get at what Randy was telling himself on his bad days, and with the two of us collaborating, we learned that Randy had, on the previous evening, walked into a grocery store and found his friend working as a stock boy.

The problem for Randy was that he had applied for the job and had not heard any more about it. Randy had always thought of his friend as just a bit less able, intelligent, and generally capable than himself. And, although Randy was not really paying attention to the things he was telling himself because they were just above the threshold of awareness, he had been propagandizing himself with some of his favorite notions. Here are some of the beliefs Randy was rehearsing in his internal monologue:

"Things should go as I want them to and when they don't, it's most aggravating and upsetting."

"It's outrageous that George got the job I wanted, and especially irritating that George *really* isn't as qualified as I am."

"Jobs should go to those who are really best able to do them and when it doesn't work this way, I have every reason to get offended."

Later, we collaborated on working out ways for Randy to change some of the beliefs he was using to upset himself. As a result, Randy stopped having "bad days" and began practicing the truth. At this point, we won't take time to look at the reasons why Randy's beliefs were false nor at the truths he learned to replace them.

The main point to note here is that Randy's emotions were shown to be responding to the beliefs in Randy's internal monologue with which he was actively, though at a low level of awareness, brainwashing himself.

If you are not yet certain that persistent negative and unwanted feelings are consequences of beliefs, you may experiment on yourself. Wait until you experience anxiety or anger, depression or nervousness. And at the moment you become aware of your bad feelings, ask yourself, "What am I telling myself right now?" You will probably become aware of thoughts which connect as closely to your unwanted feelings as Randy's beliefs connected to his emotions on "bad days."

MISBELIEFS AND MARTIN LUTHER

The thoughts which elicit such feelings are untrue. I believe Martin Luther described accurately the process we are talking about. He labeled these offending notions *misbeliefs*. In his explanation to the sixth petition of the Lord's Prayer, Luther spells it out.

> God indeed tempts no one; but we pray in this petition that God would guard and keep us, so that the devil, the world, and our flesh may not deceive us nor seduce us into misbelief, despair, and other great shame and vice; and though we be assailed by them, that still we may finally overcome and obtain the victory.

Note well the chain of events.
1. *The sources of trouble*: the devil, the world, the flesh.
2. *How they work*: they seduce and deceive us into *misbelief* (erroneous notions about how things really are) so that we repeat these notions in our internal monologues.
3. *Result*: despair (depression, hopelessness and other tormenting

feelings and emotions), shame and vice (bad behavior contrary to God's will and even to our own desires as Christians).

4. *Good news*: we can overcome and obtain the victory over the attack we are experiencing, even if we have been assisting the attackers with our own self-talk.

Misbeliefs in the internal monologue are the target of the counselor's work. The Christian counselor will be intensively involved with the counselee in trying to locate these misbeliefs, harbored and reiterated endlessly by the counselee to himself. You will be a better counselor if you know in advance what to expect.

THREE MISBELIEFS IN DEPRESSION

In depression, for instance, investigators have discovered and every counselor can confirm, that there are three standard misbeliefs. Depressives repeat these notions to themselves over and over again.

They all involve devaluating. Depression seems to be the disease of devaluating everything. Especially, depressed people engage in devaluation of the self, their daily lives, and their futures.

Look at the three misbeliefs related to depression:

Misbelief #1: "I'm no good." The belief in personal worthlessness is found in several variations. "I'm a failure." "I can't handle things as well as others." "I haven't got what it takes." "It doesn't seem possible that anyone could like me after they get to know me because I'm so dull and uninteresting," and so on. The changes on the theme of self-devaluation are endless, but the theme seems to be universally present in depression.

Misbelief #2: "My daily life is no good." The belief that nothing is really rewarding, that the activities one might engage in are all unpleasant and uninviting, that "nothing is fun anymore," that life itself is just not worth the effort is another theme nearly always present in the thoughts of those who are depressed.

Misbelief #3: "My future is hopeless." Most depressives believe, for instance, that they will not recover. The present misery will not improve. "I won't ever get over this." "I might as well be dead."

The counselor needs to understand how constant self-nagging with such misbeliefs can and does create and maintain feelings which are so miserable they may lead to suicide attempts. The processes of counseling, whatever they may be, therefore, must be such that they will lead to change in the counselee's beliefs.

Notice, please, that the misbeliefs we always find in depression are not true.

Because they are erroneous beliefs, they are subject to correction and replacement by the truth. You can look at your counseling task in these terms: You collaborate with the counselee in detecting his or her misbeliefs creating depression; you demonstrate to the counselee that his or her painful feelings result directly from the endless repetition of these misbeliefs in the internal monologue; and you collaborate with the counselee in disconfirming them and replacing them with the truth.

The end result of whatever you do should be that the counselee ceases his endless self-lacerating monologue of lies, and instead believes the truths which heal and free him.

Here we will briefly recount the truths which replace the misbeliefs of depression.

Truth #1: "You are a creature of infinite worth and value." The fact that God created you in His image and sent His Son to give His life a ransom for your freedom establishes that you have worth and value. Because of what you are in Christ and your eternal significance, you are a person of infinite interest and you have no business putting yourself down as you have been.

Truth #2: "Even a depressed person can find meaning and reinforcement in activity." One of the keys to treatment is to get the patient activated and doing things, even when he believes that the activity will be worthless and unrewarding. Nearly always the counselee discovers in the doing of the activity that it is far more rewarding than it appeared from a distance. The daily life of the Christian comes from the hand of God and is lived by God's call. It has value and worth because of that.

Truth #3: "God's Word says that the future is not hopeless." On the contrary, "we have been born anew to a living hope through the resurrection of Jesus Christ from the dead" (1 Pet. 1:3, RSV).

It is, of course, not sufficient to read Bible passages to a counselee or to simply repeat the truth in his hearing. Like anyone else, the suffering counselee can change his beliefs only on the basis of argument and evidence. You must work at changing beliefs—your own and the counselee's. Later we will discuss various activities you and the counselee can engage in which will result in change in beliefs and behavior.

HOW MISBELIEFS ARE GENERATED

A. T. Beck has described five habits of distorted thought which he calls major cognitive errors.[1] If you look carefully at them, you will

---

[1] A. T. Beck, *Cognitive therapy and the emotional disorders* (New York: Harper and Row, 1967).

see that they are common chinks in the armor of faith through which the fiery darts of the enemy can travel to pierce us where it hurts. Memorize these major errors. You will be able to detect them again and again in the faulty thinking processes of counselees as they defend their erroneous beliefs.

Cognitive Error #1: Selective abstraction. Here the sufferer is focusing only on certain details from a complex picture, using just those details to describe the entire experience.

"I just know nobody likes me," Roger complained, and then went on to give his reasons. The neighbor had failed to smile when he said "hello" that morning. Roger's secretary had forgotten to prepare coffee when he arrived at the office. A group of co-workers went to lunch without inviting Roger to join them. A rehearsal of his other interpersonal contacts for the day had revealed many positive events. But Roger, depressed, abstracted the negative from the others and used them to feed his belief that he was repulsive and unlovable.

Cognitive Error #2: Arbitrary inference. This is drawing a conclusion without evidence, or in the face of evidence to the contrary. "I know my next performance evaluation is going to be so bad I may lose my job," said Eleanor. Further questioning revealed that no one had reprimanded Eleanor at all over the period for which she was to be evaluated. "That's just it. They haven't said anything. I think they're saving it all for the review session," Eleanor reasoned in a purely arbitrary fashion. Notice that by this method she was able to argue from *the lack of criticism* that she was full of faults!

Cognitive Error #3: Overgeneralization. Drawing a conclusion on the basis of a single incident. The best example I can think of is the depressed patient who had gone to the kitchen to make coffee, turned on the burner, and found the pilot light had gone out. "Oh, the whole house is falling apart!" wailed the sufferer.

Cognitive Error #4: Personalization. This error involves relating events to oneself without clear evidence that they are so related. "The Joneses went home early, and I know it's because they can't stand me when I'm this way. I'm so repulsive it's a wonder they came at all!" Jane wailed. Questioning revealed that the Joneses stayed through a fairly long evening, did not go home until 11:30 p.m., and spoke repeatedly to Jane of the wonderful time they had had visiting with her. Yet Jane was able to conclude that the Joneses departed because they disliked her personality!

Cognitive Error #5: Dichotomous thinking. Classifying events into either/or or all/none categories when they really can be better understood as existing on a continuum. This misbelief device is very commonly used by neurotics to put themselves down. Thus, if one is not perfect, one is awful. If things don't go precisely as planned, they are hopelessly out of control. Many examples of dichotomizing will appear in the dialogues between counselor and counselees.

SUMMARY

In this chapter, you have learned that truth is the fundamental ingredient of wholeness or mental health. If you wish to be an effective Christian counselor, you must experience for yourself the freeing power of the truth. You can help others on the basis of your own experience of the freeing power of truth. Any accurate statement of the way things really are is truth. Emotions are responses of a number of physical systems to the things we really believe. When those things are not true, our emotions may go askew. Our attention must be on the counselee's internal monologue where the things truly believed are applied day and night in interpreting life. If the internal monologue is constantly processing painful misbeliefs, the counselee is miserable and needs to learn to replace those false beliefs with the truth. Counseling must involve helping the counselee to replace misbeliefs with truth. Counselees may be given insight into the devices they use for creating misbeliefs, chinks in their armor through which the enemy can drive his darts home.

FOR REVIEW AND DISCUSSION

1. Recall some common beliefs with which people make themselves unhappy.
2. What did Jesus promise would set people free?
3. How is it possible to "know" a great deal of truth and still be troubled and *un*free?
4. How can a person be the Truth?
5. Name some human difficulties from which the truth can free us.
6. What is an emotion?
7. What are some physiological events we experience when we have strong emotion?
8. Show how our beliefs enable us to determine which emotion we are currently experiencing.
9. Describe the internal monologue.
10. Discuss the relationship between emotions and the internal monologue.
11. What did Martin Luther tell us about the sources of misbeliefs?
12. Give the three misbeliefs commonly associated with depression.
13. Replace them with the truth.

CHAPTER NINE

Get a New Mind

(Sin, the Root of It All)

We have seen that sins are appropriate diagnostic entities for Christian counselors to use when discussing what is wrong with counselees. So far, however, we have remained on the surface. Counselors of all persuasions attempt to get at the root of the human condition.

Of course, most of them don't. They try, but they don't. The older therapies, psychoanalysis included, operate with the idea that something is fundamentally wrong with human beings, and they seek to take it into account in their treatment programs.

The Skinnerians and other behaviorists think that nothing is deeply wrong with man and that nothing underlies the disorders that counselees present to them for treatment. So, for them it makes sense to change only surface behaviors by manipulating reinforcement conditions. There is certainly nothing wrong with changing behaviors by utilizing known behavioral laws, but the Christian therapist will want to go deeper. He knows that, even if he desensitizes the counselee until anxiety is gone, the grip of sin, death, and hopelessness must be loosened to bring about changes with eternal value.

Most thinking people throughout the ages have disagreed with the behaviorists, and have concluded that something is radically wrong with man. *Radically* means *at the root*. Freud thought it was the fact that man's deepest instincts clashed with society's norms. Marx thought it was society's not yet having progressed through the dialectic process to the culminating revolution of the proletariat and the classless society. The existentialists have supposed that the problem is man's finitude which clashes with his infinite imagination and aspirations, forcing the existential situation of utter despair. Some secularists today believe man's basic problem is religion, especially religion like that of biblical Christianity.

According to the Bible, the root diagnosis (what is radically wrong with man) is *sin.* Not just *sins,* not just individual acts which transgress God's laws, not even merely the sin traits described in the last chapter. There is, rather, a deep, pervasive, influential disposition in all human beings which is personified in every man's selfishness. Under this strong influence of sin's power people choose what God doesn't want for them. They oppose God, remain angry with God, and desire most what God hates most. The selfishness which is at work in every man brings forth actions and thoughts which challenge God's lordship, creates misery for the sinner, and brings hurt to others.

The Christian counselor needs to make this deep and radical diagnosis: *A strong root of sin underlies whatever difficulty my counselee presents to me.* As I trace back to the origin of his pathological behaviors or misbeliefs in the present, I will likely err unless I discover, not merely what others have done to hurt my counselee, but how the influence of sin and selfishness have led him to judge, condemn, and resent those he believes have mistreated him.

Christian counselors today have sometimes been led astray by secular psychology which often removes responsibility for his condition from the shoulders of the counselee. They readily attribute counselee difficulties to some past trauma or series of traumas visited upon the counselee by others, or to hurt feelings caused by the sins of others, or to powerlessness wrought by the helpless victimizing of the counselee by demonic forces.

I have seen Christian publications blaming all counselee problems on forces outside the counselee, acting upon the counselee, forces for which the counselee has no responsibility whatever. I recently saw an instruction manual for marriage healers which attributed all the harmful behavior of people in troubled marriages to demonic spirits rather than to the individuals themselves.

Entire books on so-called "inner healing" direct sufferers to events in their past which have left "hurts" within, and fail utterly to mention the need for the counselee to discern his own sinful heart reacting to those events with bitterness and unforgiveness, defensiveness and pride, anger and lust or gluttony. This literature must be seen as belonging more to the psychological and secular realm than to the spiritual and biblical realm. The notion that whatever we do or feel or think is caused by something else finally makes us nothing but machines.

"REPENT AND BELIEVE THE GOOD NEWS"

Jesus met people with a demand that they deal first and foremost with the power of sin in their lives. And so did His apostles. Just like John the Baptist, the essence of their message to their hearers was the command to repent.

Now after John was arrested, Jesus came into Galilee, preaching the gospel of God, and saying, "The time is fulfilled, and the kingdom of God is at hand; *repent*, and *believe in the gospel*" (Mark 1:14, 15, RSV, italics added).

(Peter preached) *"Repent* . . . and *turn* again, that your sins may be blotted out, that times of refreshing may come from the presence of the Lord" (Acts 3:19, RSV, italics added).

They considered it vital for people to deal with the root of their problems: sin. Not merely sicknesses and problems, irritations and complexes, but sin. Not simply individual sins, but the deep underlying power of sin. The treatment they prescribed was repentance and faith.

HELENA

Helena's mother died when the child was five. Her father was busy with his career and had little time to care for his daughter. So she was sent to live with her paternal grandmother and an aunt. She remained in this home four years. They doted on her, lived for her, and considered her their golden-haired princess. Helena's every wish was gratified instantly, and she, in turn, sought to please her benefactors.

Soon, Helena's father saw that his daughter was learning to expect all her demands to be met. So he sought a wife, largely, he believed, for the child's sake. He chose a woman who seemed strong and able to rear his lovely little girl.

Shortly, Helena came to live with her father and stepmother. The woman and the child clashed from the beginning. The new mother saw her little stepdaughter as spoiled. She determined to force a change. She also, in Helena's view, treated the father badly. Helena seized every opportunity to escape from her and to visit her grandma and aunt, where she was treated like a princess again. She begged her father to let her go. Each time he would reply that his marriage had been undertaken for her sake, and that she needed her stepmother's influence. "Helena," he said, "I married her so you would have a mother to take care of you."

In this way, Helena learned to feel enormous guilt because she believed that somehow she was responsible for her father's unhappiness. At the same time she was filled with the stepmother's criticisms of her, and began to reflect them internally so that she was constantly criticizing herself no matter what she did. The little girl learned to shape her conduct so as to keep the four adults in her life as happy as possible and to avoid the painful criticisms of her stepmother.

Finally, Helena, as a young adult, sought to alleviate her misery through psychotherapy. By then she was so self-critical that her many successes in life meant nothing to her. Also, she was unable to remain in relationships when they began to get close. Love, to her, meant obligation! Unconsciously, she told herself she was obligated to keep those she loved happy, just as she had learned in her childhood. When any new relationship approached closeness, it looked like another yoke to Helena. So she avoided and fled such bonds. Then she invariably felt guilty for hurting the other person, and that compounded her misery.

She was unable to change. We analyzed her misbeliefs and she saw them clearly. "I know that, but I can't change," Helena said to me again and again. The truth was plain, but somehow she couldn't become free to believe it.

At last the barrier revealed itself. Deep inside Helena, almost hidden from her awareness by her powerful feelings of guilt, there was fury. She was angry and resentful, not only toward her step-mother, but toward all the other adults in her life. She felt, but did not let herself notice, great resentment toward them for repeatedly hurting her with their demands and for constricting her life with their (to her) warped love. She "hated" her stepmother, and she harbored a fleshly belief that she "needed" the doting attention of others to survive. Furthermore, she believed it was only proper that others should give her unlimited praise and gratification. When, instead, she saw others expecting that she keep them happy, she felt great conflict. Her guilt, frustration, resentment, anger, and selfish demanding undergirded the misbeliefs we had unsuccessfully attempted to change.

Helena had to deal with her own sins. It was not enough to recognize that others had something to do with her difficulties. She needed to recognize and confess her own wrongdoing, past and present, toward those very people. And she asked and received forgiveness, letting God cleanse her through the saving death of Jesus Christ on the cross. She believed God meant it! Then, as a third step, by the Holy Spirit's enabling power, she literally turned her mind around. She forgave her mother for dying and leaving her; she forgave her father for choosing and supporting the stepmother; she forgave her stepmother for the barrage of criticism and teaching her to live in unrealistic guilt; and, finally, she had to forgive her grandmother and aunt for spinning their soft sweet web of obligation around her. Then, Helena accepted, in faith and trust, the teaching of the Bible that she had been nailed to the cross with Jesus. Because she had died with Him, the power of sin was broken for her. Believing and telling herself this truth broke its power over her misbeliefs and enabled her at last to change.

HOW TO REPENT

One of the duties of the Christian counselor is to teach counselees how to repent.

Many people believe that repentance is primarily beating your breast and saying how sorry you are for your sins. They view repentance as a bewailing process which has more validity when it is loud and tearful, more force if they can make themselves feel really and truly miserable while they're doing it.

But repentance is not working up a case of wretched feelings about your sins. Though you will begin to feel pretty bad about them when you notice their effect on God, on your relationships with others, and on yourself, it isn't feeling sorrowful that is the heart of repentance.

Repentance means, literally, "getting a new mind." It is only the Holy Spirit who can work true repentance in you. Believe that when you earnestly determine to change, the Holy Spirit is at work in you, renewing and changing your old sinful, angry, unforgiving mind, and replacing it with a new mind like the mind of Christ. (Look at Philippians 2 for a discussion of this new mind.)

Here are the steps you take:

1. *Confess your sins.* Most people do not like to confess their sins. They may not mind confessing sins they don't really commit, or sins that would not be too much disapproved by their relatives and friends, but they find it difficult to confess sins with which they are deeply involved and from which they suppose they are getting some good. They resist confessing sins which are greatly at variance with their own noble picture of themselves.

Instead, they become defensive. Psychological defenses are sometimes developed unconsciously for the purpose of lying to oneself about one's sins. *Denial* is the most commonly used defense. When I don't like something about myself, when it is too far from the picture of myself I ordinarily hold in my mind, I need only deny that it exists, then hide from myself what I am doing. Then, by *repression*, I simply put the issue out of awareness and bury it. We will all energetically resist becoming aware of the sins we deny and repress.

Confessing sins to someone else, once it becomes a habit, can make us more aware of what we are really like. This may not be especially pleasant, but it will be therapeutic. Forming the habit of admitting, freely, that we have done wrong, without trying to "explain," deny, or dress up our sins, will gradually acquaint us with ourselves and alert us to the true operations of the power of sin in us. Confession implies we are convinced that God is absolutely right and we are wholly wrong, and a thorough abandonment of all excuses for sin.

Confessing sins to God is important, too. Daily, pray for the Spirit of God to speak to you about your sins, specific episodes in which you acted under the direction of the sin power. These may have appeared almost innocent to you at the time. They may even appear innocent to others. But God can show you how the root is the specific sin over which you want to gain victory. Then tell God what you did without any excuses, admitting the full impact of your sinful behavior.

It is important to confess to other people, as well as to God. The counselor should treat sin revelations from counselees as confessions. Counselees should be encouraged to confess their sins to those they have wronged when this is relevant to becoming reconciled.

Admitting sin is the same thing as confessing it. When another person calls a sin to your attention, your flesh reflexively urges, "Deny it!" or suggests you point out some evil done by the other person. "Get the conversation away from your sins!" screams the voice of the flesh. Begin, instead, to admit your sins when they are called to your attention: "Yes, I think you are right. I did do that. I have a problem with that sort of thing, and I really appreciate your calling it to my attention."

2. *Believe that God is forgiving you through the atoning death of Jesus on the cross for you.* Tell yourself the truth that God's answer for your sins is Jesus' suffering and death. He paid the full penalty for them so that God can forgive them and refuse to count them against you.

3. *Forgive others who have sinned against you or failed you.* You cannot change your sins of anger, rebelliousness, hatred, and judging others without fully and completely forgiving them for whatever you believe they have done to harm you.

4. *Believe and tell yourself that the sin habit or root within you has no further power over you.* Visualize it being nailed to the cross with Jesus. Reckon yourself dead to it (Rom. 6). It cannot compel you any longer. You can walk free from it.

5. *Each day, and on every occasion when the issue comes up, tell yourself the truth: "I'm dead to that and it cannot make me do its program."* Inwardly challenge and argue against the flesh when it attempts to persuade you to go back into old territory, or to convince you that you cannot resist its blandishments. In Christ, you have power over the flesh. Tell yourself that truth again each time you need it.

I have purposely described these steps using the second person singular "you." The reason: Though these are steps through which the counselor leads the counselee, the counselor himself must take them to heart and daily repent of his own sins in order to remain spiritually alive and vitally prepared to help others to walk away free.

The result of leading counselees through repentance and crucifixion of the sin undergirding their misbeliefs will be that they will find therapeutic change facilitated when they attempt to challenge hurtful and maladaptive misbeliefs with the truth.

SUMMARY

The root underlying maladaptive behavior is ordinarily sin. We have seen that most systems of counseling have their own theories about what lies at the root of human troubles. According to biblical Christianity, a deep, pervasive, influential attitude of sin acts with force on the behavior of all human beings. It is this that undergirds most psychological difficulties. The counselor must not be led astray by the trends in secular psychology which may lead to blaming the environment for our maladaptive behavior. Occasionally, counselees will have difficulty changing what seem to be obvious misbeliefs. Look under the surface for long-standing sinful habits of anger and resentment, unforgiveness and blaming others. In this and most other counseling programs, counselees will have to learn how to repent. Repentance means "getting a new mind," and can be worked only by the Holy Spirit within. The steps involved include confession of sins, forsaking of sins, believing in God's forgiveness for the sake of Jesus Christ, forgiving others who may have sinned against you, and believing yourself dead to the power of sin. Each day, tell yourself the truth that you are free from the power of the sin root to force its program, free to walk in the truth.

FOR REVIEW AND DISCUSSION

1. Why do secular therapies so often fail to find the true root of disordered human behavior?
2. What would Skinnerian behaviorists say about the root of disordered behavior?
3. Tell what Freud and Marx respectively had to say about what is really wrong with man.
4. What is the biblical Christian counselor's root diagnosis?
5. What is *sin*, as distinguished from *sins*?
6. How have Christian counselors frequently been led astray by secular psychology?
7. What is wrong with attributing all the counselee's disorders to spirits or demons causing him to behave the way he does?
8. Rehearse the steps in repentance.
9. Tell what you know of repression and denial and their relation to confession.

CHAPTER TEN

"In the Beginning—God": The First Interview

The beginning counselor has taken the training course. Now he knows just enough to know that he doesn't know much. Especially, he is sure he doesn't know how to do it.

He is now about to face his first counseling hour. "Hour? Oh, Lord God, how do I do it? How can I fill up a whole hour when I can't think of enough wisdom right now to fill up a millisecond?" he thinks.

Remember, "In the beginning, God. . ." (Gen. 1:1). Believe that this beginning interview is God's hour. Turn it over to Him. Believe that God will, by His Spirit, direct the interaction between you and your counselee. And above all, believe that God, *not you*, will do the work of healing. Tell yourself that it really is His hour, to do with what He wants.

TELLING YOURSELF THE TRUTH BEFORE YOU START

Tell yourself the truth based on the fact that God can use the hour—whatever you do or fail to do. Counter your counselor misbeliefs: "I don't have to bring something out of myself to solve this person's problems. I don't have to lecture. I may get anxious and want to fill up the quiet spaces with 'wise-counselor-talk,' but I don't have to. God heals through silence too. Sometimes He heals best through silence. I don't have to accomplish everything this session. I can relax and concentrate on observing because there'll always be more sessions to work it out in."

Self-instruct. Giving yourself clear instructions by faith is a technique you can use in situations where you may otherwise get carried away with anxiety, anger, or frustration. Allow the Holy Spirit to give you instructions and then direct them to yourself. Talk to yourself—something like this:

"Relax, Mary. You can calm down and handle this well. You've had some training, and you can always just wait for the counselee to continue if you can't think of anything to say at a given point. Just take it easy and you'll make it."

"Take it easy, Pete. You'll make a few mistakes, sure, but the instructor said it would happen to everybody. And there's always a supervision session coming where you can talk over the situation and get some fresh guidance and direction from the supervisor. If you make a mistake, remember, the Lord's apostle says 'we all stumble in many ways' (James 3:2). Besides, mistakes aren't usually irreversible. Sometimes God works His best through our mistakes."

This self-instruction procedure has been shown effective in reducing nervousness because it will restore a sense that God is truly in control.

FOCUS ON ASSESSMENT

Determine that you will concentrate on assessment. Perhaps you thought we had finished discussing diagnosis and assessment. The truth is that we're going to be assessing during all the hours of counseling. During the first session you have with a new counselee, aim at understanding the situation, what is going on, what the problems are, and how they relate to what you've learned about psychopathology.

Consciously resolve not to offer the counselee quick and easy solutions to his problems, not to give him a Scripture verse and tell him to go home and apply it and all will be well, not to think you have to say something so the counselee will believe he got something valuable for his time. Your target, for now, is to gain understanding. Meanwhile, you will help your counselee understand some of what he can expect from you.

LEARN TO OBSERVE PEOPLE AND BEHAVIOR

Learn to observe. Practice observing people in restaurants and waiting rooms, grocery stores and parlors. School yourself in the truth: "Behavior usually means something. I can get messages from my counselee's actions, posture, tone of voice, facial expression, even his choice of a seat." Resolve, before you begin the first session: "I am going to ask myself what it means when the counselee talks first or when he waits for me to begin. I will observe carefully how the counselee treats me and consider what his treatment of me might communicate. Are his features fixed or mobile? Is his voice even and monotonous, or is it well modulated? Are his hands wet with perspiration? Do they tremble? How about gait? Notice whether his grooming is neat or sloppy. Is the counselee clean or not? Notice whether and how he smells. You can make some reasonable assessment inferences from all sorts of observations.

HOW TO ASK QUESTIONS

Ask questions about what you don't understand, and listen to what the counselee says and how he says it. Don't ask any more questions than you absolutely must. Ask questions designed to lead the counselee to tell you a lot without your saying anything. Not "Are you feeling bad?" but "Tell me all you can about your problems."

You don't want to develop a habitual interaction pattern like the following:

Counselor: What brings you in today?
Counselee: Trouble at home.
Counselor: With whom?
Counselee: My aunt.
Counselor: What kind of trouble?
Counselee: Every kind.
Counselor: What do you mean, every kind?
Counselee: Just what I said, every kind.
Counselor: What, for instance, does your aunt do?
Counselee: She acts like nobody has any rights.
Counselor: For instance.
Counselee: For instance, she sits in our living room.
Counselor: Sits in the living room?
Counselee: Yes.
Counselor: You don't like her sitting there?
Counselee: Not all the time, I don't.
Counselor: Does she sit there *all* the time?
Counselee: You got it.

The counselor will be ready to quit after an entire hour of this kind of dialogue. Incidentally, some readers may think I'm including this dialogue sample just to be funny. Not so. This kind of tit-for-tat exchange with counselees does happen. Many counselees expect their visit to a counselor to be like their visit to the doctor. There they expose their injury or swelling, answer the doctor's questions about when, what, how, and how long, and wait for the treatment and advice they've come for. If you fall into this tit-for-tat trap, it will be by allowing a question-answer pattern to develop in your interactions with a counselee.

A SAMPLE BEGINNING SESSION

The dialogue you will now read is excerpted from an initial interview with a 24-year-old single white male counselee. Notice how the opening sets the ground rules, so to speak, for the counselee. These instructions anchor in place the expectation that the counselee will work. They prompt him to describe fully the problem from his point of view. They also make clear that the counselee is to tell the counselor what he aims to accomplish.

Counselor: I would like to use this first session to set some goals for the two of us to work toward. I'll want to hear your story, your description of the problems as you see them, and your goals. Tell me what you hope you're going to accomplish through coming here. After that, I'll give you some feedback as to whether I think your goals are workable. Also I'll discuss with you what I think we ought to do to achieve them. Is that plan satisfactory to you?

Counselee: I guess so. Sure.

Counselor: Tell me about what you have in mind.

Counselee: Yes, well, I don't know if I can tell you what I want. I guess it all seems to stem from my nervousness. (Pause) [Here the counselor thinks diagnostically: Probably neurotic rather than personality disorder, especially if the nervousness really is his major focus. Wonder what he means. Anxiety? Agoraphobia? Social inhibitions? Shyness? Looks depressed, too. I'll just keep quiet and wait for him to go on.]

Here lately I've been tense a lot. Especially when I have to present a case. I'm a medical student. This quarter I'm doing a neurology clerkship and I'm expected to present at rounds. My attending is real nice and everything, but I still find myself so tense I'd like to run.

[Counselor thinks: Sounds like he is neurotic. No way is he psychotic, and I don't imagine he's behaving badly. Most likely diagnosis is performance anxiety. It makes him nervous to have to perform before someone who is evaluating him. Likely a competitive, hard-driving person who's telling himself he'd better be great or else. Performance is a big deal for him. Wonder if he has the same problem in other situations.]

Counselor: Pretty uncomfortable at those times, huh? [Just facilitating self-disclosure]

Counselee: Well, it's not the discomfort. I have more concern about what people will think of my presentation, especially if I make a mistake of some kind.

[By now the counselor has determined that the diagnosis is anxiety related to performance situations, and will probably decide on the diagnosis: *Social Phobia*, the official diagnostic terminology for irrational fear of exposure to scrutiny when performing. The counselor knows he should look for perfectionism. He also expects deep beliefs about personal inferiority in this young man. The session continues. We pick it up toward the end].

Counselor: Sounds like you'd like to feel more comfortable when you're doing things in groups, especially when you present at rounds. And you could use some anxiety reduction in other performance situations as well.

Counselee: That would be just what I want.

Counselor: We have a goal to work toward, then. I'm hearing you say that you worry some about what others think of you. That you even worry that they'll notice your nervousness. Is this accurate?

Counselee: I wouldn't call it worry, but I do try to keep people from seeing my nervousness. And, yes, I work extra hard to keep from being caught making any mistakes. I know I think about making a good impression socially too and more often than not, I seem to think I'm not making it.

Counselor: [Accepting counselee's perfectionistic denial that he worries and willingly using the *counselee's* wording] Shall we include increased comfort in social situations as one of your goals?

Counselee: I think I'd like to work on that.

Counselor: Dating situations also?

Counselee: Well, yes. Though I haven't really dated much.

Counselor: Due to fear of girls?

[No sooner are the words out of his mouth than the counselor knows he has made a mistake. The phraseology is much too heavy-handed for this perfectionistic young man. He is going to deny it outright.]

Counselee: Not fear of girls. I just get nervous about asking people to do things. Maybe it is a little harder to keep calm about the thought of asking a girl to go out with me.

[*Counselor thinks*: I need to go easy with this man. He regularly denies the wording in my interpretations and then substitutes his own words to say the same thing in softer language. I'd better back off a little.]

Counselor: OK, you're not really afraid of girls. It's just that you'd like to feel a little more comfortable when you are asking a girl to go out with you, and when you are actually on a date.

Counselee: That's what I want.

Counselor: There may be other goals coming up later. For now we have agreed that we'll work to reduce your nervousness or anxiety at rounds and in social situations, including dating girls. Is that how you see what we've done?

Counselee: Yes, exactly.

Counselor: Are you willing to do some homework?

[Homework is an intergral part of counselee progress.

With carefully planned homework assignments, the
counselee participates in the work of getting better, treatment extends into the hours between sessions, and changes
come more readily. Homework assignments should always be agreed upon together by *both* counselor and counselee, not merely imposed by the counselor.]

Counselee: Sure, if it'll help.

At this point, the counselor asks the counselee to keep a log of his
feelings of nervousness and the times that they occur. Recording the
situations which make him anxious will facilitate treatment by exposing causes. This information will confirm or require alteration in
the diagnostic formulation the counselor has made.

PRAYER

Now commit the entire counseling procedure to the Lord Jesus,
asking the Holy Spirit to direct everything the two of you have before
you. Lay out before God the goals and problems you have noted and
the tentative course the two of you have set. Pray that He will add,
alter, or delete from the plan to make it fit His plan for the life of the
counselee. Then together praise and thank Him for His promises and
the work He is about to do in the intricate human being whose life is
the material on which you are about to work.

SUMMARY

In this chapter, you have learned that you *can* get through that
initial interview. But you can do more than that. And what you are
to do is not what most beginning counselors think: come up with
solutions or answers. Nor are you just to "be a good listener." Instead,
you listen, look, touch, smell, feel, think, and formulate. You share
your formulations with the counselee to the extent he is ready to
accept them. And you set his switches to do the work of getting better
by working with you to achieve his goals.

FOR REVIEW AND DISCUSSION

1. What are some things you need to be ready to tell yourself before
   your first session of counseling?
2. Why is silence in a session no great disaster, even if you can't
   think of anything to say?
3. What are some self-instructions which have been effective in reducing counselor nervousness?
4. What is your major goal, as a counselor, during the first interview?
5. Find some places where you can go to practice observing behavior
   and making inferences. What ideas do you have?

6. What's wrong with asking too many questions?
7. What should the counselor try to impress on the counselee during the first session?
8. Discuss the usefulness of homework. What should it accomplish? How should it be given?

CHAPTER ELEVEN

What Do You Do for a Whole Hour?

Rick was the first graduate of our last counselor training class to see a counselee. After his initial session, his classmates gathered round him eager to interview him about his experience.

"What I want to know, Rick, is how you filled up a whole hour?"

"Yeah, what do you do with all that time? Did you think of things to say?"

"Did you pray?"

"Didn't you run out of things to do and just sit and stare at each other?"

Rick was enjoying his spot at the center of attention, so he just let them talk and ask questions. But, as I overheard all this, it occurred to me that nowhere in the course had I taught them how an ordinary bread-and-butter counseling session should run. I determined to include a session on that in the next round of training; and to include a chapter in this book for mapping out the procedure for an ordinary counseling session, to the extent that such a flexible and individually-oriented activity can be ordered in advance.

LET GOD'S SPIRIT TAKE CHARGE

"Ask him about his father," the words shot through my mind like a freight train roaring through a small town and temporarily shutting out all other noises.

I had no doubt that the Holy Spirit was intervening in the counseling procedure to bring about something new. Arlyn had seen me for several hours without making much progress against his emotional-spiritual malaise. He had talked at considerable length about his mother, for whom he had little respect, incidentally. He had even discussed his grandfather, a stern disciplinarian who had participated in Arlyn's training for about two years of his life. But, come to think of it, Arlyn had never mentioned his father.

As soon as I called the omission to his attention, I knew we were onto something. His normally impassive face registered helplessness and grief. Arlyn broke into sobs, then tears, and finally we were over the hump. The ensuing conversation was a watershed. The critical turning point in psychotherapy, for Arlyn, came at this juncture.

Enough about Arlyn. Our point is that you can expect direction from the Spirit of God. Jesus' promise (John 14:26) that the Holy Spirit, the Counselor from God, will teach you all things applies, I believe, to the ministry of counseling. Expect Him to visit you.

Whatever plan you may have for the counseling hour must be tentative and flexible enough so that the Spirit can direct. If you are too intent on following a prearranged plan, program, or course, you may be teaching a one-to-one class session, but you are not counseling in the Spirit. Let your intuition be a third ear (to borrow an expression from one of the old psychoanalytic authors) through which you remain attuned to the communication of the Counselor himself.

A TENTATIVE PLAN FOR SESSIONS

Here is an outline of a typical counseling session. Remember, it is only an outline, often interrupted, restructured, and changed by the three-way interaction between the Spirit of God, the counselee, and the counselor.

1. *Feedback on the last session.*
2. *Planning an agenda for the current session together.*
3. *Working on the agenda items.*
4. *Homework agreement for next session.*
5. *Prayer, usually with laying-on of hands.*
6. *Next appointment.*

Here is what happens in each of the outlined segments of the session:

1. Feedback on the Last Session

"Please give me some feedback on our last session. What I would like to hear about particularly is your impression or evaluation of the session, about anything in it that was particularly helpful to you, or anything that hurt you or upset you. Was there something I should have done that I didn't do? Or was there anything I did which you found especially valuable?" I usually explain to my counselees what I mean by "feedback" in some such terms as that.

Then I inform them that I will be asking for their feedback at the beginning of each session, and that I am interested in negative feedback as well as positive, although I want to know about both.

Occasionally counselees will give me a report on their experiences after the session rather than feedback on the session itself. I then thank them and assure them that I am interested in anything they have to tell me. I explain again that when I ask for feedback on the session, I am interested in what they have to say about our previous counseling session itself.

THE PURPOSES OF FEEDBACK AND HOW TO USE IT

Why do you want feedback on previous sessions? The purposes of feedback are to keep you in close touch with the counselee's feelings about you and the counseling process, to pull out and enable you to deal with negative feelings, and to inform you as to what interventions seem useful to the counselee.

Frequently counselees will say such things as, "It was great," "It was positive," "I enjoyed it," "It was helpful." When such general feedback is given, you may occasionally want to ask, "Anything that you found particularly helpful?"

Other common responses: "I really appreciated the prayer—it seemed to change the way I was feeling and give me hope." "You gave me something to think about; I hadn't thought before that I was talking to myself the way my stepfather did." "It really changed the way I understood my problem when you said . . ."

You will also receive negative feedback. "I was upset because you started so late—my time is valuable too, you know." "You were unfair to me, just making the whole illness my fault like you did." "I didn't think it was spiritual enough. My problem is spiritual and you're telling me it's chemical."

Not many of your previous life experiences will have prepared you for handling feedback well. It may be unfortunate, but nonetheless it's true that we don't customarily request and receive honest feedback from one another unless relationships have hit some sort of snag.

And, sad but true, the reflex most of us have developed is to become defensive if we receive negative feedback from our families, friends, or brothers and sisters in the Lord. Equally awkward for us is handling positive feedback. Compliments often make us flustered, red-faced, and tongue-tied.

So be prepared to deal effectively with the feedback you receive in counseling. First of all, tell yourself the truth that the Lord himself may be speaking to you through the observations of your counselee at this point. "I am going to learn something through this counselee" can be valuable self-instruction. It will set the stage for you to listen carefully rather than strain yourself to come up with an adequate reply.

Which brings us to the first rule on receiving feedback. Consider whether a reply is even necessary. Usually you don't need to answer. You can just thank the counselee and move on. Your purpose is to receive attentively, not to defend yourself or show off your social graces.

Occasionally you will ask the counselee to expand, clarify, or be more specific.

Sometimes you will want to express understanding for the counselee's feelings, assuring him that you appreciate his opening up to you.

Once in a while you will clarify something about which you have been grossly misinterpreted or misunderstood. When you are doing this, you will want to assure the counselee that you can understand why he feels as he does in view of what he thought you were saying. And then tell him what you thought you were saying.

DON'T BE DEFENSIVE!

Don't fall into the trap of defending yourself! Easy to say, but so hard to do. Even experienced counselors find themselves acting defensive almost before they realize what they are doing. For example, look at this bit of dialogue. It's what you must try to avoid:

Counselor: Feedback on the last session, please, Mike.

Mike: I didn't like it. I almost didn't come back today.

Counselor: That's no way to handle things. You should have told me about it. What was wrong with the last session?

Mike: I *am* telling you about it. I didn't like you reading me all those Bible passages. It felt like you were trying to cram religion down my throat.

Counselor: I *wasn't* trying to cram anything down anybody's throat. I *told* you that before I read to you from the Word. Anyway, Mike, it seems to me that you're being pretty unreasonable not wanting to receive what God has to say to you.

Mike: I can't handle that stuff right now. I don't understand it and it just confuses me. And you do cram it down my throat whether you think so or not.

Counselor: If I were you, Mike, I'd be more concerned about my spiritual condition. You can't get better if you keep rejecting the Word of God. I think you ought to listen.

Mike: I don't think this is helping me. I'm not coming back.

Counselor: You probably shouldn't. Not until you get a teachable spirit.

Of course, this counselor appears to be defending God, God's Word, truth, and righteousness. But really, he is only defending his own poor judgment and tactical blunders. The counselee has no way of dealing with this defensive behavior, so the counselee severs the relationship and goes out convinced that there is no help for him in the office of a Christian counselor.

Let's look at the way the counselor in the above dialogue *wished*

he had handled it and how things might have gone with this counselee:

Counselor: Feedback on the last session, please, Mike.

Mike: I didn't like it. I almost didn't come back today.

Counselor: Sounds serious, Mike. Would you tell me about what upset you?

Mike: The Bible passages. I wasn't ready for that. You sat there
and read to me out of the Bible for fifteen minutes and I
didn't get it. I felt you were cramming it down my throat.

Counselor: Like I was pushing something at you before you could
handle it, huh?

Mike: That's the way it felt. It's not that I don't want you to
work with the Bible. That's why I'm here, I guess. But
it's—I don't know—it's just the way you did it.

Counselor: The timing, maybe?

Mike: I think that's it. I did have some things I wanted to say,
and I felt like you read so much I couldn't deal with them.

Counselor: Maybe I ought to check with you before I do anything like
that again. Then you could tell me if you don't feel like
it's the right time.

Mike: That sounds great. I hope you don't feel bad. I do really
want you to tell me how I can get along better with God.

CLARIFYING MISPERCEPTIONS

Here is an example of useful clarification following feedback:

Counselor: Would you please give me your feedback about the last
session, Elena?

Elena: Well, it really has been bothering me. You called me
"neurotic," and I didn't realize you thought I was so bad
off. I guess I haven't thought about much else.

Counselor: That term really hit you hard, huh?

Elena: It did. I don't know for sure what it means. Maybe if you
would explain, I could at least understand better.

Counselor: I should have amplified and clarified more last time. I'm
sorry you worried about it all week. But I'm really glad
you told me how much it disturbed you. Actually, I thought
you'd feel some relief, since neurosis is usually not a severe or incurable emotional difficulty.

Elena: It isn't? I thought it sounded pretty bad when you said it.

Counselor: My mistake for using a term you didn't understand. I
meant that your problems are related to misbeliefs, untruthful notions you have learned to believe and repeat
to yourself, making you feel bad.

Elena: Then you think I'm not a hopeless case?
Counselor: Of course you're not hopeless.

2. Planning an Agenda

After receiving feedback and dealing with whatever is necessary, you can move on to invite the counselee to work on planning the current session.

"What's on your agenda for today?" "What would you like to work on today?" "What things do you want to deal with in this session?" So I ask the counselee to give me his plans for the session.

Initially, this will surprise those counselees who have come expecting that you will tell them what to do just as soon as you have come to a conclusion about the nature of the difficulty. So they may say, "That's up to you. You're the doctor." Or, "I don't know. That's why I'm here. What do you want to talk about?"

It is very important to develop a different set of expectations in both yourself and your counselee. Not that it isn't occasionally a temptation to tell the counselee what you think should occur. But, unless you can get across the conviction that counseling is work in which the two of you collaborate, and that the counselee must work at the business of getting well, you will likely experience nothing but frustration.

Right here is a good place to begin teaching. "It is up to you to decide what you'd like to work on and then begin doing the work of counseling by telling me about it as thoroughly as you can" is the message you want to get across by requesting the counselee to give you his agenda.

Collaboration implies that you too may have agenda items. If you do, supply them *after* the counselee supplies his.

I usually record the agenda and then try to control the session so that we actually cover all items. If some are not covered, we can hold them over until next time.

Here is how an agenda might look when you and the counselee have constructed it:

- Counselee wants to report on improvements noted over the past week.
- Counselee has several spiritual experiences he'd like to have us evaluate together.
- Counselor wants counselee to present his log of self-talk recorded for homework.
- New homework agreement to be reached before end of session.
- Prayer for healing of memories of counselee's early bad school experiences.

3. Working on the Agenda Items

Dora had not expected counseling to be like it was. She felt she had done her part of the work of counseling by getting her body into the counseling session. From there on, she assumed, it was up to the counselor to keep her interested, entertained, and occupied. Her answers to questions were fragmentary. Her waiting for the counselor to say something became painful for both her and the counselor. Finally, something had to give.

"Dora, counseling is your work, not mine. I'm here to help, if I can. But I can't do your work for you. I want to get you working at your problems right here in this session," the counselor finally told Dora.

More often it will be the counselor's own behavior that communicates to the counselee what is expected of him.

For one thing, a good counselor, seasoned with experience, won't be so quick to allay misgivings, anxiety, and unease because the experienced counselor knows that it is such uncomfortable states which motivate and prompt the counselee to work.

ARE WE GETTING ANYWHERE?

For example, here is a very common counselee gambit, often employed at the beginning of a session:

Fred: Are we getting anywhere or not?

Counselor: Well—why, yes, I think we are. I do have to know a good deal about you before I can help you, you know.

Fred: I suppose. We have been having sessions for two months, and I don't really know what we've accomplished. What *have* we accomplished?

Counselor: Oh, well, we have covered your early history. I surely know a lot more about your childhood. And all that takes time, you know, Fred.

Fred: What exactly are you going to do after you find out all you need to know?

Counselor: Well, then, we'll try to decide what you should do about your trouble. I'm sure things will go just fine once we know more.

Fred: Hmm. OK. What do you want to know today?

Notice the trouble the counselor is in with this dialogue. He has assumed responsibility for allaying Fred's misgivings, probably because he wants desperately for Fred to think the counseling is helpful and the counselor is doing a good job. But he is ending up with Fred off the hook and himself on the hook. He has practically promised to produce a cure for Fred. And Fred continues to believe that he can do his part by merely contributing information. Fred has no idea how much he will have to work at discovering his misbeliefs and activating change.

In contrast, study this bit of dialogue between that same Fred and an experienced Christian counselor who knows that healing is up to God.

Fred: Are we getting anywhere or not?

Counselor: Are you having some misgivings, Fred? Why do you ask?

Fred: Well, I just wondered if you thought we were making progress. I've seen you for about seven sessions, I think, and I'd like to know how I'm doing.

Counselor: You'd kind of like an expert opinion on your progress, huh?

Fred: Yeah, I would. I don't see what's happening as well as you do.

Counselor: Well, Fred, on this one you're the expert. What have you yourself observed about your progress?

Fred: I don't know. Sometimes I think I'm better. Have you found out anything about me yet? I mean, do you have an opinion on my case?

Counselor: Sounds like you think you might be better, but then again, you're not sure.

Fred: That's about it.

Counselor: Too early for you to tell, maybe, huh?

Fred: You think so?

Counselor: Maybe you've been thinking you'd like us to move a lot faster.

Fred: Well, I would like to get well.

Notice how the experienced counselor deals with Fred's question. He tries to find out what Fred is thinking about the counseling and about their relationship instead of simply wading in and trying to set Fred's mind at ease about how the counseling is progressing. He allows Fred to remain "on the hook" so that if he wants to answer the question about his progress he, Fred, will have to look to his own experience with the results of counseling. And, truthfully, who should know better than Fred how he is doing? After all, he, not the counselor, lives inside his skin.

HOW *NOT* TO GIVE REASSURANCE

Inexperienced counselors are apt to interpret the counselee's desire to get better as a demand on them to produce results. Then they become anxious and attempt to handle the counselee's tension with reassurance so that they themselves won't feel quite so inadequate.

Observe this sample:

Counselor: Well, what's on your agenda for today, Bonnie?

Bonnie: I just want to get rid of these thoughts. They're terrible. I don't know how long I can stand them.

Counselor: You want to talk about your obsessional thoughts. OK.

Bonnie: I've already told you all about them. They're still bothering me. What can I do about them? I want to get rid of them?

Counselor: We could try relaxation training. That's very good for obsessional thoughts.

Bonnie: I've tried relaxing. It doesn't help at all. I'm just more bothered by the thoughts than ever then.

Counselor: This kind of relaxation is different. It involves learning to relax all your muscles one by—

Bonnie: I've done that. Progressive relaxation? Yes, my last therapist tried that with me. I just wonder if I have a demon.

Counselor: We could pray about it. That's the only way to find out.

Bonnie: I had prayer and ministry at summer camp. It didn't help. But I still think the problem is spiritual, and I wish you'd try a spiritual approach.

Now study the following illustration of the work of a more experienced and relaxed Christian counselor:

Counselor: Give me your agenda for today, Bonnie.

Bonnie: I just want to get rid of these thoughts. They're terrible. I don't know how long I can stand them.

Counselor: Bonnie, what's your conception of how you "get rid of these thoughts"? How do you picture that working?

Bonnie: Can't you just cast them out or something?

Counselor: Is that how you see this working? At some point I just order your thoughts out of your head for you?

Bonnie: Isn't that possible? I don't know. You're the expert. What *do* you do to get rid of these things?

Counselor: Any idea what made them come on in the first place?

Bonnie: Let's see. The whole thing started after my accident. I've always been a worrier, but this time I couldn't get out of my head that I was responsible for the accident, so I had terrible guilt . . .

Note what has happened. By refusing to try to tell Bonnie how to get rid of the thoughts, the counselor gets her working to find out for herself what changes their intensity. He allows Bonnie to remain anxious rather than rushing in to allay her discomfort *because he knows that discomfort motivates counselees to work at getting well.*

4. The Work of Counseling

After the agenda has been constructed, and as exemplified by the above dialogue samples, occasionally during its construction, the work

of counseling takes place. The beginning counselor must pay careful
attention to the following guidelines:

- Counseling, whatever its form, is to identify misbeliefs and replace them with the truth, in order to change both inward and
outward behavior and actions.
- Counseling is normally dialogue, not lecture, with the counselee doing the larger share of the work.
- Counselor activity includes:

Asking questions for clarification.

Counselee: ... And so, my roommates just seemed to be crowding me
out of the room, like, you know, it was my place, but they
were all there, all the time ...
Counselor: How many roommates did you have in college?

Asking questions to focus counselee attention on a point.

Counselee: So all this week I've been feeling angry, mostly at my
wife. Then, when she asked me to leave her alone so she
could get her work done, I lost it. I just blew up. I don't
know why I reacted that way. I felt furious.
Counselor: A little bit like you told me you felt when your mother
would push you outside to play and lock the door?

Calling attention to themes in the counselee's dialogue.

Counselor: I've noticed a theme running through your various subjects today. Have you spotted it?
Counselee: Hmm. No. Let's see, I talked about my old football
coach ... Then about work, and how I feel when my boss
comes in ... I talked for a while about how I used to be
afraid of Santa Claus.
Counselor: Sounds like fear and anger at authority figures.
Counselee: Authority figures? You know, I think you have a point. I
used to get very upset when I had to go see the dean or
an advisor at school.
Counselor: Once you told me you feel upset when you go to church
or pray. Could God be an authority figure who upsets you
too? Do you think you're afraid of God?
Counselee: Why, I don't know. (Pause) You know, I think I am. I
always feel like He's watching me and waiting to catch
me doing something wrong.

Pointing out connections between themes in the counselee's dialogue.

Counselor: From what you have just told me, I wonder if you got the
idea that you were responsible for your little brother's

accident and death. Do you think so?

Counselee: Maybe that's why I feel so guilty every time I think about him.

Counselor: Yes, it might explain that. And it also might explain why you are obsessed with the notion that you might somehow harm or even kill your baby.

Showing the connection between the counselee's pathological feelings and actions and misbeliefs in the counselee's self-talk.

Counselee: So I just don't go up to communion anymore. I'm afraid I'll have another one of those spells where I get nervous and shaky and everybody will see it and think something's really wrong with me.

Counselor: What do you do to make yourself so nervous? What's on your mind when you think about taking communion?

Counselee: Well, I think that I'd like to and I should, but then I think, "What if I fall apart up there and everybody notices?"

Counselor: Would you be nervous if you weren't thinking those thoughts and worrying about getting nervous?

Counselee: I don't know. Probably not. Actually, I think it started after I accidentally spilled some of the wine at communion once. I worried about what people might think.

Counselor: Can you see that it's your thoughts, especially your belief that it is vitally important to make sure people think nice things about you, that upset you and make you nervous at even thinking about communion?

Debating and arguing against the counselee's misbeliefs.

Counselee: Nobody likes me.

Counselor: How do you know?

Counselee: I just know I'm not likable, so nobody likes me.

Counselor: You just know. How? By divine inspiration? Did God tell you nobody likes you?

Counselee: (Laughs a little) No, of course not. I can just tell.

Counselor: How?

Counselee: The way people act. You're going to ask me what they do, right? Well, for example, the other day I had arranged for Ron to pick me up and take me to the airport. He totally forgot me. He wouldn't forget if he liked me, would he?

Counselor: I don't know Ron, but does Ron remember everything when he likes someone? Do you know that for a fact?

Counselee: Well, no, actually, he doesn't. He likes Judy and he forgot to pick up something for her at the store. But you wouldn't forget to take somebody to the airport, would you, if you liked them?

Counselor: Why do you say that? Can't you think of any instances in your experience where people have liked others and also forgotten important commitments to them?

Counselee: I guess I can, yes. Once my dad forgot to meet my mother at a bus station. She couldn't reach him by phone, so she just sat there all night. So, all right, maybe Ron doesn't dislike me.

Counselor: Then won't you have to quit telling yourself that nobody likes you? Anyway, how about God? Even if every human being in your circle of acquaintances hated you, it would still be true that God loves you and wants your companionship so very much that Jesus willingly died for you. So it would never be true to say, "Nobody likes me. Nobody loves me."

Presenting and arguing the case for the truth as it applies to the counselee's misbeliefs.

Counselor: So you've been telling yourself you have to go on an eating binge because nothing else will make you feel good and it's good for you to feel good?

Counselee: That's right. I tell myself it will be good for me to eat a whole pie and some ice cream with it. At least I won't feel so depressed.

Counselor: Then how do you feel afterward?

Counselee: Depressed.

Counselor: So the truth is, binge eating makes you feel bad, not good, even though it makes you feel good very briefly?

Counselee: I'd have to say that's correct.

Counselor: And how about your contention that such eating is good for you to do? Isn't it more truthful to say that pie and ice cream are calories, mountains of fat, and the destruction of your dreams of being thin, attractive, and stylishly dressed? Isn't it more truthful to tell yourself that, since your body is the temple of the Holy Spirit, only what makes it healthy, strong, and functional can be good for it? Isn't it really true that stuffing with pie and ice cream can never *be* good just because they *feel* good for a moment. And, remember, they don't even *feel* good by the next day!

Teaching the counselee to identify, debate against, and replace his own misbeliefs with the truth.

Counselor: So, Rhonda, next time you are at the point of a binge, I want you to take a tape recorder instead of a trip to the refrigerator. Sit down and dictate all the thoughts in your head. While you're at it, notice precisely what you are telling yourself about the situation. Then argue out loud against the misbeliefs which are prompting you to over-eat. Replace them with the truth. When you have finished, substitute something constructive in the place of binging. Call a friend, read from the Scriptures, go for a walk, go to work on your stamp collection. Agreed?

Helping the counselee devise ways of discovering the truth about specific points. Devising activities which will, like scientific experiments, help the counselee discover truth empirically.

Counselee: People always reject me.

Counselor: I would like you to begin doing some experiments to check on the truth or falsehood of that belief. For example, it would work fine if you would agree to call a friend or acquaintance every week until we agree to stop the experiment and ask that person to do something with you. Will you agree to do that? If they all reject you, we'll know your belief is true. If some of them accept your invitation, we'll know it isn't true.

Counselee: My sins are too bad and disgusting and nauseating to be forgiven. I'm not good enough to stay out of hell.

Counselor: Would you be willing to do some homework to check on whether or not that is true? I'd like you to take this concordance home with you and check all the Bible passages using the words "forgive" and "forgiveness." Better stick to the New Testament, there are so many. Write them out. And let's look at them to see if your belief is true.

Counselee: People who make mistakes are unreliable. That's why I don't like myself at all. I make mistakes where I shouldn't.

Counselor: I'd like to propose a homework assignment for you. Would you be willing to list three or four people you know and think are "reliable" and likable people? Then I'd like you to make a point of asking each of them, "Do you make mistakes where you really shouldn't?" Write down their answers, and let's look at them next session.

Counselee: Eric hasn't called me in three weeks. I guess he doesn't want to go with me anymore. He hasn't said anything was wrong. I just worry about it all the time.

Counselor: Would you be willing to call Eric and ask him? You could say, "I haven't heard from you for three weeks and I am beginning to think you want our relationship to end. Is that so? If not, what does it mean?"

5. Homework Agreement for Next Session

See above for examples of counselor behavior when suggesting homework.

6. Prayer

Placing prayer at the end of the session does not mean that prayer will not be prompted by the Spirit of God and the developments in the session at other points. It has simply happened in my practice that prayer occurs as the final and climactic event of the hour. As if all that has gone before is preparatory for a time when I will (usually) lay hands on the counselee and pray for healing, with requests related to material from the foregoing discussion.

This book is not a training manual for Christian prayer. So it is assumed that the Christian counselor will know how to pray, will be in prayer daily for his counselees, and for his own life, and will believe the promises connected to prayer everywhere in the Bible. If the reader desires to practice Christian counseling and for some reason has not learned to pray, it is very important to take some training in prayer from a person qualified to teach it to others.

The laying on of hands has biblical precedent, and seems to have observable beneficial effects. Counselees tend to feel cared for by the therapist who touches them gently, firmly, and in the context of blessing.

Professional therapists will doubtless concern themselves with the transference effects such a practice might elicit. In my own experience it seems to improve and strengthen relationships with counselees, particularly when they are aware of the power of prayer. Counselees seem to respond both intellectually and emotionally to the therapist's prayer accompanied by touch.

7. The Next Appointment

One of the unique features of counseling is that it continues. No one session has to be seen as the last chance to accomplish what needs to be done. There is always next session.

In view of this fact, counselees can be asked to avoid precipitous actions, not to lose hope, "make it" through the week, and work on getting better by carrying out agreed assignments.

For these reasons, the next appointment is an important, if brief, agenda item, and should be agreed upon before counselor and counselee take leave of one another at the end of a session.

SUMMARY

This chapter was written to give the new counselor a more precise and detailed picture of a typical counseling session. The caution should be repeated here that plans and schedules are subject to revision and change, and that the counselor needs to listen for the direction of the Spirit of God. If the Holy Spirit so orders, routines must be set aside.

Nevertheless, routines and plans can be made. The elements suggested here for the counseling session include: feedback; agenda construction; dialogue and misbelief identification, debate, and replacement; prayer with laying on of hands; and arranging of the next appointment.

FOR REVIEW AND DISCUSSION

1. Give some reasons for having a plan for sessions.
2. Why do we ask for feedback?
3. What kinds of feedback can you expect to hear from various counselees?
4. Give some examples of poor ways of dealing with negative feedback.
5. Give some examples of good ways of handling negative feedback.
6. How might feedback normally be handled?
7. Why construct an agenda?
8. Who should supply agenda items?
9. What erroneous conceptions of counseling will probably be corrected in the counselee by the regular request for agenda items?
10. What are the counselor's functions during the carrying out of agenda items?
11. Give some examples of each.
12. Try to create some more plausible assignments for counselees to do to change their misbeliefs experimentally.
13. Why might prayer at the end of the session be more meaningful than at the outset?
14. What values can you see in the laying on of hands?
15. What is therapeutic about the making of the next appointment?

CHAPTER TWELVE

Terminating with a Future and a Hope

Beginning counselors worry a good deal about how to get started. "How," they wonder, "will I ever find enough to do to fill an entire 50-minute hour?"

Few counselors concern themselves with how to terminate.

Norm, an otherwise effective pastoral counselor, didn't know how to terminate. So he just kept the counseling going until the counselee no longer showed up for sessions. Usually, counselees would just sort of fade away.

Some counselors, like Brad for example, allow the counseling to drag on and on until they themselves lose interest, forget to keep appointments, sleep through the session, and end the hours early. Counselees eventually gather through all this that the sessions had probably better terminate, and they stop showing up.

Linda chopped the process off rather suddenly. Out of the blue, one day, her counselee would be told, "Well, I don't think you need to come back anymore. Let's make this the last session, what do you say?" After recovering from the surprise ending, counselees would murmur agreement, wondering why Linda had made her decision so abruptly.

If you don't know how and when to wind up with a counselee, perhaps it's because you have never been taught. Many courses of instruction, even in graduate schools, omit lessons on how to quit. Many instruction manuals for counselors fail to discuss termination.

KNOWING WHEN TO QUIT COUNSELING

How do you know when it's time to terminate?

"The Holy Spirit will direct," answered Patty, a promising trainee in one of my classes.

"How will He show you, Patty?" I asked, pretty sure I had her stumped.

"By making clear to me and the counselee that we have reached the goals we set out to tackle under His direction," she replied without batting an eye.

An excellent response. Sometimes the Holy Spirit will override all natural indicators and, speaking directly to you, will order a change of direction in counseling, maybe even termination.

More often, He will underscore and direct your attention to the orderly indicators in the nature of the counseling process. As Patty put it so beautifully, He will make it clear to you and the counselee that you have reached the goals you aimed at from the outset.

Recall our lessons in goal-setting in Chapter 4. One of the great advantages of having set goals initially under the guidance of the Spirit of God is that you have a built-in thermostat for the counseling process. A thermostat shuts the furnace off when the house reaches the temperature you set in advance. Your initial goals can function as a thermostat to shut off the process of counseling when you and the counselee have accomplished what you targeted in the beginning.

Marie listened carefully to Patty, hesitated, then raised her hand. "What if we don't reach the goals we agreed to work on? What if the counselee just doesn't get better?" Marie asked, echoing the unspoken dread of most beginners. "Do we just keep on trying until we either reach the goals or die working at it?"

WHAT IF THERE'S NO IMPROVEMENT?

Most beginning counselors feel inadequate. "How on earth can I make anyone else get better?" they ask themselves.

And they are astonished and pleased when counselees begin to show improvement. Most counselees improve. The counselor can count on the blessing of God. And, if you practice what you have learned in this book, you will find yourself working effectively with excellent results.

At the Center for Christian Psychological Services, Roseville, Minnesota, we deliberately contacted one hundred of our counselees months after their therapy ended, questioning each one in detail to determine how close to the achievement of initial goals each counselee had come and remained. Nearly all (95%) felt that they had made progress in achieving over half the goals they had set initially.

I am not promising that your results will be the same as ours. According to Jesus' parable of the sower, we can expect different results with different hearers. This also applies to counseling counselees. Some are more motivated than others. Some have more ability to help themselves than others. Some have better and more favorable life situations than others.

Counselors differ in their skills and abilities too.

The point here is that many, perhaps most, of your counselees can be expected to improve and to achieve some of the goals they set for themselves at the beginning.

What if someone shows little or no improvement? Imagine a situation in which you and the counselee have met for six weekly sessions, and the counselee has reported absolutely no gains on any of her goals. Should you just keep slogging through the mental mud? Should you terminate? Should you tell yourself you have no business being a counselor and find some other job to do?

None of the above.

REEXAMINE GOALS

Reassess. You and the counselee should face the fact that nothing appears to be happening. Then, together, you should pray for further directions from God. What does He want you to do? After that, look again at the goals. Are they realistic and plausible? Are they truly in the mainstream of God's will for this counselee's life? Are they so vague that it's impossible to tell when they have been achieved? Are they perfectionistic, so that no one on earth would ever achieve them as they are stated?

Revise the goals, correcting them if they have been stated impossibly from the beginning. Part of counseling sometimes consists in teaching the counselee to set goals which can be achieved, thus breaking a lifelong habit of yearning after unrealistic chimeras.

REVIEW THE COUNSELING PROCESS

Besides reexamining goals, examine the process of counseling itself. Have you allowed the counselee to work hard on his portion of the change process? Have you insisted that homework be carefully completed? Or have you fostered counselee dependency and tried to do everything for him? Have you made the counselee responsible for bringing material to the sessions, or have you made yourself do his work in this regard too? Perhaps you have overlooked something of major significance, such as abuse of some substance (alcohol, marijuana, prescription drugs, sugar).

HOW IS THE RELATIONSHIP?

Check your relationship with the counselee. Has the counselee become angry at you and expressed anger by resisting change? Has the counselee formed such an attachment to you that he is threatened by the idea of improvement because it might mean the end of his relationship with you? Are your feelings toward the counselee so negative you can't be effectively helpful? Or are they so strong and positive that you haven't been setting the counselee free to grow up?

Should you consider having the counselee see a physician to eliminate possible physical causes or to be evaluated for psychotropic medication?

MAKE A CORRECTIVE PLAN

Make a plan. Having recognized lack of progress and done your best to diagnose the reason, seeking the guidance of God, you and the counselee agree on corrective action.

This may involve a decision to have the counselee do more homework, bring in a written agenda for each session, or stop calling you so often at home. It may include an agreement that you, the counselor, will refrain from talking as much as you have been doing because it seems to have prevented the counselee from working in the sessions. Your plan should have a reasonable probability of correcting whatever is holding back progress.

Once in a while, you may want to ask a psychologist, psychiatrist, or an experienced pastoral counselor to see the counselee for evaluation and consultation. This means you are asking the professional to give you an opinion as to what is wrong and what needs to be done, not that you are asking him to take over and treat your counselee. You must make this clear to the professional in advance. Such an opinion can be very helpful when you are stuck.

REFER

Occasionally you may decide to have the counselee transfer to another Christian counselor or a professional psychologist, psychiatrist, pastoral counselor, or social worker.

Should it appear that someone else might be more able to help, do not hesitate to transfer or refer the counselee! There is no room for your personal fears of failure or your pride to interfere with the counselee's welfare.

TERMINATE

At times, you and the nonimproving counselee will realize that counseling is not the answer at all, and that it is best to terminate rather than waste more time on a situation which will not improve. You should not hesitate to express your own desire to terminate under such conditions. You need not be reticent about saying that you do not want to continue the counseling because you have become convinced that you are not being helpful. You may do this even if the counselee disagrees with the decision.

PRAYER, NOT HOPELESSNESS

Again and again, it becomes clear to me in my practice of psychology that there is no such thing as a hopeless case or situation. This insight has been revealed only to Christians. I would not want to be a secular psychotherapist. At some point in nearly every case there appears a problem or circumstance that will not budge. From a purely empirical perspective, the situation is hopeless.

But not in our clinic. We pray. And we continue to pray—hard. We pray with the counselee, we pray for the counselee in his presence, we pray in intercession when the counselee is not present. I pray each day for each of my counselees by name, making specific requests of God. And we let our counselees know that we know that God can do *anything*.

Even at the point where you are ready to terminate because no progress has been made, you need not communicate hopelessness. You let the counselee know that God is still at work in his life, and that God will not let him down. You pray for God's will to be revealed to him and for his life to be ordered by God. And you pray, trust, and believe with the counselee that God is going to resolve the difficulty.

"Now that we have agreed to terminate, I won't be in your life any longer. But God will. I am discontinuing, but God is not discontinuing His work with you. We are going to terminate, believing together that God will bring you to that place where He will work to resolve your difficulty."

A TERMINATION SESSION

Most often, when it has come time to terminate, you and the counselee will know it. Nevertheless one of you must broach the subject of ending the counseling. Who will do it? Occasionally the counselee will. Most often, it will be up to you to raise the issue of termination. Here is one way to do it:

You: From what you have just told me, I conclude that you're feeling considerably better than you did when we started working together.

Counselee: Oh, yes. I think I'm a lot better.

You: How about your depression? Have you stopped feeling depressed?

Counselee: I think so. I've been sleeping fine and my appetite is back. I don't mind facing the day anymore.

You: Sounds like that's about licked. Another goal we set for ourselves was for you to initiate contacts with others rather than sit and wait for them to come to you.

Counselee: Oh, yes, I'm doing that now. I had a great week socially. Went to the ballgame with Patty and then we had dinner out. And this time *I* asked *her*. Sunday, I started a conversation with a new couple at Bible class and we made a date to get together for coffee. They work in the same building I do. And, just as you and I agreed, I made a phone call to someone daily just to initiate a chat. Worked out fine.

You: That's quite different from the way you used to deal with other people. A real change! What would you say has happened in the matter of your career? When you came in you thought maybe you were in the wrong field and that some change was in order, so we listed that as a goal. Really, you haven't talked any more about that one. What's doing there?

Counselee: You know, I think that one resolved itself. I'm quite happy at work now, and I think I know the reason. Want to hear it?

You: Sure.

Counselee: Well, I think my misery about going to work was because I didn't think anyone there liked me. And I didn't talk to any of them because I was sure they'd put me down or something. Anyway, since I've been practicing more loving and more initiatives with people, I'm having a great time with other people at work. And, lo and behold, I like my job now.

You: One other goal we had was to strengthen your relationship with God. Do you remember, you were feeling distant from the Lord when you came in? We thought at the time that you might have been dealing with Him the same way you did with other people.

Counselee: By sitting in the corner and waiting for Him to always take the initiative, and then getting angry and peeved at Him because He wasn't doing anything—I thought. Yes, I remember. And all the time I was backing it with Bible passages about "waiting on the Lord." I can see now that I was just using those passages to excuse my passivity and protect my anxiety.

You: How are things now between you and the Lord?

Counselee: Just fine. I have started having a time of prayer and Scripture reading every morning (getting up at 5:30 to do it, too). And I feel the Lord is talking to me and giving me some understandings I never had before. He's done great things for me and I know He has healed me.

You: Around here, we know that every healing is from God. And it's a delight to watch Him work. Wonder how you'd feel about terminating since your goals seem to be pretty well met?

Counselee: Hmm. There are some things I still want to work on, but I suppose I could cope with them myself. I know that God will be there working in me to get them done.

You: You think this would be a good time to wind up?

Counselee: It is a little sudden. I feel like I might need you and then what would I do? But, yes, I really think I can get along now OK.

You: You see termination as a basically good idea, but you feel a little nervous about it all the same?

Counselee: Right. I think about the mess I'd gotten myself into before and wonder if I'll get back into it.

You: Maybe we ought to aim at terminating after next session. How does that sound? It'll give us time to pick up on any loose ends and also to seek the Lord together to make sure He hasn't got something else for us to do right now.

Counselee: Sounds good, I guess.

You: Fine. Let's pray about it right now and then wind up our session for tonight. We can look at this issue again next session.

During the time between sessions, both you and the counselee can continue to pray and think about termination. It may be that one or the other of you will be led to see some reason to continue the counseling for a while instead of terminating. Normally, with goals fairly well completed, the Lord will confirm the plan to both of you. If, however, either counselor or counselee finds that termination does not appear to be quite right yet, the decision should be reconsidered. It is best if termination can occur by mutual agreement.

Normally, at the next session, the counselee will have prepared himself for termination and so will the counselor.

You: Well, have you given some thought to whether it's time to bring this to a close?

Counselee: Yes, I have. And I've decided you were right. This is the time to do it. I'm a little nervous about not having you to talk to every week, but I know I would be no matter when we quit.

You: Apart from the nervousness, how do you feel about it?

Counselee: Really good. It made me feel good to know that you think I'm ready for it. I must have made progress. I've been praying about it too, and I get the feeling that the Lord is assuring me that things will go all right.

You: Great. Tell me how you plan to use this last session? What would you like to do with it? Any unfinished business you've thought of to discuss?

TERMINATION BRINGS OUT COUNSELOR MISBELIEFS

Although you may become a skilled Christian counselor, you will never stop being a human being. You will make some progress in changing misbeliefs in yourself and your counselees, but remember that our whole lifetime will involve new applications of God's truth to our lives.

Since termination is a time of testing for counselors, it tends to bring many counselor misbeliefs to the fore.

CLIFF

Cliff had taken the class for Christian counselors and had done exceptionally well. He had learned everything set out in the lectures and in addition had read several books. When he started his supervised practice counseling, he went at it with a vengeance.

He took more counselees and saw them more often than anyone else. He even went skating with counselees and tried to coach them in social skills by observing their performance. Cliff could never bring himself to terminate his counselees, always thinking of some further horizons to attain with each one.

When Jeanette, Cliff's wife, complained about the increasing encroachment of Cliff's counseling on their home life, he brushed off her reasonable objections.

"These people are sick and miserable and I have to help them," Cliff replied. "Who else will if I don't? Anyway, things should slack off after I get Vonnie over her depression. That's what's taking all the time right now."

Things didn't slack off. They got worse, from Jeanette's point of view. She seldom saw her husband, and when she did he was on the telephone.

Eighteen months later, I was doing marriage counseling with Cliff and Jeanette. Her blood pressure was elevated (it had always been normal before Cliff became a counselor), and Cliff had stomach pains. The tests did not reveal an ulcer, but you could see it coming. What had been a peaceful and reasonably satisfactory Christian marriage was on the verge of destruction.

As we talked, it became clear that Cliff had a number of misbeliefs which his work as a counselor activated.

When counselors terminate sessions with counselees they value highly, some of the same counselor misbeliefs may be activated in them.

This is as good a time as any for you to look at yourself to determine your own counseling-related misbeliefs and go to work on them.

A LIST OF COUNSELING-RELATED COUNSELOR MISBELIEFS

- I am indispensable. So nothing should keep me from responding to a counselee's beck and call.

- If I weren't desperately needed by each counselee all the time, I would have to believe that I'm worthless and no good at all.
- I need to counsel others for my own satisfaction. If I didn't do counseling, I would feel useless.
- Counseling is a good way to buttress my shaky self-image. It assures me of my importance in life.
- Everyone else should see how vital my work as a counselor is.
- Counselees shouldn't be able to get along without me if I'm really important. They should have to call me night and day and hang onto me through thick and thin.
- If a counselee should begin to think he doesn't need me anymore, it's a sign of my lack of worth and value.
- If the subject of termination comes up, and a counselee says that he is ready to terminate, he's really telling me I'm not important to him. That's unendurable.
- Other people can't run their own lives half as well as I can.
- It's nice to pray, but real progress depends on me and my hard effort.
- My motives are all pure and selfless. I am never thinking of myself at all. I get nothing whatever out of counselees being dependent on me. I am totally loving and self-sacrificing. All I do is give. I never take. There is absolutely no ego gratification for me in counseling.
- It is vital for me that every counselee love me.
- I need lots of appreciation.

THE TRUTH

No doubt everyone can see the falsehood in most of these misbeliefs.

The truth is that our counselees do not have to have us in their lives to survive. "One thing is needful," said Jesus to Martha. And that "one thing" was not Cliff. You either. It is Jesus Christ himself.

The truth is that we are very dispensable. If God can make children of Abraham from the stones, as Jesus put it to the unbelieving Jews, He can also handle other people's problems without you and me.

The truth is that our worth and value must not hinge on the reactions of counselees but on the God who has established our value in Christ and created us in His image.

The truth is that the progress of a counselee in counseling or psychotherapy is utterly dependent on the blessing of God and on His ordering of circumstances beyond the control of the counselor.

The truth is that our motives as counselors may easily become fleshly and self-seeking, and we need to pray daily that the Holy Spirit will convict us of any such tendencies in ourselves.

The truth is that the only love and appreciation we *have* to receive is God's love and appreciation, and that it is wrong for us to use our counselees for gratification of our own needs for approval.

The truth is that we do no one a favor by encouraging counselees to become overdependent upon us rather than encouraging total dependence on God alone.

The truth is that we can take vacations, give attention to our families, and even get away from the telephone without any need to worry that our counselees won't be able to function without talking to us whenever they want to.

HOW CLIFF GOT BETTER

As Cliff began to build his sense of worth on God alone, he came to see his counselees, not as opportunities for him to prove himself, but as people he could really love in terms of their own real needs.

Cliff realized that God had already given him infinite worth and value. He came to see that his wife's needs and his counselees' needs were both important, but not as levers to hoist Cliff's self-worth.

And with all that, he began to appreciate his own need for times alone with God, for peace and quiet, for recreation, for shedding the unrealistic commitments of a misguided counselor.

Cliff and Jeanette learned to take time for one another. They restored what their marriage had lost—God as the center. And they began to discover their interest in one another growing again. Cliff found he no longer needed counseling and his counselees to give him a few shreds of self-respect and self-worth.

As Cliff and his marriage improved, his counselees did too. And they marked their improvement by terminating. No longer did Cliff find himself resenting the counselees' various ways of saying they didn't need him any longer.

Cliff even began to see termination as good news.

And it is. It is a mark of the truth and outworking of the great good news, the gospel of Jesus Christ, that God is busy working out the salvation of human beings.

Successful counseling is one channel through which God's salvation is delivered to people.

SUMMARY

In this chapter, we have discussed the indicators for termination of counseling. The most likely indicator is that the counselee has realized the goals he agreed to aim for initially. Occasionally, it becomes clear that some or all the goals are not being reached and that the counseling is not moving ahead. If this occurs, the counselor and the counselee should initiate an investigation to determine the reasons for lack of progress. Prayer for God's light on the matter will often reveal factors such as failure to involve the counselee in homework on his problems or too much "answer-giving" talk on the part of the counselor. It may happen occasionally, however, that no reason can be found. The Lord may reveal that counseling is not the way. Normally, however, counselor and counselee, on reviewing goals and their attainment, will conclude that termination is in order. Both may experience some anxiety about ending their relationship and time should be given to pray it through. Counselees should be given a chance to discuss their feelings about terminating and to raise any loose ends they wish to deal with. It is possible that termination will activate some misbeliefs in the counselor. If so, he should be willing to face them and deal with them in prayer and in the light of God's truth. Occasionally, as with Cliff, the counselor may need some counseling for help with misbeliefs activated under the stress of termination.

FOR REVIEW AND DISCUSSION

1. Describe some of the ineffective ways of terminating which may occur in counseling.
2. How do you know when it's time to terminate?
3. What does termination have to do with goals? How do goals function like a thermostat?
4. What are some reasons for different rates of counselee improvement?
5. Can you expect that most counselees will improve? Reasons for your answer.
6. What should you do if after six sessions or more a counselee has shown no improvement?
7. What might your relationship with the counselee have to do with lack of improvement?
8. List some possible plans you and the counselee might make after reevaluating the situation.
9. Why should you not hesitate to transfer or refer a counselee who is not improving?
10. What keeps the Christian counselor's work from hopelessness even where there is no improvement?
11. Who will know it when it is time to terminate?
12. Who will usually take the initiative in terminating?
13. How will you do it?
14. Even counselees who are ready to terminate may feel bad about it. What kind of feelings will likely be expressed?
15. What are some of the counselor misbeliefs which might be brought out through termination?
16. Describe how Cliff exemplified these misbeliefs.
17. Give a truthful replacement for each of the misbeliefs of the counselor.

Part Three

COUNSELING FOR COMMON DISORDERS

CHAPTER THIRTEEN

Anxiety Disorders

(When Fear Moves In)

So many people live with fear, it is hard for them to believe there is healing for anxiety.

ANXIETY, PILLS, AND BOURBON

Celia had graduated from a vocational training school as a pastry chef. She was good at her craft and had been employed at it for two years since graduation. "But I can't go on!" she told me, breaking into tears which kept flowing throughout the interview.

Shortly after she began working, Celia experienced a severe attack of panic on her job. She believed it would wipe her out. Her pounding heart and sweating palms had terrified her. She worried, "What if I should have another one? I couldn't stand it." Sure enough, the following Monday she experienced panic again. From then on her life became a nightmare of anxiety. When she wasn't actually in panic, she was filled with dread. What if another episode should sweep over her?

"How long since you've had a panic attack, Celia?" I asked her.

"To tell you the truth, I haven't had one for two months. That's because whenever I think I'm going to get one, I take several tranquilizers and a glass of whiskey to prevent the attacks. It works, but I know I can't keep going this way. I need help."

Celia had been seeing another counselor before she came to our center. I couldn't believe my ears when she told me he had suggested that she medicate herself with tranquilizers and alcohol. Either Celia had mistaken his message or he had never learned the principles involved in treating anxiety.

"You must, if you want to get well, stop using pills and bourbon,"

I told Celia. "That is because, as you will learn, the key ingredient in the treatment of fear is exposure to the thing feared. Exposure may be sudden or gradual; small doses or heavy; but if you want to get over fear, you must experience the thing you fear until the fear is gone."

NEUROTIC ANXIETY

People call it "nerves," "tension," "stress," "apprehension." But anxiety, whatever you call it, is fear. Inappropriate fear. Irrational fear. And sufferers frequently believe their fear is "foolish."

When fear keeps on occurring in diverse situations which are not dangerous, we are probably dealing with neurotic anxiety. Most often, people with neurotic anxiety have little or no idea of what they fear. They just feel the dread hanging over them. They may actually be fearful and worried about such things as rejection or disapproval, physical abuse and harm, put-downs, criticism, and failure (performance anxiety). In my experience, such fears of other people and what others may say or do are more common than any other causes of anxiety.

Anxious dread may be a signal of *guilt* and fear of punishment by parents, God, or other power figures. Or it may boil down to a pervasive *shame* or fear that other people may form a bad opinion of you. Closely related is *embarrassment*, the fear that others may make fun of you or mock you. Sometimes the dread appears to be a deep worry that everyone is going to leave and that you will be left helpless and alone.

Counselees may be so conscious of their painful fear symptoms that they have not really focused their attention on what they are afraid of. Some counselees don't know, and some are only dimly aware of the objects of their fears.

When the fear is almost constantly present, psychologists and psychiatrists diagnose: Generalized Anxiety Disorder.

PHOBIC NEUROSES

Lee hated his job. It wasn't the people he had to see daily in his work as a salesman. He really enjoyed others, and the work he had to do was more pleasure than effort. But Lee hated to go to work because it required that he call on people in office buildings high above the street. He was planning to change occupations.

Lee was afraid of high places. His *acrophobia*, as it is called, became the consideration which governed his life. He carried a huge vial of pills in his pocket. Prior to making a call, Lee would pop a pill to dampen the anxiety he experienced on any level above the fourth floor. Like many other people, Lee had a phobia.

The word *phobia* is from the Greek word for "fear." Simple phobias are fears restricted to objects or situations of which the sufferer is well aware. The fear is unreasonable, and the sufferer knows that there is little danger or threat in the thing feared. Nonetheless, the fear persists. Dogs, cars, heights, crowds, elevators, locked rooms, physical restriction, dirt, airplanes—these are common phobic objects. But a counselee can conceivably present a phobia about anything—chickens, mice, and freeways, for example.

One of the marks of phobic anxiety is that the counselee knows very well what he fears. And he exerts great care to avoid the feared object. Because of the fact that phobics can rather easily identify what they fear and avoid it, they are often able to remain fairly comfortable—so long as life does not require them to encounter the things they fear.

AGORAPHOBIA

Although the name *agoraphobia* means "fear of the marketplace," or "fear of open spaces," it has been injudiciously coined. Agoraphobic counselees are afraid of being unable to get help or to get away in case they have an attack of panic-level anxiety. It is a fear of anxiety itself and they will do all in their power to avoid it.

Most agoraphobics are women and they usually have stories similar to Gwenn's.

Gwenn, a 32-year-old married woman, had come to a counselor for help with the fears which had increasingly limited the activities she felt free to undertake.

"It all started eight years ago," Gwenn explained. "I was doing some last-minute shopping a few days before my wedding. The store was crowded, I was looking over some blouses, when all of a sudden it hit. I felt my heart pounding—like it would smash to bits. I couldn't breathe. It seemed as if there was a five-hundred-pound weight on my chest. I felt like I was having a heart attack."

Gwenn was taken to an emergency room and treated for panic. Her physician later confirmed that there was no physical disorder. Nevertheless, the episode so frightened her that she never went back into the store where it occurred.

She soon began to dread going to any store, fearing a repetition of her experience. Sure enough, it happened on her honeymoon—this time in a drugstore. There was no trip to the hospital this time, but Gwenn had been sure she would faint, or perhaps even die of the malady which had now moved unwanted into her life.

Over the years, Gwenn sought treatment without avail. Many hours of analytic therapy had failed to bring relief. The tranquilizers she was given seemed to lose their power to defend her against the seemingly omnipotent panic attacks. Even when she didn't actually have panic, she tormented herself with fear and worry lest it come again.

"I don't like going anywhere," she told the counselor. "It scares me to go to church. I think I won't be able to get out if anything happens. If I did have to leave, everybody would see that something is wrong with me."

Shopping areas and malls, checkout lines, beauty shops, automobile trips—all these and more were scenes Gwenn had done her best to avoid.

SOCIAL PHOBIA

One of the most prevalent forms of anxiety is fear of other people. How ironic it is that people seem to fear other human beings more than anything else! What they fear is not usually that others will drop nuclear bombs on them, or beat them up, or steal their bank accounts. What they fear appears to be that others will disapprove or criticize.

For many, there is nothing more dreadful than the scowl or sharp tongue of another human being. So a good deal of their energy is spent planning how to avoid:

- the evaluation of others
- the scrutiny of others
- any chance of making a fool of oneself
- any event which might prove humiliating or embarrassing

They do their best not to speak in public, contribute to a discussion group, appear before an audience, or even sit in the front row of an auditorium.

Some of these poor victims even go to the extreme of fearing and avoiding public restrooms because they might be seen by someone and terribly shamed and embarrassed!

Social phobics also fear going to parties, having to perform, doing stunts, making introductions, asking others for dates, or requesting favors. They have great difficulty making friends because of all this avoidance. And so they often feel lonely and isolated, living life almost solely on terms dictated by their fears.

ANXIETY SYMPTOMS

Sometimes the sufferer seems ignorant of what he fears. Whatever the object of anxiety, its symptoms are the same. Note them well. Some or all are presented frequently by counselees coming for counseling. The symptoms are markedly unpleasant.

1. *Purely mental events*: The counselee stews about things. Generally, he worries over the future. What is *going* to happen is nearly always of more concern than what is happening now or

what has happened in the past. Jesus hit it on the head when He related anxiety to "taking thought for the morrow."

2. *Muscle tension*: Muscles are anything but relaxed. Often, counselees are disturbed by the feeling that they can't relax. Such tension produces shakiness, tremors, and jittery, restless jumpiness. Headaches and other muscle pains may result directly from this tension chronically preventing relaxed muscles.

3. *Watchfulness*: The counselee is exceptionally watchful, attentive, and on guard. He notices each sound, each change in bodily function, or each nuance of expression on the face of another person. Therefore, it is hard to concentrate or even to sleep, and frustration tolerance becomes poor.

4. *Frightening autonomic events*: The counselee experiences reactions in his body which he believes he cannot control and which he comes to dread. Sweating, pounding heart, pallor, or flushing, chest pains, dizziness, faint feelings, unreality feelings, tingling, numbness, dry mouth, breathing trouble, weakness, upset stomach, light-headedness, twitching, diarrhea, frequent urination, "butterflies," lump in throat, and other such sensations often create a secondary round of fear—that is, fear of the fear symptoms themselves. This *fear of fear* becomes so important that some counselees, agoraphobics, for example, make it the primary symptom of their "illness."

THE EMERGENCY RESPONSE

"I don't understand why I have to feel all these terrible things!" Jennifer was irritated at the experience of anxiety in her own body. God had made a mistake, she thought, allowing her to experience such disturbing bodily reactions.

Jennifer did not know enough to appreciate what was happening when she became anxious; therefore, she was terrified when the sensations occurred.

"What you are experiencing is perfectly normal," responded her counselor. "God designed it all for a good purpose."

"What! You're trying to tell me that the feeling that I'm going to have a coronary with my heart thumping this way is *normal*?" She was incredulous. She was sure her counselor was just trying to make her feel better. Jennifer had also read articles in magazines which described psychosomatic illnesses in foreboding terms so she had gotten the impression that she might die from her emotional reactions.

"Certainly. The physiology of all this was studied in detail by the great physiologist, Walter Cannon, who determined that it was a normal bodily response to threat. Cannon called it *The Fight or Flight*

Response. And Hans Selye, who spent his life studying stress, noted that stress is perfectly normal in life and that the symptoms are part of human adaptation to stress. So Selye labeled the reaction *The General Adaptation Syndrome.* Sometimes it is called simply a state of arousal."

The counselor went on to explain that very similar (but not identical) physiological reactions occur during exercise as well as during intense pleasant emotional states. His purpose was to contribute to Jennifer's treatment by helping her lose her needless terror at her body's response to fear.

"All the symptoms are part of a feature designed by the Creator which gears your body up for action in the face of threatening circumstances. With your body in readiness, you can combat the danger, or, if that's not the best plan, you can get away. And *The Fight or Flight Response* is what God made your body do to enable it to get going," said the counselor. She then went on to explain how Jennifer could begin telling herself the truth that she had nothing to fear from the anxiety she was frequently experiencing, and thus did not need to go to such great lengths to avoid it.

"GOING TO SUCH GREAT LENGTHS . . ."

Jennifer wasn't unique.

People, and animals too for that matter, avoid anxiety if they can. All species try their best to escape situations where they experience great fear. In fact, escape and avoidance are "natural" responses to anxiety. They were designed by God, and intended to give even the least intelligent of his living creatures the impetus to get away from danger. You can understand the anxiety response as the mark of God's love for each of His creatures.

But what if the thing feared isn't truly dangerous? What if the avoidance is prompted by neurotic fear, which is fear based on misbeliefs instead of truth?

When this is the case, the avoidance is maladaptive. That is, it prevents a person from doing what God wants him to do. It is God's design operating contrary to His original intention. Incidentally, when I use the term *maladaptive* in this book, I mean "not good for you because it is not what God wills."

Avoiding other people because you needlessly fear criticism or judgment is clearly bad for you. It cannot be the will of God for a person to avoid grocery store checkout lines just to keep from experiencing a knot in the stomach. Especially when the calling God has placed you in requires that you do some shopping for food. When your calling from God involves using an elevator, it cannot be good for you to avoid elevators in honor of your fear! Think of the counselee who has become so bent on avoiding anxiety that she stays in one corner of her home and never leaves it. Daily she experiences the pain of a life so cut off from doing what her calling requires that she hates herself.

AVOIDANCE DEVICES

There are many devices for avoiding anxiety. One of them is staying physically away from the feared stimulus. Another is taking alcohol and tranquilizers so the fear response cannot happen. Still a third way of avoidance is to block out of your mind all negative thoughts and convince yourself that they are not present, even when they are down there somewhere in the lower recesses of your consciousness.

The person who, fearful of heights, refuses ever to climb a ladder perpetuates his fear by avoidance.

The counselee who, terrified of even the possibility of being embarrassed, refuses to meet new people and thus has no friends, also maintains fear and anxiety in himself by his avoidance.

You met Celia at the beginning of the chapter. Not yet an alcoholic, she was nonetheless on the way. For Celia had learned to avoid her anxiety by sedating herself with pills and booze—another sure device for preventing recovery.

"POSITIVE THINKING" AS AN AVOIDANCE DEVICE

Perhaps you have met someone like Marvin. Marvin practiced a form of denial he called "positive thinking." Really, it was not thinking at all, but the repression and denial of reality to the point where Marvin would not admit even actual facts into his consciousness if they happened to be negative.

Marvin was as successfully insulated from actuality as the counselee who stays in her room all the time. Marvin's so-called "positive thinking" was just another device for avoiding anxiety which proved maladaptive because it kept him out of touch with reality and thus unable to discern the will of God for his life.

HOW AVOIDANCE PREVENTS RECOVERY

For many years, psychologists were puzzled because people and animals didn't seem to unlearn anxiety responses. And this appeared odd because, as behavior scientists know very well, a learned response will extinguish or stop occurring when it is no longer followed by a reinforcer.

For example, a pigeon or a rat which has learned to respond to a signal by touching a key will continue responding for only so long as the response is rewarded or reinforced with a food pellet. Stop delivering the reward and the animal may touch a few times, but eventually, the response ceases or "extinguishes."

Fear responses are learned reactions to punishing experiences. If they occur a few times without punishment, they too should extinguish. So why didn't these responses extinguish when they were no longer punished?

Here is the sort of thing the psychologists observed. A dog would be placed in a box with an electric floor grid. The scientist would flash a light as a signal and then shock the dog's feet. If there was no lid on the box, the dog showed his lack of appreciation for the shock by jumping out of the box. It usually required very few repetitions of this sequence of events before the dog was jumping well in advance of the shock. And even if the experimenter never turned on another volt of current, it made no difference. Mr. Dog never stayed around to find out that the rules had changed and that no more shocks were being presented.

The dog had learned to jump when the signal light went on, and he never quit jumping—no matter how often the sequence was repeated—though it was never again reinforced with the punishing shock. It certainly seemed that fear was a response different from all other behavior. Different because it didn't extinguish.

Then an experimenter got to thinking about what might be the explanation for this peculiarity. "What does the dog 'think'?" he asked himself. "Why, of course, the dog 'thinks' that the shock is still being turned on after he jumps out of the box. The reason he thinks so is that he hasn't stayed around to discover that no more shock is occurring. By jumping the instant the signal light flashes, the animal prevents himself from learning that there is really nothing to fear anymore. In addition, Mr. Dog feels so good about getting away from the site of danger, his good feelings of relief constitute a reward for jumping.

"The dog, from his point of view, is avoiding shock. But what his avoidance really does is prevent his learning that there is no more shock and that the box is perfectly safe. Thus, the dog's fear never gets a chance to extinguish or go away *because of the dog's avoidance behavior.*"

WHY WE HAVE TO FACE FEARFUL SITUATIONS

The human being who avoids all situations where he might believe, as erroneously as the dog, that he will be harmed, also preserves the anxiety and fear from being extinguished. In order for this to happen, and for the anxiety to get better, one needs to expose oneself to the situations one has been avoiding—even if there is discomfort encountered in doing so.

The next step in the dog experiment involved closing the lid of the box so the dog couldn't jump. Then as usual, the light went on, but without shock, the dog was given a chance to jump again by the removal of the lid. But now the dog stayed in the box. It had become clear to him that the danger of shock had passed. How had he managed to learn about the safety of the box? Why, by staying where he had thought there was danger until he discovered that there was no danger.

When clinicians learned to apply similar principles to human beings, finding ways to expose them to the conditions which aroused anxiety, the treatment worked. People who had been avoiding things for years discovered, through therapeutic exposure, that nothing awful would happen to them in the situations they feared—and they recovered from their anxiety disorders.

HOW TO UNLEARN ANXIETY RESPONSES

Please note the following carefully:
- To unlearn anxiety responses people must expose themselves in some way to the thing they have been avoiding.
- You as a counselor must seek ways to help the counselee eliminate avoidance.
- The unlearning of the notion that some harmless things are truly dangerous must take place at a "gut" level. That is, it appears that just knowing, intellectually, that a kitten can't hurt him does not cure the person with cat phobia. He must experience through exposure to kittens that the little animals are truly harmless. And he must continue to experience exposure until the feelings of anxiety come to an end.

MISBELIEFS AND ANXIETY

The Bible has a good deal to say about fear and anxiety. And what it has to say on the subject is priceless wisdom. Truth. The truth, as taught by the Spirit of Truth speaking through the Word of God, can be boiled down to one sentence:

For the person who knows God through Jesus Christ, chronic intense anxiety is needless and maladaptive.

Please note what is *not* said in the above sentence:
- It is *not* said or implied in Scripture that if you happen to be suffering from anxiety of one kind or another you are an awful person and a rotten Christian.
- It is *not* implied that something is dreadfully wrong with you spiritually, that you have a demon, or that you are a counterfeit if anxiety presents problems for you.
- The counselor who condemns others for their suffering just be-

cause he perceives that they have a part in creating their own misery is not fit to counsel others in the name of Him who said to the woman taken in sin, "Neither do I condemn you. . . ."

What Scripture *does* make clear is that there is a way out! You don't have to be a housebound anxiety cripple for life. You don't have to stay in the corner by yourself if you are now missing out on human relationships because you are so terrified of the consequences of criticism, embarrassment, or shame. There is help in Christ Jesus who came to give us the truth.

At the bottom of maladaptive anxiety, you will find misbeliefs. Human beings particularly maintain their anxiety and their avoidance behaviors by telling themselves untruths—untruths which they doubtless believe with all their might and main, but which are nonetheless utterly false and plainly harmful.

As you get into counseling someone suffering from anxiety, you will discover that the internal monologue of the anxiety counselee contains two classes of statements:

1. X event is likely to occur (predictions).
2. If it occurs, I cannot handle it (evaluations).

PREDICTIONS

Celia, whom you read about above, predicted:

"I'm surely going to have one of those panic attacks if I go to work. It'll happen just when I'm doing someone's wedding cake that has to be finished before 5 o'clock!"

Jennifer predicted too:

"I just know I'm going to have a heart attack from all this emotion. The rapid beating of my heart proves it."

Here is a list of predictions I have collected from people I've counseled for anxiety problems:

"This plane will probably crash. It's a real danger to be up here in the sky."

"I'm going to go crazy and have to be locked up in the hospital if I keep experiencing these attacks of panic."

"I just know the elevator will get stuck between floors and I won't be able to get out."

"If I go to the doctor he'll probably tell me I have some incurable fatal disease."

"Someone will notice my trembling and then they'll think there's something really weird about me."

"No pretty girl will ever agree to go out with me."

"I know I'm going to fail the test."

"I'll probably be turned down after the interview."

"I'm probably going to be told my performance is unsatisfactory at the evaluation session next week."

I want you to know something right here. I have treated hundreds, maybe thousands of people who were anxiously making such predictions. And I can tell you truthfully: Not one plane has crashed, not one counselee has gone crazy or had a heart attack from anxiety; not a single elevator door has failed to open, and no trip to the doctor has resulted in the expected dreadful diagnosis. Not one of these people has been hated and rejected by a person because of hand tremors; pretty girls *do* sometimes go out with these counselees; they pass tests, succeed in interviews, and obtain good performance ratings.

Fifteen years of counseling have enabled me to hear these predictions by the dozens. I have also been around to discover whether the predictions come true. They don't. Of course, the events predicted *do* happen to people. But not very often. And, to my knowledge, not one of the fearful predictions of my anxiety patients has *ever* actually occurred.

EVALUATIONS

Celia not only predicted she would have panic attacks everywhere, but she accompanied those predictions with the firm belief that if she should panic any time or any place, it would be simply unendurable. Dreadful.

Jeremy predicted, not only that the elevator would stick, but that if it did and he had to wait to be rescued, it would be so awful he couldn't stand it.

Carla's prediction that people would reject her when she reached out to them was accompanied by a completely untested belief that she couldn't handle a rejection and that it would be such a catastrophe she couldn't afford to even think about what rejection would really be like.

When you are working with these problems, you will notice that the people suffering from them not only make predictions, but regularly overevaluate. They believe—and the belief is hard for counselors to shake—that *if* a prediction should come true, it would not be merely unpleasant, painful, uncomfortable, or undesirable. It would be *terrible*—on the scale of a major earthquake, a nuclear war, or the loss of all four limbs.

This notion that when unpleasant events happen to us it's a catastrophe has no ground at all when you hold it up to the light of the truth. A child of God is in a most fortunate position. He has the Ruler of the entire universe for a Father. He doesn't lie, and He has promised that nothing can really harm His own. He has never promised that they won't experience rough times and unpleasant events, but He has guaranteed that not one of them can do real harm to His children. Moreover, He has promised to put limits on the testing so that it doesn't exceed what His child can bear.

So when you hear your anxiety-afflicted counselee saying things like:

"It would be awful or terrible or catastrophic."
"I can't stand it."
"I couldn't handle it."
"It would be simply unthinkable."
"That's unbearable."
"That would be a disaster."
"Why, it would be a calamity, cataclysmic, ruinous, tragic, fatal, shattering, or crushing."

about his predictions and his unpleasant feelings, try to teach him from the Scriptures and from his own experiences that his belief in the ultimate badness of the events he predicts or the emotions he experiences is false.

CHANGING ANXIETY MISBELIEFS

Let's tune in on a counseling session. Phyllis, a 24-year-old newlywed, has begun her first good job after earning her master's degree in business administration. She's especially upset about the weekly oral presentations she is required to make before a meeting of officers and directors.

Phyllis: I've done it a couple of times, but I can't see how I'll do this every week. Last week, my mouth got so dry I didn't think I'd be able to finish. And then one of the directors thought a couple of my projections were too optimistic. I nearly went through the floor! If you can't help me somehow, I'll have to quit. And this is the best job I could ever hope to get. (Weeping) I couldn't sleep all night thinking about it.

Counselor: Why do you think you'd have to quit?

Phyllis: I can't stand this. I can't handle those oral presentations. I never have been able to make a presentation to a group. In school I'd get so scared I'd try to be absent when it was my turn.

Counselor: Tell me what goes through your mind when you're about to get up to present to the directors.

Phyllis: I think about getting so rattled I'll mess up somehow or forget what to say—or maybe I'll get all confused and do so badly I'll lose my job.

Counselor: And then?

Phyllis: And then I'd be a failure. This is the best job I could ever hope to get now and I can't lose it. It would be just too awful.

Counselor: So you're telling yourself that everything hinges on making those presentations well, that if you don't you'll probably get fired, and that getting fired would be such a monumental tragedy your entire life would amount to a failure.

Phyllis: You make it sound a little silly. But it's really true that I couldn't stand getting fired. I've never been able to handle failure. I wonder if I shouldn't just quit and try to find some other job. Maybe this one's just not for me.

Counselor: Quit before you're fired, huh? Why not wait and see, since the end result will be the same whether you quit or they fire you?

Phyllis: Yeah, I guess you're right. Except I don't think I could handle getting fired. Like I told you, I just can't stand failure. And I don't know how many more of those presentations I can stand either. They terrify me. You've no idea. I don't sleep for a couple of nights before.

Counselor: Sounds like you're telling yourself you're definitely going to blow it—to fail or something like failing—if you have to keep presenting.

Phyllis: I just know something like that will happen.

Counselor: And that if you do fail, it will be so terrible you won't be able to live through it.

Phyllis: Well, it wouldn't be quite that bad, but I wouldn't like it.

Counselor: No, of course you wouldn't. Nobody likes to perform poorly, but that's different from not being able to stand it. You *would* live through it. And you'd find another job? That's not impossible?

Phyllis: No, it's not impossible. I'd find a job for sure. But it wouldn't be as good as this job.

Counselor: How do you know that? Are you certain you are in touch with all the possible opportunities God might open to you in the future? You don't know for sure that you wouldn't get an even better job than the one you have now. Do you believe that God is in control of your life?

Phyllis: Yes, I do. I'm a Christian and my life has been placed in His hands. So why am I telling myself that if He lets me lose this job, it will be a tragedy? Good point. I think I see where this is going. I really have been making myself upset by believing that God would let something go so terribly wrong, I'd never recover from the awful effects of it.

Counselor: Right. And we could point out too that your prediction that you're going to fail on account of anxiety is likely false too. Generally, although anxiety *can* impair your performance to some extent, it's not likely to do so to the extent you're envisioning. In fact, the most likely prediction is that through repeated presentations, you'll become less and less anxious. Especially if you don't avoid thinking about it or doing it just because you're uncomfortable.

Phyllis and the counselor completed the session with a plan to keep Phyllis working at her presentations even if she became nervous for a time. In addition, they would do some systematic desensitization, a procedure with an excellent record of decreasing uncomfortable anxiety of various kinds. Notice that the focal ingredient in the counseling is to modify Phyllis's beliefs that her anxiety would devastate her and get her to agree to "stay in the box"—to be exposed to the frightening situation—until her anxiety diminished.

The counselor's efforts were then repeatedly directed toward Phyllis' misbeliefs. The counselor knew that even if Phyllis should lose her job, she could recover from that setback as have many, many others who are now happily employed. He also knew that Phyllis' anxiety was partially produced by her misbeliefs, and that when she stopped telling herself how awful her presentation sessions were, and how terrible it would be if she did not do every one of them perfectly, she would experience less and less discomfort and finally be able to present without fear. Indeed, five sessions later, the desensitization was discontinued, since Phyllis reported that she was enjoying her presenting immensely and was receiving considerable reinforcement for the quality of her work.

"I'LL PROBABLY DIE OR GO CRAZY OR SOMETHING . . ."

One of the most common misbeliefs harbored by anxious people is the notion that their anxiety will become so potent it will kill them. Or, sometimes, they are convinced they will lose their minds. The truth is that neither of these things is likely. The following dialogue might serve as a model for you:

Ron: I'm in terrible shape. I haven't been sleeping at all. I'm just too sick from this to work or anything.

Counselor: Trouble sleeping, huh? What's going on when you're trying to sleep?

Ron: I just lie there with all this stuff going through my head.

Counselor: What, exactly, goes through your mind at those times?

Ron: Last night I thought about dying. If I don't get better pretty soon—well, my heart starts to pound, and I can't breathe. I feel like I'm going to choke.

Counselor: Do you think you will suffocate?

Ron: Maybe. Something will happen. I think I might have a heart attack or something. I can't stand this much longer.

Counselor: Then what?

Ron: What do you mean?

Counselor: What will happen when you can't stand it anymore?

Ron: I don't know. I guess I'll have a coronary and die. I wouldn't be able to get help. I don't know.

Counselor: But you tell yourself that if this keeps up you'll suffocate or have a heart attack?

Ron: Or maybe a stroke. Something's got to happen. It's an awful feeling. I can't go on like this. I've got to get over this pretty soon. And if I don't get some sleep soon, I'll collapse. I almost passed out at work.

Counselor: Sounds like what you do when you're in bed is tell yourself horror stories about what's going to happen to you as a result of your anxiety. Right?

Ron: Right—and I know if I keep getting worse, something's bound to happen. It just can't go on.

Counselor: What makes you think you'll die from anxiety?

Ron: I just know it can't go on. If it gets any worse, something terrible will happen. Something's gotta give.

Counselor: How do you know it can't get worse without you dying from anxiety?

Ron: Well, isn't it so?

Counselor: Absolutely not! Nobody dies from anxiety! But let's take your prediction for the sake of discussion. Suppose you do die—tonight?

Ron: Hey—what? Gosh—

Counselor: No, really. I want you to think about it. What happens next?

Ron: Well, I don't know ... I ... I don't know. Guess I'd just be dead.

Counselor: What's so awful about that?

Ron: Are you kidding? I don't want to die!

Counselor: No, you don't *want* to. But you're telling yourself a whole lot more than that. It sounds like you're telling yourself that if you should die, it would be just terrible. And I'm wondering why you think that's the case? Are you a Christian?

The session continued with an exploration by Ron and his counselor of Ron's habit of failing to tell himself the truth about eternal life. He saw for the first time that he was making his anxiety worse by threatening himself with grotesque imagery about death and keeping out of his thoughts the truth that even death can't separate him from the love and presence of Jesus Christ.

IN ADDITION TO TALK

You can help your counselee change misbeliefs, not only in anxiety, but in other syndromes, by activity, as well as by talking with you. Here are some suggestions for counselee homework:

- When the counselee believes he will die from anxiety, he might be asked to call or visit a trusted physician who will explain that there is no objective physical danger from anxiety.
- For treatment of airplane phobia, the counselee may agree to research the comparative probabilities of fatal accidents in flying vs. driving. Or, he might compare the probability of death from cancer or heart disease with the probability of death from aircraft accidents.
- For the counselee whose fears are based on the belief that other people generally don't like him, it might be useful to ask others for their feedback. He might agree to ask three people something like: "I'm working on learning some things about myself. Would you be willing to give me some feedback? What do you think are my most positive strong points?"
- The counselee may be telling himself he can't live without someone else (a friend who is moving, a spouse or sweetheart who is rejecting him, for example). Ask him to recall specific occasions in the past when the other person was not yet a part of his life in which he was exceptionally happy—proving he does not absolutely *need* that other person to exist, or even to exist happily. "One thing is needful," according to Jesus, and that one is Jesus himself. No one else is absolutely essential to any of us.
- The counselee who fears and dreads foreseen failure can be asked to write out exactly his memories in connection with some past failure and how he recovered from it in order to demonstrate beyond doubt that failure is not the absolute end of everything, but an experience that can be survived and even utilized as part of God's chastening and training program.
- Ask the counselee to engage in study of Scripture for homework, to build a case against his own fear of death or loss; or to write out a scriptural argument against his anxious misbeliefs.
- Ask the counselee to observe his own thoughts in the midst of anxiety, and to write them down in a log. He is to notice that there will be two classes of statements in his thoughts: (a) statements about how things are (e.g. "My palms are wet."), and (b)

statements which predict some dire event (e.g., "I'll probably pass out."). Then use the material to show that the "a" statements are generally true, while the "b" statements are always false—they haven't happened yet. Counselee can then practice reminding himself that "my 'b's' are misbeliefs, so I don't have to let them upset me."

- A very simple tactic which the counselor can employ is to work out life situations with the counselee in which he will likely experience anxiety. Then make an agreement that he is to enter those situations, progressing week by week from those which are easier to the more difficult, until he finally completes the list.
- *Modeling*. People learn by observing another person doing what is to be learned. This process is known as *modeling*. The counselor can often arrange to model anxiety-reducing behavior for the counselee. The counselor can let the counselee observe him handling the snake or kitten, climbing the ladder, entering the elevator. The counselee is then asked to copy the model's behavior.

Anxiety will be reduced as this process is repeated.

You may also choose to model things the counselee might say to others when the counselee might benefit from truthful confrontation and is fearful of it. How to ask others to do things, how to accept compliments, how to decline when others ask. These and other interpersonal tactics may be modeled where the counselee fears doing them.

BEYOND THE SCOPE OF THIS BOOK

Some of the most commonly used clinical treatments for anxiety are beyond the scope of this manual. The counselor who wishes to learn them might obtain more information and supervised instruction from a psychologist in clinical practice. A brief description of these procedures follows, but is insufficient as a basis for practicing them.

Systematic desensitization has an excellent track record. This is a method of presenting to a relaxed person a graded series of scenes to be rehearsed in the imagination. The scenes all share the capacity to arouse anxiety and they have been put together by counselor and counselee in order based on the amount of distress the separate scenes elicit. The easiest are presented first, and are repeated in imagination until the counselee stops feeling anxious. Then more difficult scenes are imagined. The process continues over perhaps fifteen to twenty treatment sessions or more until the entire "hierarchy" has been completed.

Implosion, another way of exposing counselees to their feared situations, is done by presenting the very worst anxiety-arousing situation possible for the counselee to envision, and keeping the counselee's attention on it until the anxiety dissipates.

Both *systematic desensitization* and *implosion* can sometimes be done *in vivo*, that is, by exposing the counselee in actuality to situations he fears. An example: taking a counselee with height phobia to the top floor of a high building and just staying until the level of his anxiety drops from high to low.

DOING THE TRUTH

In the work of overcoming anxiety the counselee and the counselor will discover that the scriptural teaching that the truth is to be *done*, not merely understood, is true to life.

Misbeliefs in anxiety must be corrected and changed, but this will not occur as a purely intellectual exercise. The counselee must actually *do* the thing he fears; expose himself to the anxiety, if need be. And, like the dog in the shock box, he will learn at a "gut" level that there is little or nothing to fear. His anxiety will extinguish.

The counselor should see his work as that of getting the counselee to identify and change his misbeliefs connected to anxiety. A part of this can be done through dialogue and argument. Usually, just enough change can be wrought this way to prime the pump. Just enough truth may get through to enable the counselee to go out and *do* the thing feared. When this is successful, more truth will be apprehended. Experience itself will work with the counselor, the Holy Spirit, and the Word to create in the counselee a new awareness of the truth that he need not fear anything, even fear itself.

MISBELIEF IDENTIFICATION

At first, you, the counselor, must identify the counselee's misbeliefs. And you may have to argue and persuade him to accept your contention that they are false. For he truly believes that he *is* headed for disaster, that his emotions *are* catastrophic, and that he really *cannot* stand any more.

After the counselee has been trained to recognize his misbeliefs as contributing to his misery, you can assign homework: "Would you be willing to pay careful attention to your internal monologue during the next week? I'm especially interested in what you tell yourself when you're in an anxiety-arousing situation. I think you'll notice that you make a number of predictions. Would you be willing to note them carefully and log them on paper as they occur? Then we'll work together to help you to change some of the notions that are causing your pain."

The counselor asks for agreement on homework, and treats the counselee as a collaborator, not as a subordinate.

At the next session, counselee and counselor go over the counselee's homework, working at each misbelief until it is perfectly clear that there is no truth in it. For the following session, the counselee can be instructed to again log his misbeliefs, but this time to add to them the truth as he vigorously challenges his mental nonsense and replaces the misbeliefs with truth.

The object of all this is to train the counselee through practice to notice his misbeliefs *when they occur* in his internal monologue and to immediately clobber them for the untruths they contain, replacing them with the truth he has learned through dialogues and experience.

SUMMARY

In this chapter, the nature and treatment of anxiety have been discussed. You should have learned something of the dynamics of anxiety, as well as becoming acquainted with the kinds of misbeliefs counselees are likely to reiterate to themselves to make themselves anxious. In addition you learned that the key element in all treatment for anxiety must be exposure to the feared stimulus. In some way, the counselee must be induced to try the thing he fears and experience the truth that it will not total him out. The counselor can bring this about by helping the counselee identify, challenge, and replace with truth the misbeliefs which lead to anxiety.

FOR REVIEW AND DISCUSSION

1. Explain some reasons why pills and alcohol are not good treatments for anxiety.
2. What is generalized anxiety disorder?
3. Tell what you can about phobias.
4. List some common phobic objects.
5. What is agoraphobia?
6. How does agoraphobia sometimes end in incapacitation?
7. Why do people fear other people?
8. What things frighten the social phobic?
9. What are the four classes of anxiety symptoms? Describe some of the frightening autonomic events people experience when they are anxious.
10. What was Cannon's term for this state? How about Hans Selye's?
11. Why can you say that the state of arousal is normal? What is God's purpose in creating us with the capacity for experiencing this state?
12. Give the two classes of misbeliefs in anxiety.
13. List or recount some common anxiety related misbeliefs.
14. Tell about the principle of exposure.

15. Rehearse a method for helping the counselee identify and overcome misbeliefs in anxiety.
16. Why shouldn't you "bawl out" the counselee for being a bad Christian when he presents his untruthful fears to you?
17. Why shouldn't you tell another person that there is nothing at all wrong with being irrationally anxious?

CHAPTER FOURTEEN

Depression

(When Feelings of Sorrow Refuse to Leave)

"Is there anyone in this audience who has never been depressed?"
Over the past few years I have asked this question before thousands of people in audiences the country over.

And the result is always the same. Not a hand goes up. Not one person in all those thousands has claimed a life without depression.

Granted, I have usually inquired before defining depression precisely. And granted, the word depression admits of many possible interpretations. Then, too, there is, in any audience, a social pressure effect which influences what people are willing to admit by raising their hands.

Nonetheless, though the experiment is far from a scientific study, it seems very likely that depression is universal among humans. Any phenomenon as common as that deserves attention. Particularly since depression is so miserable. We *all* know something about depression from our own unpleasant experiences with it.

DEPRESSION—AN AFFECTIVE DISORDER

For one thing, we know where depression hits us. It is called an *affective disorder*—a disturbance primarily in the mood or affect of the sufferer.

You should learn the terms used in psychological diagnosis. Several categories of depression are distinguished. And these distinctions have a bearing on what is to be done to help.

1. Major Depression

This type of depression is sometimes called *reactive* depression. That is because it occurs in reaction to life events. These events have often been described in terms of loss.

PRECIPITANTS

A person important to the counselee has died, the counselee has lost his job, he has been robbed of his self-respect or reputation, he has lost a great deal of money, or some dominant life concern has been taken from him. Sometimes the loss amounts to frustration, as the counselee is prevented from progressing toward an important life goal.

Events like these are called *precipitants* to signify that they are not necessarily the main cause of the depression, but that they are the "straw that broke the camel's back," in that they furnish an occasion for a predisposed person to develop a depression.

Counselors should inquire for precipitants when diagnosing depression. If you discover a precipitant, you have reason to diagnose the problem as a major depression.

DEPRESSION VS. GRIEF

People frequently ask, "Isn't it normal to feel bad when you have lost the thing or person most important to you? Why give grief a fancy psychiatric label?"

Strictly speaking, you should not label ordinary grief or expected bad feelings after a loss as depression. Depression implies exceptional or disproportionate bad feelings. When feelings of loss are *disproportionate in intensity and duration*, it is appropriate to diagnose depression.

PREDISPOSED TO DEPRESSION?

Since some people react disproportionately and with unusual behavior to certain losses, while others react normally, it is reasonable to assume that certain people are predisposed to depression. This appears to be the case. Clinicians have noticed that depression *can* occur in almost any type of person, but most frequently it appears in those who are especially conscientious (to the point of nit-picking), dependent, unable to express their feelings directly, and prone to deal with hurt by becoming helpless and passive.

SYMPTOMS OF DEPRESSION

Here are the symptoms of this most common disorder. They include spiritual downers as well as physical and emotional ones. All the various depressive diagnoses include some of these symptoms.

Spiritual symptoms: Counselee feels far from God and cannot imagine that He is near. Prayer and Bible reading are especially difficult. The counselee will say he cannot pray, and describes a sense of spiritual dryness. A spiritually sensitive diagnostician will detect in the counselee's spirit a deficiency of joy in God. The agony of the depressed counselee is often compounded by the belief that God is irreparably angry with him and that his sins are too great to be forgiven.

Mood symptoms: Acts listless, feels lonely and dejected, looks, acts and feels helpless, weeps for very little reason.

Other symptoms: Watch for appetite changes. Counselees often lose or gain weight. Sleep difficulties are almost always present in significant depressions. Usually sleep is impaired, and the counselee has difficulty falling asleep or wakes frequently or early. Sometimes the sleep problem becomes one of hypersomnia rather than insomnia and the counselee sleeps more than normal. Tiredness and lack of energy are common. There is loss of interest in one's normal activities so that what was engrossing and challenging before the depression now seems blah and useless. Counselees say that nothing is pleasurable. They cannot believe that even activities normally pleasurable for them will be rewarding anymore. Depressed people frequently complain that their thinking is slowed, their concentration impaired, and their ability to make decisions gone. Some are troubled by recurrent thoughts of death or suicide.

The reader might, at this point, turn back to chapter seven and compare the ancient description of the sin of sloth with the symptoms of depression just given. John Cassian's (fourth century) definition of sloth appears to be a spiritually oriented portrayal of depression.

2. Dysthymic Disorder

This diagnosis is used when the depression is less severe than in major depression. Sometimes this is called neurotic depression. It is rather difficult to specify how you can differentiate dysthymic depression from major depression. That is because there are no exact signs for telling the two apart. You will just have to become accustomed to noticing that some people are depressed to a milder degree than others.

3. Bipolar Disorder

Bipolar disorders are also discussed in chapter 19, where the focus of attention is on the manic or "high" pole. Here we will briefly review the problem from the perspective of depression. You should be able to identify this one because it is particularly responsive to medication and therefore counselees who suffer from it must be referred to a physician or a psychiatrist for help with the chemical disorder involved. Be sure to make clear to the doctor that you intend to continue counseling the counselee, so the referral is *not* for psychotherapy.

The term "bipolar" refers to the fact that these counselees have mood swings which represent opposite poles on the elation-depression dimension. Some are "high," some are "low," and some are "high and low" at the same time!

In *bipolar disorder, mixed,* the counselee presents a mixture of elation and depression. Manic and depressive ends of the mood pole are present at the same time. Later we will discuss the symptoms of mania. For now, it is sufficient to say that these mixtures are rare. They bubble actively, perhaps even hyperactively, but nonetheless own up to gloomy mood and hopeless feelings. Along with rapid pace in their movements, they speak of feeling sad and down.

Counselees who are having a manic episode are described as suffering from *bipolar disorder, manic.* We will discuss mania in chapter 19. Here, we can note that little can be done with these excitable counselees until medicine has brought them "down." Then psychotherapy and counseling are appropriate. Deliverance is often attempted with these counselees, usually without alteration in the symptom picture, because it is the result of biochemical factors. Where deliverance is effective demonic spirits have mimicked the manic symptoms.

When the counselee's history, taken by the counselor in every case of depression, shows that the counselee has had one or more manic episodes but now is in major depression, the appropriate diagnosis is not major depression, but *bipolor disorder, depressed.* Remember, this one is distinguished from other kinds of depression by the presence in the counselee's history of recurrent episodes of mania and depression.

Treatment for the bipolar disorders is medication. For the depressions, antidepressant medication is indicated. In intractable severe depression, electroshock may be used by the psychiatrist. Readers who are accustomed to hearing negative rumors about this treatment will perhaps be surprised to learn that shock or electro-convulsive therapy has a record of 80% remissions when used with exceedingly resistant depressions. If the counselee is manic or the depression is in remission, lithium, administered with careful medical monitoring, will prevent recurrence. Lithium has no effect on existing depression.

Counseling may be used in conjunction with medication, since these people often have difficult life problems to deal with, as well as spiritual setbacks with which they can use help. Counseling will rarely result in cure for manic or depressive symptoms in bipolar disorder.

4. Involutional Depression

This is a major depression which typically occurs after age 40–55 in women and after age 50–65 in men. Its onset coincides roughly with the period of the so-called "change of life." Counselees often wear a distressed, worried, even angry expression. They are frequently agitated in their depression, and will wring their hands and pace the floor, unable to sit still. The counselor accustomed to seeing his interventions bring relief to counselees with reactive depression will probably be uneasy with these counselees because their moods ordinarily fail to respond even momentarily to the things said to them. Their faces don't light up at all. This depression can be differentiated from bipolar disorder by the history of no previous episodes. Insomnia, guilt, and anxiety are prominent. Sometimes depressive delusions are prominent. Involutional depression occurs three times more often in females than in males.

The involutional period brings menopause and a series of stressful biological and social changes. Women with this disorder speak of feeling useless. They sense that they have lost physical beauty and much of their self-esteem. Children have left home and life seems pointless.

Males speak of loss of self-esteem due to occupational frustrations, retirement, lowered sexual potency, health, strength, and intellectual speed. "I've gone about as far as I can go in life," the counselee tells himself.

Most often these counselees have showed compulsive personality traits throughout life, including difficulty accepting any changes or unplanned events. Typically they have cultivated no hobbies, no outside interests that truly absorb them, and they have exhibited a lifelong fear of death which has never been dealt with as a spiritual issue. They have a sense that time is short, there has been little achieved, and they are usually rigid and hard on themselves.

5. Psychotic Depression

When depression becomes sufficiently intense to include a break with reality, it is diagnosed *psychotic depression*. These counselees may exhibit delusional beliefs. Such beliefs are not subject to change by evidence, argument, or persuasion. And in depression their flavor is always self-depreciating. Counselees believe they are being persecuted because of their sinfulness or their own inadequacy. They cannot seem to believe in the overwhelming love of God for *them personally*, and no amount of assurance seems to get through to them. They may be certain they have cancer (contrary to fact), or that they have been reduced to abject poverty when nothing of the sort has happened.

MEDICATION: YES OR NO?

Recent improvement in antidepressant medication has resulted in the likelihood of improvement in as many as 70% of depressives who are given the newer drugs. With such a high probability of rapid improvement, it is my belief that counselors should refer all depressives to a psychiatrist or physician for adjunctive treatment.

Since many people have the notion that medication for psychological problems creates more difficulties than it solves, we will give some thought to the issue. Medication: yes or no?

While it is true that most tranquilizers for anxiety have little to commend them, are ordinarily quite addictive and habit-forming, and may even perpetuate the anxiety they purport to cure, it seems likely that the Christian counselor will rarely encourage or support their use. It is possible that medications for anxiety will be developed without the drawbacks of presently available tranquilizers. As this chapter is being written, one preparation gaining wide usage appears to be non-addictive. If so, there might, in some instances, be reason to use it.

Sleep research has demonstrated to my satisfaction that sleep medications actually create insomnia, as well as unwanted side effects. This is another class of drugs the Christian counselor will likely not advise his counselees to use.

The newer antidepressants are a different story. Current understanding of the physiological substructure of depression suggests that biochemical imbalances in the brain are regularly present. Specifically implicated are the neurotransmitters. Five of the many neurotransmitting chemicals especially involved are: dopamine, acetylcholine, epinephrine, norepinephrine, and serotonin. The effect of antidepressant medications seems to be to redress the balance among these chemicals in the brain.

These medications are non-addictive, have few side effects, and nearly always bring some immediate positive benefits. Sleep and appetite begin to improve almost at once. Mood improvement may not appear until the medicine has been taken for a week or two.

Since depression occurs with misbeliefs in the self-talk, it should rarely be treated with medication alone. Counseling for change in beliefs and behavior ought to be a part of treatment. Currently available research suggests that, though medication is as effective as counseling in lifting depression, counseling to change misbeliefs has the additional effect of preventing recurrence.

DEPRESSION AND THE INTERNAL MONOLOGUE

In an earlier chapter we saw how an emotion is a response of a person's physical systems to a stimulus and that the stimulus usually consists of words in the internal monologue. As a man "thinketh in his heart, so is he," says the Bible (Prov. 23:7, KJV). I believe that the "heart" in the Bible is virtually equivalent to what we mean by the "self-talk" or "internal monologue." The internal monologue seems to continue night and day. Much of what it does is to interpret events, attribute meaning to them, and talk to a person about that meaning. Thus it serves as an eliciting stimulus for emotions and actions.

Furthermore, it is universally true that depressives think depressive thoughts, as the Bible says, "in their hearts." Depressed mood and symptoms are universally related to certain notions or beliefs in the self-talk of depressed sufferers. When you understand how intimately these characteristic misbeliefs are related to depression and its agony, you will understand better why, in the words of Psalm 51, God "desires truth in the inward parts." In depression, as in other persistent maladaptive emotions, the internal monologue pours forth virulent untruth.

THREE UNIVERSAL DEPRESSIVE MISBELIEFS

It might be well, at this point, to review the section on misbeliefs related to depression in chapter 8. There you will recall that the research on misbeliefs in depression has demonstrated that depressives typically harbor and repeat to themselves three devaluative misbeliefs. To summarize, people devalue or deny the worth of:

• Self
• Daily life
• Future

Their misbeliefs in these three areas include some version of:

• I'm no good.
• My life isn't worth living.
• My future is without hope.

Counseling treatment for depression must aim at change. The counselor and the counselee together work to alter these self-clobbering untruths and replace them with truth.

CHANGING MISBELIEFS BY DIALOGUE

You can help counselees change misbeliefs by means of dialogue, arguing, and persuasion. But you can also change misbeliefs by getting the other person to do new things. And in the final analysis truth learned must be done, practiced, obeyed.

We will look at a sample of counseling dialogue directed at the goal of changing some depressive misbeliefs.

One common notion encountered in depressives is the belief that suicide is a good idea. "I'd be better off dead since life isn't worth living and there's no hope for the future."

Dialogue like the following may be found frequently in the opening sessions of treatment for depression.

Counselee: I can't handle things anymore. What's been on my mind has me scared, so I thought I'd better talk to you.
Counselor: You've had some pretty disturbing ideas, huh?

Counselee: Yes. I've been thinking about—well—I just don't feel like trying anymore—like going on.

Counselor: You've thought about killing yourself?

Counselee: Well, yes, I have. Oh, I don't think I'd actually *do* it, but I have come sort of close. Pills look good sometimes, and I think about how it would put an end to this misery if I could just lie down and fall asleep and never wake up.

Counselor: You think your troubles would end if you killed yourself?

Counselee: Yes, well, I guess so.

Counselor: How do you know?

Counselee: Huh? What d'you mean? I'd be dead. Out of it. That's it. Gone.

Counselor: What do you think that will be like?

Counselee: Just having all those problems over would be nice.

Counselor: What makes you think you'd have finished with your problems if you killed yourself?

Counselee: Well, wouldn't I?

Counselor: I wouldn't be too sure. Killing yourself is taking a life, something the law of God forbids. And in this case there wouldn't be much likelihood of repentance. There's some chance you could find yourself in hell, isn't there?

Counselee: Oh, no, I don't think I'd go to hell. Do you?

Counselor: I don't know of any promises from God that assure us that we can die by means of a sin and still go to heaven. It's pretty risky, isn't it? Assuming you wouldn't go to hell?

Counselee: Well, I never thought of it like that. Maybe it isn't the best answer. Anyway, I don't think I'm ready to do it.

Counselor: I want you to agree with me formally that you won't. I don't feel like working hard with you only to have you put an end to your life before you're all over this thing. Will you make a contract with me in which you agree not to kill yourself? At least for as long as we're still working on your difficulties?

Counselee: I guess so. OK. Agreed. But I still don't see how I'm going to keep on.

Counselor: You're depressed right now. And one of the components of clinical depression is the belief that nothing is worth doing. Another is that the future is totally hopeless. Both of these beliefs result not from the facts but from your depression. And neither of them is true. I can assure you that you will get better. Depression always improves. And meanwhile we'll begin to work on the things you now believe and tell yourself which keep you feeling down.

The counselee now believes it is worthwhile to go on, especially since counseling has begun and maybe, just maybe, there is hope. Notice that the counselor has given reassurance that things will get better. This is not whistling in the dark. Depressives have an excellent prognosis and will almost certainly feel better. But they seem to be unaware of the facts about recovery. It is therefore truthful and appropriate to give them a strong statement to the effect that they will recover.

"I'M A TOTAL FAILURE!"

Now let's examine some sample dialogue on the issue of devaluation of the self. "I'm worthless, no good, a failure," the counselee will say in some form. Nina has just said she's a total failure.

Counselor: A failure? At what?

Nina: At everything. I can't make friends, not real friends, and it's because I'm so worthless. Who would want me for a friend?

Counselor: You're a failure because you're such a social dud? Nobody would like to have you for a friend?

Nina: That's right.

Counselor: Because you are such a poor excuse for a friend yourself?

Nina: Right.

Counselor: Tell me, Nina, what are the qualities that make a person a good friend? Better yet, write a list for me of the ten qualities you'd like most in a friend. Will you do that right now?

Nina: Sure, I guess so. Can you give me some paper?

[Nina now lists the following traits: loyal, kind, thoughtful, warm, friendly, dependable, frank, intelligent, easy to get along with—and she couldn't think of anymore.] Here.

[Hands list to counselor who looks it over and then says—]

Counselor: Now, will you please take the list and put a check beside each of the traits you think describes you?

Nina: Sure.

[Counselee checks for a while, then looks up.]

Counselor: Finished? Which one did you check?

Nina: (A little abashed) Well, I checked all of them.

Counselor: All of them are characteristic of you? And these are the traits you believe most important in a friend?

Nina: Yes. I do have all of them and they are the traits I would most like to find in a friend.

Counselor: Then it looks as though you have what you believe it takes to make a person a worthwhile friend?

Nina: I guess so. Yes, I do. (Smiling) I can't be as bad as I thought I was! Hmm. Maybe I'm not totally worthless, after all.

I have chosen this dialogue to illustrate, using a maneuver of

Beck's, how the cognitions of worthlessness can be changed in the counseling session. It is also possible to use Scripture when counselees maintain they are without value:

"I'M UTTERLY WORTHLESS!"

Counselee: I just feel worthless. I've done so many things that prove I'm no good.

Counselor: What have you done that's so bad it proves you're no good?

Counselee: Oh, I just haven't lived up to my responsibilities, you know.

Counselor: For instance?

Counselee: For instance, I haven't been able to earn enough so my kids can go to college without having to work night and day to pay their way.

Counselor: And that makes you worthless, valueless?

Counselee: Yes, compared with other fathers, it does.

Counselor: Because you should have acted more responsibly in regard to money?

Counselee: Yeah, I could have done more and probably saved more, if I'd been really responsible.

Counselor: Do you recall the story Jesus told about the son who wasted money until he ran out and had to come home with his empty hand out?

Counselee: Uh huh, I remember.

Counselor: He must have felt pretty worthless. Remember, he said to his father, "I am no more *worthy* to be called your son." Not worthy means worthless, doesn't it?

Counselee: Uh huh.

Counselor: How did the father respond?

Counselee: He brought out the best robe and a ring and made a feast. Wanted to show the boy he was still loved, I guess.

Counselor: Did the father consider the son worthless?

Counselee: No, I guess not. Not worthless at all. He loved him.

Counselor: Who does the father in the story stand for?

Counselee: God.

Counselor: God is saying something to you through the story. What is it?

Counselee: That in His eyes I'm not worthless. He loves me.

Counselor: But you've been telling yourself night and day that you are worthless, valueless. So who's right, you or God?

Counselee: Well, God, I guess. He's always right.

Counselor: Then can I get you to agree to stop that voice inside which is propagandizing you with nonsense about your lack of worth and value? Will you challenge it after this and confront it with the issue whether God or that nonsense-laden voice is going to be the source of truth for you?

Counselee: I guess I could try.

"MY LIFE IS NOT WORTH LIVING"

The life of the child of God has a call from God upon it. Many people do not know that God has called them *even if they are not employed in the church's public ministry*. Counselees often must be told that God has called them to be fathers, mothers, sons, daughters, husbands, wives, carpenters, storekeepers, sales persons, and teachers. The contention that life cannot be worth living is thus fundamentally untrue for the Christian. It may well be true for the non-Christian. However, his remedy is to come to the place of knowing Jesus Christ and receiving the Holy Spirit that God may call him and fit him out with gifts for performing his calling.

Sometimes, though, the counselee who is depressed will say, "I know all that, but it just makes things worse. I'm not doing what I'm called to do or anything else. I'm accomplishing nothing."

Study the following dialogue. It illustrates initiating the mastery and pleasure schedule.[1] This is one procedure specifically aimed at countering the notion, "I'm accomplishing nothing, so life isn't worth living."

Counselee: I'm not doing anything.

Counselor: What do you mean by that?

Counselee: Just what I said. I'm not doing a thing. I might be worth something to God, but I'm sure not worth much to myself. Or to anybody else, for that matter.

Counselor: Why do you say that?

Counselee: Because I don't get a thing done. I seem to just putter. Nothing works. And what I do is no fun anymore. It's all just effort, painful effort.

Counselor: Are you serious when you tell me you're not doing *anything*?

Counselee: I'm serious. I can't manage anything anymore.

Counselor: Did you tell yourself all that this morning when you were thinking about getting up?

Counselee: I did. I think these things every morning—all the time.

Counselor: What did you do after you got up?

Counselee: Shaved. Took a shower. Dressed.

Counselor: Did you do all that yourself, without help?

Counselee: Of course I did. (Smiles a little) What are you getting at?

Counselor: Looks like, in spite of what you told me, you do accomplish

---

[1] A.G. Beck, *The Cognitive Therapy of Depression* (Guilford Press, 1979).

some things. And you did dress yourself, quite appropriately, too.

Counselee: Oh, but I don't get much done, I'll guarantee you.

Counselor: And you don't find anything rewarding either, you said.

Counselee: Right. It's all hard.

Counselor: Sometimes depressed people underestimate how much they do. And they also talk themselves into believing their activities are less rewarding than they actually are at the time they're doing them.

Counselee: Not me. I'm getting nothing done, and what I absolutely have to do isn't the least bit rewarding.

Counselor: Nevertheless, I'd appreciate it if you'd do some on-the-spot recording and reporting. Would you be willing to keep a mastery and pleasure schedule of your activities this week? I'll show you how.

Counselee: I guess. It can't hurt. What am I supposed to do?

THE MASTERY AND PLEASURE SCHEDULE

The counselee now agrees to keep a record for one week of all his activities. On this record he is to rate each activity twice on ten-point scales. One rating estimates the sense of mastery he feels in doing each activity. The other estimates the amount of reward he experiences when he does the activity. How pleasurable is it? Mastery is the sense of having accomplished something worthwhile. Pleasure is the feeling that what you are doing is somewhat positive and rewarding to you.

For example, the counselee notes on his log that he walked the dog at 6:40 a.m. Since he had never been able to get himself to even get up before 7:00, he (to his surprise) felt a rather clear sense of mastery, of accomplishment. He gave himself a 6 on the mastery scale. He did not particularly enjoy the walk, so he gave the dog walk a pleasure rating of 2. By contrast, watching television was quite pleasurable for him, but produced little sense of accomplishment or mastery. So, he rated it 1 for mastery, 7 for pleasure.

When this counselee brought his schedule to the next counseling session, there was concrete evidence which refuted his own predictions. He had many items rated higher than 1 for accomplishment so he could no longer say he never did anything worthwhile. And many items were clearly rewarding, in direct contradiction to the depressive misbelief that nothing is any fun anymore.

The counselor then asked the counselee to review his own evidence, conclude that he had been telling himself straight nonsense, and agree to challenge vigorously any self-talk sentences asserting that his life was worthless and empty. In addition, the counselee agreed to deliberately increase the number of activities he would engage in.

LOGGING SELF-TALK

One of the reasons counselees are unable to help themselves when they are afflicted with persistent unwanted emotions, depression, for example, is that they do not know that they are rehearsing misbeliefs to themselves. They are literally unaware that they are making themselves feel bad and haven't the faintest idea how they are doing it.

Frequently, depressed people picture their depression as "coming on," as "coming back," as attacking them, and have no idea that they themselves are endorsing misbeliefs sufficiently devastating to make the happiest person alive descend into gloom.

The counselor can introduce self-talk logs early in the process of counseling.

Counselor: Would you be willing to work at home to tune in on your internal monologue and see how it causes you to be depressed?

Steven: I guess so. But I can't see why I would want to make myself depressed. I just think it's because I haven't got what it takes to handle setbacks.

Counselor: I know you think that—and also you think you are a wretch, a fool, a failure, and a fraud. You've told me all that. I want an on-the-scene, blow-by-blow account of you beating yourself up until you feel depressed. So I'd like to have you log your self-put-downs when they occur. Will you?

Steven: Yes, but I don't see how it's going to help.

Counselor: I realize that, and it may or may not alleviate your depression. But at least we can see how you cause yourself to feel bad; and then if you want to change, you'll see what you must do differently.

Steven: I know other people have tried to tell me I'm not all that bad, but it hasn't helped. I'll try it though. Nothing to lose. What do you want me to do?

Counselor: Throughout this week, please notice when you're feeling bad. At those moments, stop and ask yourself, "What am I telling myself right now?" You'll find, if you tune in, that there are some pretty negative sentences in your head. You probably believe they're true, though they aren't. Please write down how you feel and what you are at that moment telling yourself. Please make a note, too, of any environmental event which may have set the whole thing off—like a disappointment, or some conflict with another person—whatever.

Steven: OK. I'll give it a try.

At subsequent sessions, the assignments can progress. Using the log, the counselor can help Steven see how he scuttles his own ship, so to speak. Furthermore, he can debate with Steven, countering and defeating specific misbeliefs introduced into Steven's thoughts by the enemy. Additional assignments can include logging, not only the counselee's misbeliefs, but also his efforts to counter them with evidence, Scripture, and logic, as well as the truth with which he replaces them in order to experience recovery.

A completed log should include, for each episode of misbelief identification, the following items of information:

1. *The precipitating environmental event.* What happened to "set you off"? Example: Car wouldn't start. Wife seemed crabby. No one said "good morning."
2. *The negative feeling.* How did you feel in reaction? Example: blue, down, sad, worthless.
3. *Misbeliefs in the internal monologue.* Example: "Told myself the car wouldn't start because I'm inept and guilty; can't handle machines or anything else; so guilty I don't deserve a car that starts."
4. *Countering and challenging arguments.* Example: "Jesus died for my sins and I've repented. It's a lie that I'm so awful and guilty. God says the opposite. And I *can* handle machines. I fixed the washer the other day just beautifully."
5. *Truth to replace misbeliefs.* Example: "I don't have to knock myself down with all this baloney. I'm a child of God. I'm free from the lies of the enemy if I want to be, and I do. How dare I put down and berate a child of God of whom God has said, 'I value and love you'? And I'm not going to keep telling myself how inept I am. I'm going to think of the things that, by God's grace, I'm quite able to do and do well."
6. *Expected outcome.* What new feelings do you anticipate as a result of the truth replacing your old depression-generating misbeliefs? Example: sense of worth and value, positive outlook even when something goes wrong.

ACTIVATE

One last point about depression. Research has shown that counselees who are depressed reduce their activities. Depressed people tend to sit and stare at the wall or do things in which they are mostly passive. The result of this activity reduction is that the counselee does not experience the normal rewards which accrue to us all when we get out and do things in the service of God and our neighbor. Thus, the depressed person continues to feel bad in part because he does nothing which might make him feel good.

Meanwhile, the counselee insists that doing things would be useless since nothing would make him feel any better.

In actual fact, this too is a misbelief. Depressed people *do* experience reinforcement or reward when they do activities which were pleasurable for them before the onset of the depression.

Therapists of all kinds therefore try to get patients with depression to get up and do things.

Even if the counselee says, "I can't pray. It doesn't go anywhere," God will be faithful. Christian counselors therefore try to get counselees to agree to a schedule of prayer and Scripture reading which will be carried out for homework. This schedule can be graded in terms of length and difficulty. Don't start out with four hours of Bible reading a day. Begin with perhaps five minutes and increase the length and difficulty of the assignments.

If the counselee has been avoiding going to work, get him there any way you can. You may hear strenuous objections. "I just can't do anything even if I go to work."

"Even if you do nothing but sit and twiddle your thumbs, I want you to agree to go to work each day, rather than stay at home as you've been doing," the counselor will reply. Gradually increase the amount of agreed activity at work as the treatment goes on. Focus on the fact that work is service to God and man, not just a burdensome and time-squandering necessity.

Depressives avoid their friends, let recreation and exercise fall into oblivion, and neglect their families. Systematic graded task assignments can get them activated in all areas. Once activated, the reinforcers they've been missing will flow again.

SUMMARY

Depression is the major component of several diagnostic syndromes. The counselor will do well to learn to identify what type of depression he is dealing with and discriminate those who are likely to need medical intervention from those who can respond to counseling alone. Even in the latter group, a number can be helped by adjunctive medication. Three misbeliefs, all devaluing, are found in depression, whatever its cause. In these notions, counselees systematically and endlessly devalue themselves, their lives, and their futures. Measures to counteract these misbeliefs include argument and dialogue as well as various homework activities to be done by the counselee.

FOR REVIEW AND DISCUSSION

1. What is a major depressive episode?
2. Describe the various types of bipolar disorder?

3. Discriminate major depression from dysthymic disorder.
4. What is involutional depression and how is it related to sex and age?
5. Describe some of the techniques used in the chapter for changing depressive misbeliefs.
6. Enumerate the three misbeliefs found in various forms in all depressives.
7. How is antidepressant medication different in principle from tranquilizers and sleeping pills?
8. Tell how to use the mastery and pleasure schedule.
9. Tell how to use logging for homework.

CHAPTER FIFTEEN

Anger

(When Negative Feelings Take Control)

THE BIBLE AND THE PROBLEM OF ANGER

The problem of anger is not restricted to counselees with a particular diagnosis. It may appear in counselees with various symptoms, carrying a variety of diagnostic labels. Or, it may be the only problem the counselee presents.

The counselor himself is likely no stranger to some of the painful consequences of anger—his own or someone else's. When anger is uncontrolled or poorly channeled, the counselee's life will suffer—spiritually, socially, and emotionally.

Thomas A. Tutko, professor of psychology at San Jose State University, is an expert on the effects of anger. He tells how unmitigated anger may impair the performances of athletes. "If you get so mad that you'd really rather punch the judges," says Professor Tutko, "you're going to be off your game." As a case in point, Edwin Kiester Jr., writing in *Psychology Today*, recounts the story of Pat Ahern, champion in Nordic skiing at the 1984 Winter Olympics. The judges disallowed two of Ahern's jumps, both apparently medal winners. Ahern was understandably angry and it hurt his performance. His next jump was off, and he finished 17th in the cross-country event.[1]

Like an erupting volcano, burying itself and its surroundings, intemperate angry outbursts leave the counselee and those around him weighed down under their fallout. For want of the skills needed to control anger, relationships with God are seriously impaired,

---

[1]Edwin Kiester Jr., "The Uses of Anger," *Psychology Today*, July 1984, p. 16.

marriages are shattered, jobs are lost, friendships are destroyed, children are taught fear, depression, and other neurotic behaviors.

To learn how to apply the truth against anger, we begin with the Scriptures. The word of truth by which God gave us new birth to begin with is a reliable source of power in the control and management of angry impulses and feelings. For instance:

> Of his own will he brought us forth by the word of truth that we should be a kind of first fruits of his creatures. Know this, my beloved brethren. Let every man be quick to hear, slow to speak, slow to anger, for the anger of man does not work the righteousness of God. Therefore put away all filthiness and rank growth of wickedness and receive with meekness the implanted word, which is able to save your souls (James 1:18–21, RSV).
>
> Therefore, putting away falsehood, let every one speak the truth with his neighbor, for we are members one of another. Be angry but do not sin; do not let the sun go down on your anger, and give no opportunity to the devil (Eph. 4:25–27, RSV).
>
> The fruit of the Spirit is . . . self-control (Gal. 5:22–23, RSV).

From these and other materials in the Scriptures, we can learn the following facts about helping counselees with the management of anger:

1. It is possible to be angry without sin, since anger is an emotion created by God for certain adaptive purposes. Jesus, himself, became angry on occasion—of course, without sin.
2. Counselees should be taught to deal with the issues giving rise to anger as soon as they notice they are angry (before sundown, as Ephesians puts it). Perpetuating anger and not dealing with it creates opportunity for the devil to achieve gains.
3. Not all anger is sinless. Some human anger may inhibit and retard God's righteousness in one's behavior.
4. Such sinful anger is irrational and pointless, accomplishes nothing but strife, and should be dealt with immediately by the application of the truth.
5. Self-control is a primary issue here. The Christian ideal is not the all-too-common imperative: "Let your anger out!" but rather, "Develop self-control in all things, especially in matters of anger."

Truths about anger which are related to the above verses:

1. Some anger is to be expressed to the person whose behavior provokes. Here, speaking the truth in love, we seek to involve the other person in changing elements in our relationship which cause difficulty for us.
2. Some anger is not to be expressed, but managed within

ourselves. Here, speaking the truth to ourselves, we seek to eliminate our angry feelings and responses, and to replace them with more God-pleasing and effective attitudes and behaviors.

3. Often, the Holy Spirit will lead us to do both of these things, speaking the truth to ourselves until we are no longer angry, bitter, and resentful so that we can effectively speak the truth to the person whose behavior causes problems for us.

In this chapter, we learn how to help counselees whose difficulties include failure to manage anger well. Such counselees must be taught to apply the truth to their own personal internal monologues to prevent themselves from becoming angry, to stop anger once it has begun, and to enable effective action when they are provoked.

UNDERSTANDING ANGER

One domain of truth opened up by the Word of God and the Spirit of Truth is the working of one's own mind. Knowing the truth about their own reactions helps counselees grow, even when that truth is not totally positive. If they are to change, counselees must know what they are doing and what they need to do differently. Now take a look at anger.

LEN

Len came home whistling. He thought he hadn't a care in the world. It was Friday night, a week's hard work was over, and now for a weekend at home. "Ah, home! A man's home is truly his castle," thought Len to himself. He planned to work on the 1956 Chevy he was restoring. And maybe to spend a little time playing with the kids. And—well, who could tell what pleasures might present themselves? Len was happy and at peace with the world, his expectations high.

No sooner did Len walk in the front door than grim reality intruded. Big Boy, the family mutt, in his zeal to defend the house against the postman, had pulled down the drapes at the front window, tearing gaping holes in the sheetrock. A half day's work? More? When Len went to the garage to check on the supply of patching materials, he found his tools scattered all over the garage floor. Tim! When would that kid learn to consider others? Rachel heard the clank of the tools being put back into the tool cabinet and rushed to the garage. "Oh, Len, you're not going to spend the whole weekend working on that car again, are you?" There was exasperation in her voice.

That did it. Len blew his top. He shouted. He cursed and swore. He threw the tools at the tool box. The kids were scared. Big Boy ran under a bed. Rachel cried. Dinner was a nightmare. Len was ashamed and sore and the weekend was ruined.

Len wanted to learn to control his anger. As we discussed this and other episodes in Len's anger log, the anatomy of Len's anger became clear. As is the case with everyone, each episode of anger Len described involved three categories:

1. *Environmental events.* These are the events we usually (mistakenly) think *make* us angry. Events occur which violate our expectations. Others act contrary to our desires. Someone else criticizes, nags, puts us down. In Len's case, the torn-down drapes, the scattered tools, and finally the disapproval of his wife over his most enjoyable activity were the environmental events to which Len responded with an explosion of rage.

2. *Under-the-skin events.* These take place inside us, and are of crucial importance. These events we often ignore in our eagerness to establish that our anger is someone else's "fault." They include:

- *Internal monologue or self-talk.* We have already been introduced to this crucial element of our personal makeup. We could not become angry without it. It is here that we tell ourselves what the behavior of others means to us. And when we tell ourselves that another person's actions are violating our expectations, hurting us, or meant to harm us we are on our way to becoming angry. Our assessment of the meaning of events may thus help precipitate an angry explosion.

  Evaluation of the other person's actions also occurs here. When we tell ourselves that the behavior is outrageous, or excessive, or too much for us to take, terrible, awful, totally unacceptable, etc., we prime ourselves for anger.

  Len, for example, told himself that his expectations were being shattered, that others in the family were ignoring his needs, and finally that Rachel was viciously attacking him. It was this kind of assessment which enabled him to go on and tell himself that it was simply too much to take, so outrageous that it was perfectly right for him to be angry.

- *Feelings.* The feelings or emotional events we call anger occur next, and these are elicited directly by the provocative statements, beliefs, and evaluations of the internal monologue. If this sort of self-talk continues, the anger is prolonged. Sometimes, the internal monologue of anger-arousing evaluations and assessments continues for hours, days, perhaps even years, with painful and harmful results.

- *Autonomic events.* A number of under-the-skin physiological reactions accompany the emotion of anger. Rapid heartbeat, elevated blood pressure, flushing, sweating, rapid breathing, increased circulating adrenalin, increased muscle tone, clenching of fists, and other internal responses of the autonomic nervous system occur to enable action.

3. *Actions.* How did Len express his anger in actions? At first, he attempted not to express it. When he learned about the drapes, he felt somewhat upset, but said nothing, did nothing to express his dismay. When he encountered the scattered tools, Len again suppressed any expression of distress. Nonetheless, the internal events described above were occurring. At last, when Len told himself that Rachel was attacking and criticizing him, he also told himself he had reached his limit. And so he yelled, shouted, swore, and attacked Rachel verbally. In Len's case, the expression of anger really resembled an explosion.

People may express anger in many kinds of behavior. There may be no expression at all. In that case, the anger occurs mostly under the skin. Mild verbal expression, strong verbal attack, physical violence against objects (Len threw the tools around), or physical violence against a person—all are varieties of behavioral expression.

One variety that is particularly disruptive to relationships and difficult for others to cope with is *passive-aggressive behavior.* Here, the angry person gets even in passive, indirect ways which may not even be recognized for what they are by himself, let alone by the person against whom they are directed. Silence, pouting, stubbornness, burning the dinner, being annoyingly late for an appointment are only a few of the literally infinite number of ways of passively expressing anger against another.

Passive-aggressive behavior does not resemble the explosion of gunpowder or the eruption of a volcano. Therefore, passive-aggressive people often deny that they are angry and persuade themselves that they are hurting no one. In actuality, their anger is as destructive as the explosive kind, if not more so. The deceptive, contorted, indirect aggression these people turn against others is more like the relentless eating-away of a bath in corrosive acid than the concussion of a bomb blast.

PEOPLE ARE MORE LIKELY TO GET ANGRY WHEN . . .

Sometimes a particular set of events occurs and we handle it without becoming angry. At other times, the same events elicit an angry explosion. Why the difference? Some things that make us more likely to become angry are:

- *Tension.* When you are uptight, tense, and nervous, you are more likely to become angry at a particular provoking situation than when you are relaxed, at ease, and calm. Counselees should be helped to identify the conditions which lead to tension for them personally. They can then make allowances for themselves when things are likely to be more difficult, perhaps avoiding events they know will be stressful for the time being. Such conditions as tiredness, hunger, and premenstrual or menstrual upset are commonly associated with increased tension. High humidity and/or temperatures bring increased suscepti- bility to irritation and anger for some people.

- *Expectations.* When you expect someone to provoke you, to be hostile, to be difficult, you are more likely to become angry in interaction with that person than when you have no particular prior expectations. Counselees should be taught to counter their negative expectations with the truth. Example: "I don't have to tell myself that so-and-so will try to provoke me. I can just as well concentrate on keeping my cool and see what actually hap-' pens. I know I can handle it, whatever it is, as long as I don't blow my top."
- *Depression.* There is some evidence that people become angry more readily when they are depressed than when they are feel- ing normal.

Any serious effort to help a counselee overcome a habit of reacting with irrational anger should be accompanied by measures to reduce tension, change negative expectations, and resolve depression and other sources of negative feeling.

But the primary target of efforts to change must be the internal monologue with its anger-arousing assessments and evaluations. We will see that these assessments and evaluations are misbeliefs. That is, though the counselee believes them wholeheartedly at the time, they are untrue and can be countered by the truth of reality and God's Word.

MISBELIEFS IN ANGER

Len made himself angry. He would have said that Rachel did it. Or that Big Boy did it. Or, he might have noted that it was a com- bination of external events, including Tim's dispersal of Len's tools all over the garage. But, as we study anger carefully, we will see that what kicks it off is not some event outside ourselves, not some action of another person, but *our beliefs about that action and our interpre- tation of its meaning and importance.* None of these environmental events could have made Len angry, since none of them hurt him in the slightest—*until Len started telling himself certain things about the events.*

It wasn't Rachel's words, but Len's assessment that they were an attack against him that made him angry. The drapes and the tools couldn't cause anger, but Len's evaluation of those events as terrible and thoughtless acts resulting in abuse to Len led to Len's upset feeling.

Help your counselee see clearly that when he is angry, he has made himself angry by telling himself misbeliefs like the following:

- He is putting me down, ignoring me, insulting me, belittling my importance.
- She is trying to cut me to ribbons, attacking me, slashing at me verbally.
- He did that intentionally and meant to upset me by doing it.
- Her being late means she doesn't think my time is valuable and therefore that I'm insignificant.
- If he thinks I'm unimportant, small, and insignificant and that my time does not matter, I must really be unimportant, small, and insignificant. (Therefore I should get furiously angry to let him know he can't get away with it. Then he'll have to consider me important.)
- His wanting to buy a new car means he doesn't care about my needs, just his own, and that I'm always going to come out second, third, or last in his view of things. (Maybe if I get good and mad he'll see that I have to be considered and my needs do matter.)
- Her treatment of me is unfair, terrible, unjust, outrageous, awful, intolerable, and infuriating.
- He shouldn't be doing what he is doing to me and I have a right to be exempt from that kind of treatment.
- These circumstances, or any circumstances contrary to my perfectly reasonable expectations, shouldn't occur and it's therefore extremely lamentable that they did occur.
- I should get upset about this.
- I have a right to be furiously angry over this.
- I'd better get angry or this will keep occurring.

The misbeliefs involved in making ourselves angry usually include four components. People get angry by telling themselves the following things about some external event or circumstance:

1. This event or circumstance means something hurtful to me.
2. This event or circumstance shouldn't happen. He shouldn't act that way. She shouldn't do that. I have every right to live in a universe where such things don't occur.
3. It's outrageous, terribly bad, awfully unfair, ultimately unjust that this has happened.
4. I have every right, and every reason to become aggravated, angry, upset, and aggressive because this has happened. In fact, I'd better get angry to prevent it happening again.

THE TRUTH

The anger-prone counselee must learn that he makes himself angry by telling himself untruths and lies invented and propagated by the enemy. He can become non-angry by becoming convinced of the truth and energetically informing himself of that truth at the time of provocation and after.

The truth is:

- Nobody can put me down, make me unimportant, or cut me to ribbons verbally. I alone can make myself feel like a nothing by (1) telling myself that the other person means to slight me and hurt me; (2) believing and reiterating that if the other person means to slight me, I must be insignificant; and (3) therefore I should react intensely to what I believe to be slights, insults, and put-downs.

- It is seldom true that the words or actions of others have the sole purpose of slighting and hurting us. People rarely have a vested interest in telling me that I am insignificant.

- Even if it can be proved that the other person ignored, hurt, or insulted me *intentionally*, I do not need to lose my cool, get upset, hurt, provoked, or angry unless I choose to tell myself it's catastrophic for him to do so. While I may not particularly like to discover that another person is trying to upset me, I definitely do not need to upset myself over the whole thing.

- When I interpret another person's actions or choices (being late, buying a new car for himself instead of a washing machine for me, interrupting me, etc.) as commentaries on *me*, I am *personalizing*. Such personalizing interpretations are nearly always erroneous. People do what they do for their own reasons, and these seldom center on me.

- Although I may not like someone else's behavior toward me, I don't need to tell myself how terrible, awful, and infuriating it is. Instead, I can tell myself that there is no particular reason to expect that others will always behave in ways that I consider best for me. The fact is that people are sinners and are quite likely to do wrong, even toward me.

- Nowhere in Scripture is it recorded that I have a right to be exempt from bad treatment by others. As a matter of fact, I have been told rather clearly by Jesus and some of the writers of the Scriptures that I can expect that at times others will treat me badly. Why should I tell myself such things are shocking and unbelievably dreadful when in reality they are par for the course?

- Nowhere in Scripture is it recorded that I should expect that circumstances will always go my way and that if they do not, something is amiss in the universe, or God is dead.

- I do *not* have to get upset over this or anything else. "The fruit of the Spirit is . . . self-control."

- It is silly for me to claim a right to be angry and upset, since getting upset and staying that way harm me more than anyone else. Why should I want a right to give myself ulcers and high blood pressure? Why should I want a right to give myself a knot in my stomach? Why should I want a right to be miserable myself because I believe someone else did wrong?

• What Jesus teaches us to do instead of claiming a right to be upset and stay that way is to forgive. Forgiveness to a brother or to an enemy for hurting us is the Christian alternative to becoming angry and remaining bitter. Counselors should teach any counselee with an anger problem how to go before God and, in prayer, solemnly forgive the person who has hurt him. It is unlikely that real spiritual progress against anger will occur until the counselee has made a point of actively forgiving before God each person against whom he harbors any grudge at all.

Suppose some event occurs which would normally provoke you. Can you imagine telling yourself the truths we have just heard in place of the infuriating garbage you rehearse to make yourself angry and miserable? Can you appreciate how much less irritated you would feel if you did that?

"Certainly," you say, "but I get angry before I even realize what I'm doing. How do I get myself to recall and install the truth in place of my misbeliefs in that split second before I lose my temper? And how can I expect my counselee, whose temper is on a hair trigger, to do it if I can't?"

THE TREATMENT OF ANGER

A good question! And the answer is to take the measures God has provided for changing behavior.

One possible cause of intractable anger is demonic bondage. Occasionally, outbursts of rage are simply expressions of control by an evil spirit interfering with the counselee's freedom to choose his behavior. Christian counselors may or may not have experience with deliverance ministry. If you are not experienced in this area, you would do well to locate someone who has a proven ministry, including discernment, in deliverance from evil spiritual powers.

Most people, however, who have problems managing anger, are not possessed by demons, but experiencing the effects of their own sinful flesh. Begin the treatment of anger with repentance and the crucifixion of the flesh with its anger against God and man. It might be well, in this connection, to review chapter 9, where the issue of repentance is discussed.

Having done these things, and in a context of daily repentance, the counselee must *learn* the habit of managing anger. And this calls for practice. Here is how to train your counselee to practice handling anger with the truth.

HOW TO PRACTICE TELLING YOURSELF THE TRUTH
AGAINST ANGER

The principle of thought practice. If you want to form new thought habits, you can do it by repeatedly thinking the new thoughts you desire to install in place of others. To generate new thought habits in your counselee, teach him how he can practice them in his imagination for use in real situations.

The Apostle Paul urges thought practice when he writes, "Whatever is true, whatever is honorable, whatever is just, whatever is pure, whatever is lovely, whatever is gracious, if there is any excellence, if there is anything worthy of praise, *think about these things*" (Phil. 4:8, RSV).

How to do it. Here is a step-by-step practice schedule for working on anger problems. Counselees will need to practice daily for a while, so they should set aside 15–20 minutes, preferably at the same time each day, to work on replacing anger misbeliefs with the truth. Tell the counselee, "It's important that you set aside this time, devoting it totally to your work. So arrange to be unavailable for answering the phone or the door. And no interruptions from others in the house! Find a comfortable chair or recline on your bed."

Then teach the following seven steps in anger control practice:

1. Take a deep breath. Inhale slowly, filling the bottom of the lungs and expanding the abdomen rather than the chest. Exhale slowly and easily, feeling your body relax as you expel the air. Repeat this three times.

2. Relax all the muscles of your body. Begin at the top of your head and relax muscles in turn until you have reached the muscles of your feet and toes.

3. Think of the last time you became angry at someone and re-create the scene. Notice particularly the under-the-skin events which took place, especially the assessment you made and the evaluation you did, as well as any other anger-arousing and untruthful self-talk you rehearsed for yourself. Notice also what you did to express your anger in actions. Run the whole event through like a movie in your mind.

4. Now, rehearse the scene again, but with some changes. As soon as you are aware of feeling provoked, say, to yourself, "Cool it, George. Just calm down and look at this a minute. You can handle this without getting upset if you want to."

5. Next, replace your anger-arousing misbeliefs with the truth, saying the truth to yourself convincingly. For example, "I don't really have to believe that she did this to get my goat. And even if she did, I don't have to upset myself over it. It's not terrible and outrageous. I've known for years that other people are imperfect, so why get myself an ulcer over it? I can calm down right now and think about how

I want to respond to bring about a constructive result."

6. Next, imagine your actions or words of response. In working this out, remember the Scriptures teach that "a soft answer turns away wrath."

7. Finally, tell yourself that you did well and hear the Holy Spirit say, "Well done, good and faithful servant." Remember, your behavior change is approved by God himself!

This sort of practice will lead to the replacement of habitual and anger-generating self-talk. Instead of telling himself untruths which cause him to become highly aroused and inflamed emotionally, he will tell himself those truths which result in self-control. The result: healthier, happier, more loving, and more effective interpersonal relationships.

THE ANGER LOG

You will want to know exactly what your counselee does when he is angry. And he will need to find a number of typical anger scenes to rehearse and correct in his practice sessions. Also, you will want to keep track of his improvement. For these reasons, have your counselee keep an anger log.

For this, a notebook is needed, preferably one the counselee can carry in with him. *Every* episode of anger should be recorded here. The counselee should include events in which he is successful in lessening or overcoming anger, that is, events which would have caused him to become upset before he began working on his anger. Include events which cause only slight irritation as well as those which infuriate. A carefully written account of internal speech, especially assessment and evaluation of the situation, should be included. Finally, the counselee should describe the behavior with which he expressed or otherwise handled his feelings.

As counselees continue working on anger, their notebooks will provide records of improvement, and they can note the decreasing frequency of their angry episodes from week to week as they continue working. They may also discover that the emotional reactions to these situations will become less and less intense.

"IF YOUR BROTHER SINS . . . GO AND TELL HIM HIS FAULT . . ."

Earlier in this chapter it was pointed out that anger is not only a matter of internal events in reaction to some environmental situation. In addition to the internal response, anger usually includes some behavioral expression. Angry people say or do angry things. Even when we try to repress our anger and deny its presence, it often gains expression in our facial tension, our crabby mood, or our sarcastic voice tones.

Counselors should make counselees aware of the importance of appropriate behavioral expression of anger.

There will be times, of course, when our irritation and anger are so obviously based on our own nonsensical assessments that *no* expression of it is appropriate. Rather, in these situations, it is only one's self-talk that needs alteration. It is of the utmost importance that counselors do *not* teach counselees to lay it on someone else every time some little thing irritates. Learning, by telling ourselves the truth, to put up with small and insignificant irritants in others, is a necessary part of living together.

There are times, however, in which it is appropriate to act. When the other person's behavior truly hurts us, or is sinful, for example. Jesus' words in Matthew 18:15 give invaluable instruction for the management of anger. There we are taught to go to the person and tell him what it is he is doing, how it hurts us, and what we would like him to do differently.

> If your brother sins against you, go and tell him his fault, between you and him alone. If he listens to you, you have gained your brother (Matt. 18:15, RSV).

Training counselees to do this is not simply a matter of telling them that Jesus says they must. Most people do not know how to speak to another person in this situation. It is therefore vital to get the counselee to role play scenes with you, developing what to say to people in his environment at whom he becomes angry or frustrated. Encourage the counselee to practice his conversations with you playing the role of the other person in his dialogues.

Some key principles for the counselee to learn and incorporate into his practice session:

- Calm down before you talk to your brother! This is no place for emotional excesses. Just telling yourself, as you begin, "Cool it, Joe. You can handle this much better if you don't get all shook. Keep it calm and no personal attacks, no matter what he says. You can handle it if you just keep control."
- Tell the other person without sarcasm, angry looks, personal affronts, or indirect insults, what he has done or is doing to hurt you, how it hurts you, and what you would like him to do differently. Keep your speech in terms of tasks and behavior, issues and events, and do not become personal.
- Don't get defensive, even if your brother does. Expect that he will defend himself. Most people have never learned any better. Don't get drawn into an argument, but just quietly repeat your request for change. Don't get involved in his defensive statements.

  As an example: You go to your brother to ask him to stop playing his tuba at 1 a.m., since you can't sleep with all that noise. He replies that you once had a party which kept him awake. He is being defensive, but don't get involved in that. You merely say, "Perhaps I have been thoughtless at times, but I would still like you to keep your instrument quiet from 11 p.m. until morning. Would you be willing to do that?"

- Work toward an agreement or a compromise, stay on target until you have a compromise, and don't forget: no put-downs; keep it issue-oriented.

By attempting to deal effectively with sources of frustration, as well as with the self-talk which prompts and elicits angry feelings, your counselee can learn to overcome his difficulties with anger and be on his way to more rewarding interpersonal relationships as well.

BUT, WHAT ABOUT THE NEED TO LET YOUR ANGER OUT?

Many people today believe that exploding in rage is healthy. They may even have been taught in lectures or books that it is bad for you to "keep it inside" and that the "pressure will build up if you do." They may have heard, from mental health professionals who really should know better, that it is therapeutic to pound on something—pillows, punching bags, or bobo dolls—to take your anger out on something. And they may believe that the consequences of not venting their wrath are terrible.

Unfortunately, mental health professionals have, occasionally, propagated this nonsense. For nonsense it is. There are reams of research reports demonstrating that such activities only increase and reward aggression. They do not "release" it and thus dampen or decrease anger.

From a psychological point of view, therefore, the counselor should never encourage counselees to explode for therapeutic purposes. The Christian point of view clearly discourages this notion. Review again the words of James at the beginning of this chapter.

The suggestions for learning self-control and constructive action to deal with sources of anger and frustration given in this chapter are far superior to the old, discredited "let your anger out" theory. The counselor must never reward or encourage the counselee's intemperate angry behavior. Screaming, swearing, breaking things, hitting people, even kicking the dog are poor ways of dealing with anger. They do not "ventilate" or "release." Instead, they intimidate others and create guilty shame in the perpetrator.

The counselor who does not believe this or needs to convince a counselee who does not believe it may consult the exhaustive account of social learning research on aggression cited by Bandura.[2] This

---

[2]A. Bandura, *Aggression: A Social Learning Analysis* (Englewood Cliffs, N.J.: Prentice-Hall, 1973).

work demonstrates unequivocally that you can't help an aggressive person become less aggressive by merely encouraging him to ventilate his feelings.

SUMMARY

The problem of anger appears in counselees with every kind of diagnosis, and may need work. Working with counselees on anger involves training them in certain kinds of self-control. The Scriptures teach that self-control, not unmitigated expression of rage and anger, is the work of the Holy Spirit in us. Anger involves environmental events which precipitate it, internal events which elicit emotional reactions, and behavioral expression of the anger. Counselees need to be taught to replace these misbeliefs with the truth in order to stop becoming irritated and angry as well as bring an end to long-held bitterness. Counselees also need to be taught to forgive those who have wronged or hurt them as an important step in anger control.

Practice in dealing with self-talk can be taught with the techniques of thought practice, and counselees should be trained to do it daily. In addition, counselees need training in dealing with others who have done something to hurt them. The counselor will give this training by actually having the counselee practice effective ways of carrying out Matthew 18:15, Jesus' teaching about what to do when another person wrongs you. Under no circumstances should the common notion that it is good to ventilate your anger by emotional explosion be encouraged. Both scriptural and research evidence suggest that this notion is incorrect.

FOR REVIEW AND DISCUSSION

1. Discuss the meaning of the spiritual fruit of self-control. Review Galatians 5:23 and context.
2. What has self-control to do with anger?
3. Describe areas in your own life where anger is a problem.
4. Show that it is possible to be angry without sin.
5. True or false: We should never express our anger. Give reasons for your answer.
6. What are the environmental events which play a part in anger episodes?
7. What are under-the-skin events? List some of them.
8. What are some of the different individual variations in action-expression of anger?
9. Give a number of conditions which make people more likely to get angry.
10. Tell why it is impossible for anyone to make us angry.
11. Give some common misbeliefs found in anger.

12. Give the four parts of anger misbeliefs.
13. Counter each misbelief you gave in #11 with the truth.
14. Outline a training program you can use to teach counselees to handle anger better.
15. Start your own anger log and notice when and where you are likely to get angry. Keep it for several weeks and see if you can decrease the frequency of anger episodes in your own life.
16. Describe the training of counselees for dealing with others who have done something to hurt or upset them.
17. Is it true that people need to let their anger out by yelling or hitting something? Explain your answer.

CHAPTER SIXTEEN

"My Doctor Says It's Psychological!"

(When Mind and Emotions Hurt the Body)

Lorna was furious. She had been referred by her physician for counseling when she had gone to him for help. Her backache was real. Why couldn't she just have something for the pain?

"He oughta have my back pain," she said. "He'd find out it isn't 'all in my head.' "

Like many people, Lorna believed that when she was advised to get psychological help for her condition, she had been put down. She thought it was a thoroughgoing disgrace to have her illness labeled "psychological," and she was having a hard time forgiving her physician.

She probably misunderstood too.

When a physical disorder is diagnosed as "psychogenic" or "psychological" or "psychophysiological" or "psychosomatic," your physician isn't playing games to see how well you can spell these big words. And he isn't putting you down.

This diagnosis doesn't mean that an illness is not "real" or that the patient's imagination is playing tricks.

Nor does it imply that a person has nothing more wrong with him than an evil spirit of some sort which needs only to be cast out for all to be well again.

A psychosomatic diagnosis is another way of reflecting the well-documented fact that life stresses can create and/or worsen physical illnesses. Another fact: Counseling can help a person recover when psychological stress has produced physiological symptoms.

STRESS

We are frequently told that we suffer more from exposure to stress than any generation in history. Such assertions are usually accompanied with vague references to nuclear war and the rapid tempo of modern life.

Such statements betray either a sketchy knowledge of history or a poor understanding of stress. During the fourteenth century, for example, bubonic plague wiped out well over half the population of Europe. Imagine the stress of living in the midst of such a threat!

But the notion that stress is purely and simply external events acting upon us is also wrong.

Psychological stress is caused, not by events, but by the meaning we attribute to events. Events don't affect us. Our beliefs about things do.

How upset we become when we believe the other person intended to insult us! And then when we discover later that what was said was actually meant as a high compliment, we recover quite nicely: the same event with two interpretations or meanings. It is the meanings which make all the difference.

Vernon calculated his income tax and thought he owed the government an enormous amount. All night he was tense, restless, sleepless, and despondent. When his accountant informed him that he'd made an error and that he owed nothing, he felt like a new man. The tax facts hadn't changed. But Vernon's interpretation did, and it was the meaning which produced—then lifted—Vernon's stress.

When people go through life believing and telling themselves that certain events would be awful, terrible, dreadful, and catastrophic, the bare possibility of those things happening creates overwhelming stress. Other people experience the same events, telling themselves that they are merely inconvenient or unpleasant but survivable. For these folks, the identical events which "throw" those in the first group cause little or no stress.

ATTRIBUTION AND STRESS

Attribution, or the meaning with which we ourselves interpret events, determines how stressful they will be for us.

We cause events to be stressful by the meaning we give to them. This is the law of attribution.

Almost any event to which we assign woeful meaning can be a stressor. Common stressors encountered in counseling others are: separation or divorce, quarrels with others, death of a spouse, suicide of a loved one, contracting a large debt, losing a job, suffering a physical illness, financial setbacks, problems with children. No surprises in that list. But some readers may be shocked to learn that positive events can be stressful too. Getting married, being promoted, finishing school, getting an advanced degree, increased income, taking a vacation are examples of events commonly involved in stress. Change may be the major ingredient of stressful events—change for the worse or for the better! When we attribute threat, horror, or demand to any event involving change, that event becomes stressful.

Remember, the events of life can be *made* into stressors. All we have to do is attribute to any of them the attributes of a mortal blow and talk to ourselves that way.

MISBELIEFS AND STRESS

With misbeliefs like the following running through our heads, it's possible to actually measure the physiological changes in heart rate, blood pressure, stomach acid secretion, and intestinal peristalsis (as well as other physiological changes and events):

- I *must* hurry! Delay is absolutely *intolerable*. I can't stand waiting. Time is money.
- People who make me wait are terrible and inconsiderate, downright infuriating.
- I must be first in everything, absolutely tops, and to be outclassed in anything I do is unbearable. I can't stand being second.
- People are all critical and waiting to catch me doing something they can judge me for. *Watch it!*
- Good, better, best
  Never let it rest
  Until the good is better,
  And the better best.
- If I don't think about my job day and night, I might not get ahead, and that would be woeful.
- It's important to be super alert so I don't have an accident, get cancer, have a heart attack, slip up somewhere, get somebody upset with me, or get killed. Any of those things would be too bad for me to tolerate. I just couldn't. I must make *sure* they don't happen!
- I know life will never be worthwhile again since my divorce.
- I'll never be the same since _____ died. He/she is all that made life worth living.
- It's essential to remember to have fun on this vacation. It's costing *so* much money! I've *got* to enjoy myself!

STRESS REACTIONS

God created us with built-in mechanisms for response to threat. If you turn back to chapter 10 you can review some of the physical events our bodies automatically activate under stress. These events, known as the *general adaptation syndrome,* the *fight or flight response,* or the *arousal syndrome,* prepare us for coping with danger. But when we attribute danger to events which are not dangerous, or attribute awful threat to events which cannot really do us all that much damage, we are liable, by our attributions, to fill up daily life with threats. Then the physical events designed for meeting real danger are made to occur frequently or constantly.

Another way to put it: if the internal monologue pours out a constant torrent of threatening predictions, negative evaluations, imperative demands, and doom-filled judgments about our affairs, we will experience a good deal more tension and arousal than God created us to handle.

If Satan can finagle until his lies saturate our internal monologues, he can make us sick—sick with stress. Sick in body, soul, and spirit. Psychological stress can produce reactions in our emotions and in our bodies only through the internal monologue.

Here is a partial list of physical systems which can be made sick with stress. Notice that all of them proceed from events which are included in the arousal syndrome.

System	*Symptom*
cardiovascular system	palpitations (rapid heart beat)
	high blood pressure
	migraines
respiratory system	asthma attacks
gastro-intestinal system	stomach ache
	ulcer
	colitis
	diarrhea
	constipation
musculoskeletal system	headache
	back pain
	muscle aches and spasms
skin system	neurodermatitis

genitourinary system	impotence
	lack of orgasm
	frequent urination

The above list is only partial. Furthermore, almost any physical illness can be made worse through stress. And when you consider the emotional pain stress can visit on us, you can begin to see what extraordinary power can be wielded for good or evil by our beliefs.

The range of human illnesses which can be precipitated by stress is wide. Not only can stress aggravate most physical problems, it can also bring on depression, anxiety, frustration and every other emotional difficulty discussed in this book. One of the chief interests of the counselor in initial interviews ought to be to determine what the stressors were which, combined with misbeliefs and misinterpretations in the self-talk, pushed the counselee into illness.

In practice, counselors most often encounter both physical and emotional problems in the same individual's reaction to stress. Depression, anxiety, and worrisome ruminations of major proportions are frequent among people who suffer from stress-related physical illnesses. Keep this in mind even though in this chapter we are concentrating our attention on physical consequences of stress.

IMPORTANT DISTINCTIONS

If you think back over the path we have traveled in this chapter, you'll see that we've come a long way from Lorna's notion that doctors thought her illness was "all in her head." Far from it. The sicknesses we have been discussing involve the whole person, not just the head. And they usually involve real, measurable, organic changes in body organs and systems.

Although we cannot venture far into a discussion of them in this book, there are some other physically manifested emotional problems you ought to know something about.

Most patients with these conditions vigorously resist any suggestion that they need counseling. Therefore we can afford to omit a lengthy discussion of them. They are fascinating, but space is limited, so we will be content with merely naming them and clarifying how they are different from the truly physiological stress illnesses we've been discussing.

1. *Conversion symptoms* (hysteria): These were evidently much more popular in the nineteenth century than they are today, presumably because *Good Housekeeping*, *Redbook*, and *Time* keep the population relatively sophisticated regarding medicine and physiology. These symptoms depend on lack of understanding or insight.

Such syndromes always involve impairment of sensory or motor functioning in some area or organ. At the same time, there is *no* organic difficulty whatsoever. If any group of illnesses can be said to be "all in your head," it is this group.

These patients manifest paralysis, blindness, deafness, mutism (inability to speak), numbness, tinglings, and lumps in the throat (imaginary symptoms all). Often the impairment seems to be "motivated"—that is, the patient has a purpose which is fostered by the development of symptoms.

Here is an example: A young woman became paralyzed after giving birth to a baby. Eventually she revealed a wish to escape from the responsibilities of marriage and caring for the child. But her wish made her terribly guilty. So she developed paralysis one morning and thus "solved her problem." She could not carry out her responsibilities because she could not walk. She didn't have to leave her home. And she could punish herself through illness for her guilt. How much better for her when she discovered a personal relationship with the truth, who is Jesus. Here was a real solution for guilt and a new source of power and motivation to serve Him by doing her duty. Though she had been lying to herself to bring about her condition, this young woman was not fully in touch with her own mental processes, and had therefore enabled herself to believe her own lies. She was not a malingerer.

2. *Hypochondriasis:* The counselee talks of nothing but his illnesses, his body, his symptoms, his pains. When he has few or none, he worries about what diseases he might have. When he is given a benign diagnosis by the physician, he often becomes disturbed by the physician's "carelessness" or "lack of skill in missing what's wrong with me." Relatively few of these counselees seek psychological counseling. Those who do are generally referred by others. They seldom participate very intensively for very long once the discussion no longer focuses on their bodily concerns.

3. *Malingering:* This is to be distinguished from conversion by the fact that the malingerer is deliberately and knowingly faking. Generally there is money to be made from disability payments or victory in a lawsuit and the malingerer tries to convince others of the genuineness of his pain or disability.

4. *Munchausen syndrome:* These individuals present themselves for hospitalization with faking of symptoms. They often have considerable medical knowledge, sophistication, and imagination, and can convince surgeons to operate on them. Their one goal appears to be hospitalization, and their entire life is marked by successive hospitalizations, often for major surgery which is not needed. Although these individuals too are lying, it is not for external gain, but is evoked by deep dependency and other underlying personality traits. They are truly psychologically disturbed. Rarely are they seen in the counseling clinic.

This disorder has proved, for all practical purposes, untreatable, since the patients leave care as soon as the diagnosis is communicated to them. The Christian physician is much more likely to encounter these poor people than the psychologist or counselor. It would seem to be an occasion to witness to the Lord Jesus as the one great Physician toward whom the patient can realistically direct his massive dependency needs.

COUNSELING FOR STRESS AND STRESS-RELATED ILLNESSES

Had this book been written a few years ago, there would have been no section on the direction to take in counseling with persons suffering from tension and tension-related illnesses.

Pat phrases were directed at these people, but they rarely did any good: "You're working too hard." "You have to take it easier." "You need a vacation." "Don't get so upset." "Think positively." "Cheer up. Laugh a little."

Or they were given tranquilizers.

Sometimes they medicated themselves with alcohol or barbiturates. This, of course, only compounded their problems.

Expensive psychotherapists would analyze them, sifting through their unconscious mental contents, recovering the repressed material of the past. It is not certain that this was helpful. In my opinion, this procedure was effective only when the patient's stress-prolonging misbeliefs happened to get changed in the process.

It is now possible to instruct counselors in a procedure which will reduce stress if it is utilized collaboratively by counselor and counselee. Here it is, in outline:

1. Explain to the counselee how it is not events, but his interpretation of events, which is causing his stress symptoms and tension. His present attributions are misbeliefs.

2. Work together to locate the counselee's stress producing misbeliefs about events. These erroneous attributions will at first seem utterly true to the counselee.

3. Dialogue with the counselee, challenging and defeating misbeliefs and breaking his hold on the lies of the enemy which have been swallowed and incorporated into the counselee's system of attributions.

4. Work together on change. Counselee and counselor together devise activities the counselee can engage in to bring about changes in the stressful attributions he now uses.

5. Collaborate with the counselee in the search for truth to replace the misbelief-laden attributions you have challenged and found erroneous.

6. Teach the counselee to vigorously battle and halt his repetition of stress-producing attributions, replacing them with truthful and stress-reducing attributions. Example: Instead of, "How outrageous

it is when anyone keeps me waiting—it makes me feel small and unimportant and I can't stand that," the counselee learns to think, "I can handle waiting and keep calm while I'm doing it. After all, I don't have to force people to act as if I matter. God says I matter. I feel better not having to insist that others constantly affirm me."

HOW IT WORKED WITH LORNA

Lorna, whom you met at the beginning of this chapter, was referred for counseling by her physician who thought that much of the pain she was experiencing from her arthritis was related to stress-induced muscle tension.

Lorna: I do worry a lot, I guess. Could worry produce all this pain? My arthritis is real. I've seen X-rays of the calcifications.

Counselor: If your worrying is accompanied by increased muscle tension, you could cause your pain to become quite a bit worse by upsetting yourself.

Lorna: Upsetting myself? What do you mean? I don't want to worry so much. I just can't help it.

Counselor: Maybe we could talk about what it is you think when you worry.

Lorna: That's easy. My job. I was promoted last June, and—come to think of it that's when my pain got worse—anyway, the new job is real responsible and all, and I just wonder if I've got what it takes to do it. I guess I'm afraid they'll think I'm not good enough.

Counselor: Why do you think that?

Lorna: Well, I've got this new supervisor. He's a perfectionist, I think. And he never says anything positive. I can't seem to do anything to please him.

Counselor: So you tell yourself you're not good enough, just because you don't manage to please your supervisor?

Lorna: I guess that's what I've been doing. If your supervisor doesn't like your work, it can't be worth much.

Counselor: Really? Your supervisor is infallible?

Lorna: That's not what I meant. He is in charge, though, and he can fire me.

Counselor: Is that what you think will happen?

Lorna: Well, no, I suppose not. But I might get demoted—back to my old job, maybe.

Counselor: The job you were happy with before you were promoted?

Lorna: Well, I didn't think of it that way, but, yes, I guess I was happy with it. I certainly didn't have this pain you claim is related to the new job.

Counselor:	What would be so terrible about getting your old job back, the job you liked well enough to stay relatively free from worry and tension.
Lorna:	Nothing, I guess. It wouldn't be terrible. It might even be a great relief.
Counselor:	Yet you've been upsetting yourself over the possibility, as if it were the worst of woes! Can you see now how a person can cause herself to be distressed and disturbed about some future possibility even when that event, if it happened, might not be so evil? Besides, it sounds as though your supervisor never says anything positive to anyone.
Lorna:	No, he doesn't. Everyone feels the same way about him. Nobody can please him.
Counselor:	Then why do you think the problem is yours at all? And how can he demote you without firing everybody? Wouldn't you be more in line with truth and reality if you told yourself that you would certainly like to please your supervisor, and as a child of God you'll give it your best shot, but if he is the kind of person who can't be happy with anyone, there may not be much you can do about it? And meanwhile it's highly unlikely you'll be demoted.
Lorna:	That would be quite a bit different from what I've been thinking. But I can see it's so. I think I'll try it.

Lorna and her counselor continued to engage in dialogue similar to the above. And as the dialogue progressed, Lorna became skilled at doing as the counselor did. She learned to locate her tension-generating misbeliefs, test them for truth, reject and challenge them, and replace them with the truth.

As she went along, Lorna discovered what many others have learned: that the misbelief at the bottom of the heap—the one on which the others mostly rest—is the notion that God isn't in charge or that God will do something that is bad for His children.

This is the final "what if" that all worriers must face.

Lorna:	You've helped me see that I probably won't lose my job. But I still wonder about it. What if I should? I wouldn't know what to do.
Counselor:	OK, let's face that. What if you should lose your job in spite of the fact that it's not very likely? What then?
Lorna:	I don't know what I'd do then. I'd feel like my life was ruined. I can't face that one.
Counselor:	You think God wouldn't be able to stop him if the crotchety supervisor decided to fire you, huh?
Lorna:	No, of course not. God can do anything.
Counselor:	Even provide a new job for you?

Lorna: He could do all that and more. But what if He didn't? How do I know He will? Maybe He won't want me to have another job or something.

Counselor: Maybe not. What if He didn't want you to? Wouldn't He be able to meet all your needs anyway? Or wouldn't He want to?

Lorna: Yes, I guess He would take care of me. Sure, He can do it and I suppose He wants to. He wouldn't let me starve, I know that. But I'd still feel terrible and defeated.

Counselor: If He did allow you to lose your job and not provide some other, better job right away, but took care of you so that you made it through, would He just be playing games with you or would He be working out some really good plan in your life?

Lorna: Well, He wouldn't play games. And He wouldn't do anything bad. And I guess there's no question that He is and always will be in control.

Counselor: So how could you be so defeated?

Lorna: You know, you're right. I've been telling myself that if the worst happened, my life would somehow be getting away from God and His plan. But it wouldn't at all. I'm going to tell myself that God is in control, and that even if I get fired or something like that, God will see me through and it will be made good in my life.

Lorna began to smile and her face brightened for the first time. As she began repeating the truth to herself she was able, for those moments, to experience the release of tension in her body and the release in her emotions which are brought about by the fundamental truth that God is in charge for good.

Two Fundamental Misbeliefs:
1. **God is not in charge**
2. **God is not truly good**
Therefore, something can go terribly wrong and I should worry about it.

I don't mean to imply that Lorna was totally finished with stress and tension from that moment on. But there was a clear result and release when the truth broke through into her self-talk. The habit of telling herself misbeliefs had to be broken. Lorna had to go home and actively battle these and other habitual misbeliefs. She did so, and was able to report markedly lessened joint pain as a result.

MORE STRESS-PRODUCING MISBELIEF-ATTRIBUTIONS

Here are some more misbeliefs commonly found in the attributions of people suffering stress symptoms in their bodies:

- My wife is pregnant and we'll never be able to make it. I can't support the family we have now. This is terrible.
- I'm sure our sex difficulties mean one of us is horribly messed up inside. I feel like just giving up.
- It's absolutely crucial for me to succeed at my new job.
- All my children have moved out and I'm useless. I might as well die.
- Now that I've retired I'm useless. I might as well die.
- Our daughter-in-law doesn't seem to like us. That makes me miserable.
- Every problem has a perfect solution and I've got to find it.
- I can't stand the way my neighbors act.
- I can't get over my anger and bitterness toward my former wife. If you'd been married to her you couldn't either.

OTHER TREATMENTS FOR STRESS

While it seems evident that the most excellent way in the treatment of stress is to help the counselee change the world view or philosophy of life reflected in his self-talk, there are other treatment techniques the counselor should be aware of. It is possible to refer counselees to appropriate professionals for these supplementary stress interventions. Some of them the counselor might learn to do himself under appropriate training and supervision. Detailed discussion of these procedures is largely beyond the scope of this book. Here is a list:

1. *Acquiring effective interpersonal behavior.* Although I take a dim view of the usual assertiveness training programs because they aim at assertion of the self and the flesh, nevertheless, many people could benefit from learning more truthful and effective ways to talk to others. Much of the tension treated in the psychological clinic occurs in people unskilled in dealing with others. Much stress in relationships results from widespread failure to act on Jesus' teaching in Matthew 18: "If your brother sins against you, go and tell him his fault. . . ."

2. *Learning relaxation techniques.* There are numerous methods for training people in relaxation skills. These have been demonstrated to be effective for reducing stress. With these methods, which can be very powerful when combined with the acquisition of new self-talk, stress is combatted on the physical level as well as in the internal monologue.

3. *Cardiovascular conditioning exercise.* This type of exercise, also

known as aerobic exercise, has been demonstrated to be effective in reducing stress, anxiety, and depression. Exercise for stress reduction must involve some repetitive movement (running, bike riding, rowing, jumping, swimming) which causes the pulse rate to increase and remain rapid for at least twenty minutes. Pulse rates appropriate for age and physical condition can be suggested by physicians knowledgeable about aerobic exercise. Counselors suggesting exercise to counselees should urge them to consult their physicians. This is especially important for counselees with known physical problems or over forty years of age.

4. *Medication.* Although medication for stress has frequently been advised, I am cautious about suggesting such an approach in most cases. There are several reasons for caution. First and most important is that stress symptoms are frequently God's signs of a need to change something. To dampen those signs by simply taking a pill will, in the long run, create more problems than it solves by postponing behavior change. Second, medication for stress has usually been rather highly addictive or habit forming. Most Christians will not want to be "hooked" on anything or dependent on anything other than God. Nevertheless, there are some drugs which are not habit forming, and there may be individual cases in which the counselor will feel that medication is a useful adjunct for reduction of tension generated in a period of temporary and unusual stress. If so, this impression may be checked with a Christian physician skilled in the use of psychotropic medications.

SUMMARY

Psychological or emotional stress, we have come to understand, is generated within our internal monologues, and is not a property inherent in circumstances. In other words, we are stressed by our *interpretation* of events rather than by events themselves. Please note that we are not talking of physical stressors such as a streptococcus infection or a hemmorhage. It is not likely that the effects of such events is mediated by our self-talk. Stress from our attribution or misbelief-filled interpretations of events can produce any number of physical symptoms and can make virtually any illness worse. A number of typical stress-related illnesses can be listed and will likely include such diseases as some kinds of high blood pressure and headache.

Psychophysiological illnesses should be distinguished from conversion, hypochondriasis, malingering, and Munchausen's syndrome. Psychophysiological, or stress-related symptoms, may be treated effectively by Christian counseling. The target is misbelief change, and the counselor aims to teach the counselee to locate and change her untruthful attributions, particularly as to the stressors in her life.

Often a fundamental change must occur in the counselee's philosophy of life. Counselors should consider referral for other methods of stress reduction in certain instances. Relaxation and exercise are both known to be effective.

FOR REVIEW AND DISCUSSION

1. Explain the meaning of the statement: Stress results from attributions.
2. List some life events which commonly prove stressful.
3. List some common misbeliefs which generate stress.
4. Describe some of the physical consequences of stress.
5. Give the fundamental misbeliefs generating stress.
6. How can those misbeliefs be countered?
7. Locate some Scripture passages which directly counter them and which could be used by counselees in changing.
8. Why should one be cautious about using tranquilizing medications for stress symptoms?
9. Have you been able to reduce your own life stresses by working on your misbelieving attributions? Can you be specific?
10. Describe and differentiate conversion, hypochondriasis, malingering, and Munchausen's syndrome.

CHAPTER SEVENTEEN

Obsessive-Compulsive Disorders

(When Perfectionism Defeats)

Counselees suffering from obsessions or compulsions believe they must perform certain actions (such as excessive washing) or think certain painful thoughts.

Let's begin our look at these puzzling disorders by first comparing some of the misbeliefs commonly found in counselees suffering from them to a section of the letter of James in the New Testament. Comparison of some of the symptoms may make this disorder more identifiable than a short definition.

James 1:16–27	The obsessive-compulsive misbelief as an answer
Do not be deceived, my beloved brethren. Every good endowment and every perfect gift is from above, coming down from the Father of lights with whom there is no variation or shadow due to change. Of his own will he brought us forth by the word of truth that we should be a kind of first fruits of his creatures.	• I can't stand it if it isn't perfect, so *I* have to do my utmost to make sure. • And how dreadful that things aren't perfect. I can't stand that either. • Change? I don't want any change that is not a result of *my* plans. I can't stand change unless I can control it. • His will? *I* have to control things or else I can't be sure they'll come out right. So I hate to let go!

Know this, my beloved brethren. Let every man be quick to hear, slow to speak, slow to anger, for the anger of man does not work the righteousness of God. Therefore put away all filthiness and rank growth of wickedness and receive with meekness the implanted word, which is able to save your souls.

But be doers of the word, and not hearers only, deceiving yourselves. For if anyone is a hearer of the word and not a doer, ... he observes himself and goes away and at once forgets what he was like. But he who looks into the perfect law, the law of liberty, and perseveres, being no hearer that forgets but a doer that acts, he shall be blessed in his doing.

If any one thinks he is religious, and does not bridle his tongue but deceives his heart, this man's religion is vain. Religion that is pure and undefiled before God and the Father is this: to visit orphans and widows in their affliction, and to keep oneself unstained from the world.

● If I stop controlling my thoughts long enough to listen, I might hear something which will upset me terribly. I can't stand that.
● Anger, filthiness, wickedness? Save my soul? I'm afraid I'm going to hell. I'm afraid I'm lost. I can't concentrate on the Word. I've probably committed the unforgivable sin.
● "Rank growth of wickedness. . . ." Yuk! How contaminated and nasty it sounds! That's me, all right!

● What if I'm deceiving myself?
● What if I'm a homosexual?
● What if I'm not saved?
● What if I. . . ?
● I just don't know myself at all.
● What if I'm not even me?

● It is so important to think, ruminate and cogitate, I don't have time to act, to write my paper, to do my housework, to visit the sick, or anything.
● That's what I'm afraid of—how do I know I'm not deceiving myself? That's my problem. Oh, this is upsetting me terribly!
● I feel guilty. I am guilty. And I can't get my mind off my guilt.

I JUST CAN'T HELP IT!

Carla: I wish you could help me. I'm not sure anyone can. I'm having trouble getting to sleep. Doesn't God say He gives

His beloved sleep? He must not love me. He's not giving much sleep to me.

Counselor: What do you do after you go to bed?

Carla: I think about—this will probably sound so weird—I think about whether or not I turned off the light in the basement.

Counselor: And you worry so much you can't fall asleep?

Carla: I don't really worry. I think about it though and finally I go and look to make sure.

Counselor: And then?

Carla: And then it's always out, just as I should have known, but I start wondering again, almost as soon as I settle down. Lots of times I'll have to get up again to go and see if I really turned it out. It becomes a big issue. I don't know why. I might have to run downstairs two or three times more before I think, "Yes, it's out. I know it is." Then I can fall asleep. But all this might take a couple of hours.

Carla's belief that her thoughts and actions were out of control was a diagnostic clue to obsessive-compulsive disorder. Other familiar obsessive-compulsive themes were right up front too.

SYMPTOMS OF OBSESSIVE-COMPULSIVE DISORDER

Notice how, in the first brief sample of conversation with Carla, she reveals a number of traits characteristic of people with these disorders.

NEGATIVE PREDICTIONS

For instance, Carla makes clear right from the start that she isn't sure anyone can help her. The cheerless conviction that things aren't going to work out very well or that every venture is bound to fail is almost always prominent in the misbeliefs of this group of people. Somehow they can't seem to expect the best from self, others, or, for that matter, from God.

PERFECT EVERYTHING

Nevertheless, and this paradox is a source of endless misery, these counselees invariably believe that everything must be perfect or it's literally unbearable. If something is less than 100%, it's zero for these folks. They don't seem to have any space between all and nothing. In their "two-category-thinking" everything is either flawless or foul, perfect or pitiful, terrific or terrible, unexceptional or unacceptable, totally everything or totally nothing. Their thermometers seem to read either hot or cold, their fortunes boom or bust, their reality either radiates or rots. And, as you can readily calculate, most often their evaluations of all reality are on the down side.

CONTROL

Because they have to guarantee that everything turns out fantastic, they have to have control so that they can rule out all chance of anything going wrong. Life theme: "Be sure to make *sure!* If I have to leave one base uncovered, I can't stand it!"

Counselors will notice that people in this group, like Carla, often have to revise every attempt to interpret their feelings. If you call their behavior "worry," they will reject your word and substitute another one. And their substitute will mean the same thing. But they have to have their "perfect" word.

DIRT

Themes of dirt, contamination, mess, and money are common in their concerns. Sometimes compulsive behaviors have to do with avoiding germs or toxins.

FEAR OF CHANGE

Change is frightening because it might mean a loosening of control and these counselees have trouble giving up control. Of course, paradoxically, the symptoms they present always consist of thoughts or actions of their own which they deem beyond their own control.

COMPLAINTS

These counselees will complain about obsessive thoughts or compulsive actions or both.

OBSESSIVE THOUGHTS

David: It all started when I read that passage about the sin against the Holy Spirit. You know, where Jesus says that whoever blasphemes against the Holy Spirit won't ever be forgiven.

Counselor: And you think you've done it.

David: Well, not for sure. I get into these thoughts, though, and I can't get them to stop. I read that passage about eight months ago, and all of a sudden it popped into my mind—the thought, "To hell with the the Holy Spirit!" It scares me just to tell you. And then I just thought, "Now you did

	it! You'll go to hell now, and there isn't any hope for you."
Counselor:	So that worry has been with you ever since?
David:	It comes and goes. Like, last week I talked to a pastor who said a person hasn't committed the unforgivable sin for sure as long as they're concerned enough to be worried about it. And that helped for a few days. But then I thought about what he said, and it came to me that I might not really be worried enough about it. How do I know I really and truly mean all this? Maybe I'm just putting on an act. So now it's all back on my mind again and I can't seem to get rid of it. I thought you might be able to tell me something that would help.

David was *obsessing*. The thought which nagged and threatened him was the suggestion that he had truly committed blasphemy against the Holy Spirit, and was therefore irrevocably outside the reach of God's saving love.

"I KNOW I CAUSED THE ACCIDENT": GUILT

Shirley was obsessing about a minor accident on the freeway a whole year after she was involved in it. Perhaps it is too much to say that she was involved. The police did not think so. She had been driving at rush hour in a crowded, bumper-to-bumper lane. She touched her brakes, the car behind her stopped suddenly, and the second car back rear-ended the car behind Shirley. As far as the law was concerned, the accident was totally between the two drivers behind Shirley's car and had absolutely nothing to do with her. She hit no one and nobody hit her.

But that wasn't enough for Shirley. Inundated with guilt, she was seeking therapeutic help. Her guilt was quite typical of the obsessional personality. They seem to reach out for opportunities to consider themselves guilty. Though Shirley had violated no law, moral or otherwise, she persisted in blaming herself.

"I caused it. I know I caused it. I shouldn't have touched my brakes so suddenly." Shirley had received mountains of reassurance, to no avail.

Why? Shirley's need to believe in her control of all circumstances around her was so great that she wouldn't allow herself to admit that she didn't have control here; and if control, then responsibility and guilt.

Frequently, the irrational guilt these people carry is related to their misbeliefs about control.

OTHER OBSESSIONS

Not all obsessions are the same. Some people obsess about questions like, "What is love? Do I really *really REALLY REALLY* love my child?"

Or, "How do I know what reality is?"

Other doubts are more threatening, "I'm not sure that I'm not a homosexual," or "Perhaps I've unwittingly killed someone with my car."

Some obsessions are just worries beginning with the classic phrase, "What if . . ." "What if my boyfriend is dating someone else without my knowing it?" "What if nobody really likes me and everyone is just pretending?" "What if my husband gets bored with me and falls out of love?"

COMPULSIVE ACTIONS: HANDWASHING

Gina: It's just that I'm afraid of certain things getting on me. So I try to avoid them. And I wash.

Counselor: You wash what?

Gina: Mostly I wash my hands a lot. And I can't feel like I'm getting them clean. I wash them once, then I think, "Well, what if there's still the tiniest bit of dirt or germs still on them? Did I get everything?" So then I think I better wash them again. Anyhow, this goes on for quite a while. My folks are complaining that I spend too long in the bathroom.

Counselor: How much time does it take to wash your hands?

Gina: It varies. Sometimes about five minutes. But the other day it was three hours. I just couldn't convince myself they were clean enough. It seems silly, I know, but I couldn't. I kept thinking I'd better wash a little more in case.

CONTAMINANTS AND CHECKING

Compulsions, or compulsive behaviors, like Gina's handwashing, are usually connected with thinking about some contaminant like germs, dirt, urine, feces, or sperm. Sometimes they involve the strong desire to keep checking and checking again to see if doors are locked, ash trays are empty, lights are out, or faucets are tightly shut off.

Compulsions may take the form of rituals. Don, for instance, had to do everything in threes. He would go to get the paper and then remember his ritual. The ritual of threes would require him to add two more tasks such as getting the mail and emptying the trash at the same time. Don had a rule that required him to do all three things in the space of one trip out of the house. He told himself he couldn't open or close the door again until three tasks were finished. Sometimes Don would doubt whether a task was truly separate, truly discreet, and therefore whether it "counted." For instance, was getting the mail separate from getting the paper? Or should he add another task before he went indoors just to make sure? Often, Don would remain outside for long periods trying to make up his mind.

Even normal people become involved with compulsive behaviors. A common example is the notion that you must not step on sidewalk cracks ("Step on a crack—break your mother's back"), or the thought that you have to touch every other fence post as you walk along the street.

This ritualistic thinking is so similar to magic that it is often called "magical thinking."

Symptoms like these are interesting because people usually believe they cannot help their pathological obsessive and compulsive actions. They feel as though they are *compelled* to obsess and to do their strange, ritualistic acts.

Often they convince others too. But the truth is that no one has to do these behaviors. Counselees are able to resist the impulse to execute a ritual or wash off supposed dirt and germs. As will be seen later, treatment now involves enlisting the counselee's cooperation in giving up these symptoms and choosing not to do them. To everyone's surprise counselees are usually able to do this.

ARE OBSESSIONS AND COMPULSIONS DEMONIC?

Because of the common impression that people cannot help compulsive behaviors, many have concluded that they must be demonic in origin. This is no doubt the case, in the sense that all lies and misbeliefs originate with the enemy. But obsessions and compulsions are not usually the direct possessing activity of the devil. They are the person's own behavior *for which he is responsible*. And, let's say it again for emphasis, counselees *can* cooperate in a treatment program in which they voluntarily eliminate these things from their lives.

THE PERSONALITY OF THE OBSESSIVE-COMPULSIVE

Some counselees don't really have the blatant and troublesome symptoms we have described. But they are troubled by their feelings, thoughts, and inefficient living. These are obsessive-compulsive personalities.

Detail-conscious, excessively neat, nit-picking to a fault, they may nevertheless paradoxically be in trouble for procrastinating rather than finishing critical work. Or they may tell you that they have a closet or desk drawer that is crammed with junk—anything but neat.

Time-conscious, they are ordinarily early for appointments and have little tolerance when others are not on time. However, some may be routinely and compulsively late. And they often waste a good deal of time getting around to deciding to do things.

Decision-making is a problem. Often they take extra time completing true-false tests like the MMPI. It is sometimes possible to diagnose them in our clinic by just observing how long they stew over each answer while they are being tested. Career decisions often seem more than they can handle. They cannot come to a conclusion about what they are to do in life. Going to graduate school, they have trouble choosing a major field. Deciding to marry, choosing a person to ask for a date, and selecting a hobby are all so difficult as to seem literally beyond reach for some.

So they want counselors to give them advice. Notice, however, that advice leaves them no better off than before.

"OH, PLEASE, TELL ME WHAT I SHOULD DO!"

Stewart: I'm trying to find myself, to find out who and what I am. Somehow, I just haven't been able to get my feet on the ground, and I'm not sure why.

Counselor: Feeling a little confused?

Stewart: Well, not exactly confused. I don't know how to put it. I just . . .

Counselor: Just not too sure what you want to be, huh?

Stewart: Partly. But that isn't all. I don't know who I am now. I wanted to find out if you think I should marry the girl I've been going with for eighteen months or not. [Here Stewart describes the relationship and concludes:] We do get along well, but I just haven't been able to decide. Can you help?

Counselor: Sounds like you care about each other and have a fine relationship. You're both serious Christians. Why don't you go ahead and get married?

Stewart: You think so? Really?

Counselor: Yes. Why not?

Stewart: I keep wondering if maybe I'm supposed to marry somebody else. What if I get married to Jan and someone comes along that I like better? I just don't know.

Counselor: Well, then, why don't you and Jan break up for a while? If you're not sure, you could set each other free to be open to other opportunities.

Stewart: Well, yes, but I'm afraid I'd lose her. She's a sharp girl, and other guys would be waiting in line for her. I'm afraid to break up with her. I just don't know what to do. I thought maybe you could help me, but I guess I'll have to figure it out myself.

Notice that the counselor, while not allowing himself to give direct advice, has inquired about the possibility of choosing each course of action, and Stewart has rejected them both. It is unlikely that advice (of which this man had already gotten plenty from his friends) will resolve this or any other of his dilemmas. Like most obsessive-compulsive personalities, Stewart wanted to answer yes and no to all decisions.

Incidentally, the counselor would have found it more fruitful to direct the conversation toward Stewart's indecision and the reasons for it, aiming to uncover and expose Stewart's misbeliefs about decision-making. Next time Stewart requests that the counselor decide for him, the counselor will be apt to counter with something like, "What keeps you from making this and other decisions? What thoughts go through your head that give you so much trouble?"

The Apostle Paul specifically rejected this wavering stance toward decisions as one that is not appropriate for Christians to hang onto.

> Do I make my plans like a worldly man, ready to say Yes and No at once? As surely as God is faithful, our word to you has not been Yes and No. For the Son of God, Jesus Christ . . . was not Yes and No; but in him it is always Yes. For all the promises of God find their Yes in him (2 Cor. 1:17–20, RSV).

Counseling with Stewart must elicit his collaboration in the detection and destruction of the misbeliefs underlying his vacillating. What are they?

COMMON OBSESSIVE-COMPULSIVE MISBELIEFS

Stewart believed these things:
- There must be a perfect answer, solution, choice, or alternative. Always.
- I must always find the perfect answer, solution, choice, or alternative.
- If I should choose something that is only good and not the very best, it would be a tragedy.
- I couldn't stand it if I made a choice and found out later that what I chose wasn't perfect.
- I can't trust my judgment to know which alternative is the perfect alternative.
- I can't count on anyone else's judgment either.
- As long as I don't know the perfect answer, it's better to give no answer.
- For all the above reasons it's terribly frightening to make choices and decisions, so I should usually postpone them and see if issues will settle themselves. Maybe someone will turn out to be omniscient enough to tell me exactly what to do.
- It's best to avoid anything frightening.
- Never take a chance.

Like Stewart, others who have obsessive-compulsive characteristics typically believe things of this kind:

- I have to make sure of everything—past, present, and future.
- If there's anything I'm not sure about, I have to regard it as
  threatening and worry about it.
- It's best to cover all bases, to provide in advance against any
  possible mischance, take *no* risks!
- Save it, hang onto it. You never know when you'll wish you
  hadn't gotten rid of it. It would be woeful to give something
  away and later wish you had it.
- You never know!
- It's vital to be in control at all times. Control is the biggest
  thing in the world.
- Being emotional is bad because you lose control. So strong feelings are awful.
- Commitment is bad—to man or God—because you lose control.
- It's terrible when people are late, because then things are out
  of control.
- Dirt, germs, messes, and details undone are things out of control.
- It's far better to feel wretched and guilty than to admit that
  some things have happened that were out of my control.

THE TRUTH

- There are no perfect choices in this sin-corrupted, imperfect
  world, except the choice for God and His kingdom.
- There are no perfect answers except the statements of the Bible,
  and they were not written to tell you exactly whom to marry,
  what career to choose, or what topic to select for your term
  paper.
- While it is certainly nice to be able to choose the best occasionally, it is not terrible to find that what you have chosen is merely
  good.
- It's nice, but not vital, to find the perfect solution for everything.
  It is enough to discover a merely workable solution. And even
  if you blow it occasionally, you can and will recover.
- You have to give up demanding perfect solutions before you can
  trust anybody's judgment, including Solomon's—and especially
  your own.
- You only need to trust your judgment enough to act on it. You
  don't have to believe you will always arrive at error-free decisions.
- It's important to choose, more important than to choose perfectly.

- It's better to give an answer than to wait forever for a perfect answer.
- When you wait for issues to settle themselves, they usually will. But you may not like the way things turn out.
- Just because a course of action is frightening is no reason to avoid it.
- You can't be sure of much of anything except God. Therefore it isn't necessary to be sure of anything else.
- Even if you're not sure, God is. Therefore, the unknown is not threatening.
- If you try to cover all bases, you spend all your time and resources covering bases, and you have no resources or time left for living. Life without risks is also without interest.
- It's not important to keep control of everything at all times.
- Commitment does mean you lose control. You agree to let God have it. And when He has control, and you don't have to, you can make commitments, you can stand messes, and you can permit others to be late without getting upset.
- Even if bad things happen as a result of your choices, they can't wipe you out because your life is grounded on a Rock: God himself.

COUNSELING OBSESSIVE-COMPULSIVES

Counselors should discuss their misbeliefs with counselees at length. You must teach the counselee how to debate them and replace them with the truth. In your dialogue with these counselees, it is often useful to observe the following:

Don't promise obsessive-compulsives complete recovery. Nothing, in their view, is ever quite complete enough to be perfect. A promise of "complete recovery" will only be used as another unreachable perfectionistic standard. Tell them instead that they must *not* expect that their counseling will free them from all their troublesome traits and symptoms. But they can expect some improvement.

Affirm the strong points associated with this personality pattern. And there are strong points. These people are often the most loyal, reliable, dependable and careful. They try hard to do what they do well. If you are looking for a friend, employee, or mate who practices virtues related to stability and stick-to-it-ive-ness, you might do worse than find someone with an obsessive-compulsive character.

I tell my compulsive and obsessive patients that they are the sort of people who hold the society together. In a culture where it seems almost standard practice to be late, they can usually be counted on to keep their appointments. Others may make "commitments" with little sense of being bound to them, but these people can be counted on to keep their promises. If they say they'll do it, they do it—even if it kills them. Others may give their word lightly, but compulsive types "mean what they say and say what they mean."

Expect them to disagree with you, to find (usually minor) flaws in your statements to them, and to be a little picky about your work with them. Don't get upset with them when they harp on their lack of progress. They hate to tell you they are getting better, even if they are, for fear you'll think they are satisfied with their progress and try to terminate. Remember, they have never been utterly satisfied with anybody, including themselves and God, so why should they start with you?

Tell them what you can about their disorder. They like to understand things. But an even more useful reason for explaining the disorder thoroughly is to be able to refer to it in your dialogues with them. When they are stewing and worrying about themselves and about their doubts, you can lighten their load a little by informing them that "that's a typical obsessional symptom; obsessionals usually think that way." The timing and manner of this must be such that you don't make them feel you aren't taking their anguish seriously.

REATTRIBUTION

The procedure of interpreting worrisome concerns as merely signs of stress is called *reattribution*.

Here is an example:

Counselor: So you've been telling yourself you've committed the sin against the Holy Spirit again. How do you say it to yourself?

David: What do you mean? I think it. I don't say it.

Counselor: Yes. How do you think it? What words do you use in your mind?

David: Oh. Well, I just think, "God doesn't have any time for you. You're as good as damned."

Counselor: Over and over? Same words over and over?

David: In my thoughts, yes. Pretty much the same words.

Counselor: That's not the way your mind processes facts. When a thing is a fact, you don't keep running over and over the same words in your mind. What you are doing is obsessing. And obsessions aren't facts.

David: They aren't? I guess I never thought of it that way. Tell me more.

Counselor: When people are under pressure, they do different things. Some get knots in their stomach, some get high blood pressure, some become psychotic. Some people obsess. And lots of them choose frightening things to obsess about, like the sin against the Holy Spirit.

David:　　You mean other people think they've done it too?

Counselor:　Counselors and therapists see them fairly often. And they're usually people with your personality type who are under stress. They begin to tell themselves things like you think about, or maybe other things. The striking thing about obsessions is that they aren't true or factual; just threatening. Perfectly fine people begin to worry about maybe killing somebody. Others fret that they may hurt themselves with a knife or scissors. Still others stew about being sexually deviant in some way, though they have nothing wrong with their sexuality at all.

One of the counseling maneuvers most helpful with obsessional counselees is reattribution. Notice that these counselees begin by attributing their troublesome thoughts to some terrible reality. In other words, they would probably tell you that the reason for their obsession about the sin against the Holy Spirit is that they have really committed that sin; that the reason they worry about being homosexual is that there is something to the notion, and so forth.

The truth is otherwise. The reason for their obsessional thoughts is that they are under stress and this is their way of experiencing stress. Some people develop ulcers. Those in this group obsess.

Another example:

Lana:　　I can't get it out of my mind. I'm afraid I'm going to kill my baby. It just keeps going through my head! I'm scared.

Counselor:　Do you wish you didn't have the baby?

Lana:　　Oh, no! I love her. I want her. I don't want to kill her. I feel terrible. There must be something hideous inside me that wants to hurt her. I hate myself so much.

Counselor:　So you think this idea in your head means you're a vicious, bad, murderous person, is that right?

Lana:　　Don't you? What else can you think?

Counselor:　Why should I judge you by your obsession? You've never done anything vicious or murderous in your life, have you?

Lana:　　No, but I'm so afraid I might.

Counselor:　Do you intend to hurt or kill someone? Are you laying plans to commit homicide?

Lana:　　Oh, no! I can't even stand to think such things. That's why this thought scares me so much.

Counselor:　And that's why this thought means only that you're obsessing.

Lana:　　You keep saying that. What does it mean exactly.

Counselor:　Some people get frightening ideas in their heads when they're under stress, and we call them obsessions because they have nothing to do with what these people are really

	like. Some people get hysterical paralysis under stress. Some of them become psychotic. You obsess.
Lana:	And that's all this means? I'm not going to slip and kill her?
Counselor:	Of course not. It's just a symptom of the stress you've been under since your mother died and John lost his job so that you've had to go back to work for a supervisor you don't care for. That's quite a load. And on top of all that you have a new baby. No wonder you're obsessing. It doesn't mean any more than tension headaches. You wouldn't be terrified if you had a headache, would you?
Lana:	Oh, no. I get them frequently. They're just irritating. And you mean that's all my thoughts of hurting my baby are? Just a tension symptom?
Counselor:	Sure.
Lana:	Oh, wow! That's a relief! I hope I can remember it tonight.
Counselor:	I'd like you to practice telling yourself the truth about your obsession. We call this process *reattribution*. Practice attributing your frightening thoughts, not to some deep mysterious drive to kill someone, but to the excess stresses you're under. Lots of people obsess when they have too much tension, and you're one of them.

AVOIDANCE BEHAVIORS

Some perceptive readers will have noticed the fact that obsessive-compulsive traits and symptoms perform the same functions as avoiding fearful situations. Phobics stay away from the elevators or heights they fear, and thereby avoid anxiety. Obsessive-compulsives are also trying to avoid excess anxiety.

Perhaps you can see, if you think about it, how many threatening situations these people keep themselves out of by their symptoms. Decision-making, situations where they have diminished control, potential loss or adversity—the traits and symptoms in these disorders clearly function as avoidance behaviors. They prevent anxiety, to some extent, but at great cost. The anxiety they produce seems, in some cases, greater than the anxiety they prevent. Furthermore, it is predictable that, as the counselee gives up some compulsive symptom, he will experience a certain amount of anxiety because he has stopped his avoidance maneuver.

These things should be communicated in therapeutic dialogue during counseling. They will fill out the counselee's understanding of the meaning of the puzzling thought or actions over which he is troubled.

ELIMINATION OF COMPULSIONS

It was thought at one time that counselees could not manage to omit their compulsive actions from their repertoires, and that compulsions were only symptoms of a deeper disease process. But it has recently become clear that people can stop doing their compulsive washing, cleaning, and checking, as well as other compulsive habits and rituals. Furthermore, deliberate omitting of the behavior is the best treatment available for compulsions.

There are times when the assistance of relatives may be needed, and there are cases in which the prevention of the compulsive response might better be done in a hospital where the staff persons are familiar with this type of treatment.

However, in many, many instances, the counselee can simply go home and prevent himself from doing his compulsive rituals or other behaviors.

He should be prepared by careful explanation of the avoidance nature of compulsive behavior. It is possible that he will experience increased anxiety due to exposure to the conditions he has been avoiding through his compulsions. Over time that anxiety will diminish, provided the counselee refuses to give in to the urge to do his compulsions.

One important caution. The counselee must not omit a given compulsion only occasionally. Nor even most of the time. Omission must be complete, because if the behavior is repeated, even only rarely, this will tend to restore to great strength the desire to repeat. The compulsive counselee, giving up a compulsive behavior, might see himself as a little like the alcoholic in remission. No way can the alcoholic return to drinking even one drink because of the risk of reinstating old drinking patterns. Similarly, the counselee allowing himself occasional repetition of his compulsions is likely to create even greater difficulty for himself.

After you have helped your counselee understand response omission and its therapeutic use, work together with him to determine one compulsive action or symptom to be eliminated first. Then you and the counselee reach an agreement that the counselee will not perform the symptom during the time until your next session. No matter how strong his urge to repeat the response, he is to resist it and go about his business. If there is anxiety, he is to keep a log of his mental contents and misbeliefs during the anxiety periods so that the two of you can work on them during the next session. He should also know that he needs to tolerate some anxiety in order to eliminate it. It will diminish.

In this way, you and the counselee collaborate to eliminate progressively the compulsive rituals and behaviors the counselee has found so defeating in his life.

SUBSTITUTE ACTIVITIES

When you are asking the counselee to practice response omission, he may suddenly discover that the void in his life caused by the omissions is very great. Encourage and train him for substituting activities which are more creative, positive, rewarding, and God-pleasing than useless, time-wasting rituals and cleansings.

Here is a list of examples. Work with your counselee to determine a list from his own life situation which meets his needs.

- *Prayer.* Time rescued from symptoms can be spent in effective and potent prayer. For this, the counselee should be instructed and taught in the meanings and skills of prayer and Bible reading.
- *Relaxation.* As with other groups, training in deep relaxation skills may be given, perhaps by a psychologist to whom you refer the counselee *for that procedure only.* There is no reason why you can't acquire books and tapes through which you can learn to help your counselee improve his relaxation skills, if you and your church see this as consonant with your counseling activities.
- *Play.* Obsessives and compulsives must learn to play. They are usually resistant to play. Dead serious types, they grow up thinking of play as wasteful and unnecessary. Jesus took hikes with His disciples. They camped out, sailed, and chatted for rest and recreation. Play should be seen as any activity the counselee prefers, so long as it isn't work, and so long as it doesn't have a goal-oriented purpose (a second job is not play).
- *Hobbies.* Help your counselee to acquire hobbies. Social hobbies often involve sports or playing games with others. Individual hobbies involve absorption in activity for personal restoration and reconstitution.
- *Exercise.* An excellent and therapeutic substitute for compulsions. "Instead of doing your ritual, go out and run" is the message. As is noted elsewhere in this book, there is empirical evidence that aerobic exercise reduces anxiety and depression. Obsessive-compulsives can use that!

It is usually not sufficient to just give your counselee a bit of advice. For example, "You really ought to take up a hobby." These people are resistant to change. Furthermore, they work best when things are thoroughly structured. Take time to break the new habit down into steps and make agreements each session detailing steps the counselee will take this week in acquiring the new behavior. For example:

- This week, counselee agrees to visit three hobby shops in the city and to write a list of at least ten activities which might make interesting hobbies for him.

- This week, counselee agrees to choose one of the hobbies on his list and acquire beginning materials. He will read about the hobby too, noting directions, procedures, and particularly, how to get started.
- This week, counselee agrees to begin taking a specific unit of time for initiating his hobby, actually doing the activity chosen.

Counselors using response prevention should be aware that it is not always successful in bringing about improvement. About 3% of counselees exposed to the increased anxiety which results when responses are eliminated become sensitized rather than desensitized and extinguished. These counselees will become worse. It's not known why this occurs in a few, and there is no way to determine in advance which counselees will succeed and which will not.

TREATMENT FOR OBSESSIONS

In addition to dealing with misbeliefs, obsessionals can be helped with the same activity-related life changes suggested above for compulsives. They too discover that as they give up obsessing, they aren't sure what to do with the time now made available. If you ask them, "What would you do with your mind if you didn't obsess?" they are apt to look startled and reply, "Why, I never thought of that. I just don't know what I would do."

There are several specific behavioral procedures for controlling obsessions which, though they are not strictly speaking counseling, could be done by a Christian counselor without requiring great additional skill training. They are *thought stopping, thought modification,* and *thought substitution.*

THOUGHT STOPPING

After explaining to the counselee exactly what you are going to do, ask him to relax and close his eyes.

Instruct him to think his obsessional thoughts and when he is aware that he is obsessing, to raise a finger.

When the counselee signals, the counselor shouts, *"STOP!"* The counselee will be startled, so it is essential you take the trouble to tell him in advance that this will occur. The obsessional thoughts will stop on this command.

Tell the counselee to relax again, repeat the above procedure, and at the proper point say "Stop!" again, but not so loudly.

Next, repeat and have the counselee say, "Stop!"

Last, repeat and have the counselee think "Stop!" in his mind, but not say it aloud.

Repeat the above procedure several times, and instruct the counselee to practice it at home. He is then to think the word "Stop!" whenever he begins to obsess.

THOUGHT MODIFICATION

This process involves training the counselee in the manner described above. But instead of thinking "Stop!" he is to change his obsessional thought by modifying it until it is nonthreatening.

For example:

- Instead of "I'm probably going to kill my baby," counselee practices thinking, "I'm never going to kill my baby."
- Instead of "I just know I committed the sin against the Holy Spirit," the counselee can learn to think, "I know 'I committed the sin against the Holy Spirit' is a thought Satan tries to use to upset me, but I don't believe it."
- Counselees can be taught to substitute truth from the Word of God for their obsession: "I am a redeemed child of God, and the Spirit of God dwells in me. I don't have to be spooked by these thoughts."

Work with the counselee to plan meaning-changing alterations he can add to his obsessional thoughts to change them into truth.

Assign thought modification practice periods for homework.

THOUGHT SUBSTITUTION

After stopping or modifying obsessional thoughts, counselees are left with a functioning brain which doesn't know quite what to do with itself.

Collaborate with your counselee in planning for deliberate substitution of creative and rewarding thoughts to replace the old obsessive nonsense. Counselee should deliberately instigate the new thinking following the thought stopping.

Spiritually uplifting and edifying truths, gardening plans, vacation plans and daydreams, thoughts about hobbies, intercessory praying for important causes or people can all fill the void left by stopped obsessions.

MEDICATION

At this writing, there is a specific medication which has been demonstrated as effective in treatment of obsessive compulsive disorders. Although this drug has not yet been licensed for use in the United States, it is available in Canada and many other countries. There is suggestive evidence that certain anti-depressant medications are helpful in reducing obsessional thinking. These medications are not tranquilizers. Counselors should consult with a psychiatrist or physician to determine whether referral for medication would be advisable in specific cases.

ALCOHOL AND TRANQUILIZERS

Like counselees suffering from the anxiety disorders, obsessive-compulsive counselees may already be medicating themselves with alcohol and tranquilizers when they come in to see you. Where this is the case, it is necessary, I believe, to eliminate the chemicals (or radically reduce intake) *before* treatment can begin. Readers will differ on the morality of using alcohol or tranquilizers. It is, however, a therapeutic essential that counselees who drink do so only as a social custom and have no more than three drinks per day. Counselees who have been hooked on valium and will not eliminate it should reduce their dose to no more than 10 milligrams per day. Occasionally, medical supervision is required for withdrawal from specific drugs. For these counselees, it is my opinion that total elimination of tranquilizing chemicals is ordinarily the preferred choice.

The reason for this is that alcohol and tranquilizers are often used as escape or avoidance maneuvers which prevent the counselee from either experiencing anxiety in order to extinguish it or changing his maladaptive behavior and misbeliefs underlying the anxiety.

SUMMARY

Obsessive-compulsive disorders involve the prevention of anxiety by engaging in senseless or ritual actions, or repetitive, worrisome, threatening thoughts. Counselees believe they can't help their actions or thoughts and can't prevent them. This is normally not the case. Treatment must include efforts to prevent compulsive actions from occurring, and obsessional thoughts from being rehearsed. These people are generally rather serious and tense, expecting the worst from others, themselves, and God. They insist that things should be perfect and believe that they must maintain tight control over themselves and their lives at all times. Guilt is frequently a theme, and they seem to prefer feeling guilty over events they actually couldn't have prevented rather than yielding their false notion that they can and must control everything. Counseling should involve efforts to change misbeliefs and replace them with truth, as well as efforts to prevent and stop compulsive actions and obsessional thoughts. Alcohol and tranquilizers should be eliminated or much reduced.

FOR REVIEW AND DISCUSSION

1. Look again at James 1:16–17 printed out at the beginning of this chapter. Tell how the passage counters and points up obsessive-compulsive traits and beliefs. Be specific.
2. What is perfectionism? How do people in this group show perfectionistic beliefs?

3. Describe the place of the control issue in the thinking of this group of counselees.
4. Why do you think these counselees are so often concerned with dirt, germs, or toxins?
5. What do you think might be the reason for compulsive rituals?
6. See if you can come up with a list of "normal" compulsions and obsessions. That is, compulsions or obsessions which occur in normal people; for example, many people may try to touch every other fence post while walking.
7. Why do these counselees often wonder if they are possessed by an evil spirit? Are they usually?
8. What is the difference between symptomatic obsessive-compulsives and obsessive-compulsive personalities?
9. List the best things to do to help each group discussed in this chapter.
10. Describe common misbeliefs in this group. What is the truth in each case?

CHAPTER EIGHTEEN

Schizophrenia

(Departure from Reality)

Lon had spent far too much time at the computer taking his tests. When a counselee labors for six hours to complete a two-hour test battery, we fear his illness has impaired his thinking.

Lon's tests and subsequent interview confirmed the suspicion that Lon was psychotic. This means he was out of touch with reality.

PSYCHOTIC THINKING

Counselor: What would you like to accomplish here at the clinic, Lon?

Lon: I need to accomplish a lot more. I'm going to hell. And I don't know for sure if . . . can you help me?

Counselor: Could you tell me more about the problem?

Lon: More about the problem? Well . . . my folks say it's the music I play, but I don't know. Maybe they don't like it because it's too loud. I don't know . . ."

Counselor: Are you working these days, Lon?

Lon: I'm working at Marshall Equipment, but they don't think I'm accomplishing enough. I might not be working there. They might let me go. They might want me to leave and get better.

Counselor: They've noticed you're sick?

Lon: I—don't—know. Maybe I told them. I'm not sure. I wish you could help me? Will I go to hell?

Lon's impairment had interfered with his ability to contact reality. He was out of touch with the way things actually were.

The mental illnesses we have discussed previously are very likely learned disorders. Although they can be accompanied by considerable misery, they are also most often recoverable, and prognoses range between fair and good with psychological counseling. Our work with patients indicates that counseling based on the truth as taught in the Scriptures plus prayer improves the outlook for these problems even more.

The psychoses are more difficult. They are diseases causing disruption of more areas of the patient's personality. Especially, these illnesses play havoc with a person's thinking processes in ways we have not seen in the other disorders covered in this manual.

Here is a list of the most common psychoses: psychotic depression, involutional psychosis, manic-depressive psychosis, acute psychosis, and schizophrenia. These are the most common of the functional psychoses.

These conditions interfere more than most others with the counselee's ability to function. When the counselor interviewing Lon noticed the looseness of Lon's thinking, he inquired about whether Lon was working. The counselor hoped to determine whether others had found him functioning poorly in the affairs of daily existence. At its worst, a psychotic condition makes it almost unthinkable that the counselee could "get it together" sufficiently to meet the demands of life.

We have studied neuroses and how they are grounded in misbeliefs and disproportionate evaluations. We have seen how neuroses work their major effect in the emotions. When you talk to a neurotic counselee, you will notice that, though he presents numerous gigantic misbeliefs, his thinking processes are intact.

Not so with the poor psychotic. It is as if his thinking equipment had a wire crossed or a few cells nonfunctioning. The counselor often feels that he and the counselee just "can't get through" to each other.

TWO USES OF THE WORD "PSYCHOTIC"

As you read literature on counseling and abnormal behavior, you will find the word *psychotic* applied in two ways. A person may be diagnosed psychotic in the sense that he is suffering chronically from one of the illnesses classified as psychoses.

On the other hand, you may hear a counselee's current condition described as "grossly psychotic" or "not currently psychotic." This second way of using the term indicates whether the counselee's thinking is or is not "out of it" at a given moment. In this second sense, the word "psychotic" merely signifies that the counselee is, at this moment, in very poor contact with reality.

You should know that counselees fluctuate in this regard, and will typically manifest better or worse reality contact depending on many factors.

ORGANIC AND FUNCTIONAL PSYCHOSES

Some psychoses are organic. For example, we are hearing a great deal these days about Alzheimer's disease, or dementia. This condition causes psychosis, and the psychosis is due to organic damage: brain cells are atrophied.

When no organic cause exists, the psychosis is described as *functional*. Today, the notion that some psychoses are purely functional (having no organic or chemical basis in the brain) is quite out of fashion, and for good reason. Evidence is increasing that some psychoses labeled functional may be constitutional and biochemical, at least in part.

Here are some examples of conditions which are currently labeled "organic" psychoses: senile and presenile dementias; Korsakoff's Syndrome found in later stages of severe alcoholism; alcoholic hallucinosis; drug-induced psychotic states.

Here are some examples of conditions which are currently labeled "functional" psychoses: schizophrenia, manic-depressive psychosis, psychotic depression, involutional psychosis.

We will focus our attention on the most commonly seen functional psychoses: schizophrenia and manic depressive psychoses. We will discuss schizophrenia in the remainder of this chapter, and in the next chapter, we will consider bipolar disorders or manic depressive psychoses.

SCHIZOPHRENIA

Most Christian counselors will see a large number of schizophrenics in their work, more than any other group of psychotics. You should have very little trouble recognizing this condition after awhile. The illness is common. One percent of the general population is afflicted with schizophrenia. Twenty-three percent of first admissions to mental hospitals are schizophrenic. Fifty percent of all resident psychiatric patients are schizophrenic.

Many years ago, a physician named Eugen Bleuler wrote the classic book on the subject of schizophrenia. Bleuler coined the name of the disease, but it is a misnomer. The word means "split personality." However, schizophrenics do not ordinarily have split personalities.

BLEULER'S FOUR A'S

When you are trying to decide if a counselee has this disease, it will help you to recall Bleuler's four A's, representing the four primary symptoms of schizophrenia: *association, autism, ambivalence, affect.*

1. *Association is impaired.* Look for loose connections between thoughts. Paul Meehl has called this "cognitive slippage," implying

that the connections between thoughts are functioning as loosely as a slipping clutch on a car. This is the "crazy" thinking people often connect with mental disease.

2. *Autism is present.* Autism is the name for the schizophrenic counselee's withdrawal into a world of his own. There he remains preoccupied with that world's peculiar concerns while he excludes some or all other reality. Sometimes, when you interview a patient with this disease, you get the feeling you are talking to someone far away, in another world, behind a veil through which there is no real emotional contact.

3. *Ambivalence is present and strong.* Here we are not dealing with obsessive vacillating and inability to choose. Ambivalence is intense love and intense hatred for the same person at the same time. It is very characteristic of schizophrenic relationships. It will appear sooner or later in the counselee's relationship with you, and you will need the love and direction of the Holy Spirit to deal with it sensitively.

4. *Affect isn't right.* The counselee's emotions are inappropriate or flat. It is as if you are hearing a song in which the music does not fit the words nor the occasion. Or, with flat affect, it is as if there is no music at all.

SOME EXAMPLES OF SCHIZOPHRENIC BEHAVIOR

1. *Associative difficulties.* Here are some examples of thinking difficulties of various types taken from a text by Ephraim Rosen and Ian Gregory:[1]

- *Paralogical thinking*: These are logical bloopers, fallacies. Vigotsky found that schizophrenic patients tend to identify objects with one another on the basis of identical predicates. Two objects with common properties are construed as the same. You have a *head* and so does a *screw*—so you are a screw.

  The girlfriend of a schizophrenic patient became pregnant by another man. When she told the patient, she neglected to mention the other man. The patient and the girl had not had intercourse. He concluded that she was the Virgin Mary and he was God. Notice the schizophrenic predicate logic he employed: (1) Mary conceived without intercourse. (2) His girl conceived without intercourse. (3) The girl must be the Virgin Mary, and that being the case, he must be God. To him, identity on the basis of having common predicates made good sense.

- *Concrete thinking*: Like children, mental defectives, and people with brain damage, schizophrenics have difficulty with abstraction.

---

[1] Ian Gregory and Ephraim Rosen, *Abnormal Psychology* (Philadelphia: W.B. Saunders Co., 1965).

A patient was asked, "Is something weighing heavily on your mind?" Answer, "Yes, iron is heavy." Proverbs are commonly used to test for schizophrenic thinking because they require abstraction. Here are some examples from life:

What does it mean to say, "A rolling stone gathers no moss"? Answer, "The stone keeps rolling endlessly." Another response by a different patient, "It won't grow any grass."

What does it mean that "people who live in glass houses shouldn't throw stones"? Answer, "Because they'd break the glass."

What about "a new broom sweeps clean"? Answer, "No, it doesn't, because the bristles are stiff."

● *Bizarre or peculiar thinking*: A student reported that he was unable to decide whether to organize his books by title or author, so he decided to do it by the colors of the spectrum.

Other bizarre thinking may involve adequate logic, but use of words which are not customarily chosen in the given context. Bleuler reports the definition of *hay* given by a patient: "a means of maintenance of the cow." There is nothing logically wrong with the definition. What grates on our ears is the choice of words seldom used in this context.

2. *Autism.* The counselee's speech reflects concerns and information which you really do not and cannot share, although it sounds to you as though the counselee assumes you do know and share his peculiar autistic world.

For example, after a pause, a counselee began talking about someone named Renaldo, who had never once been mentioned in our interviews. And clearly the counselee assumed I would know all he knew about Renaldo without being told. I eventually gathered that, in the counselee's thinking, Renaldo was an agent of a foreign government working on creating a dossier of information on the counselee.

Autistic withdrawal. Here, the patient pulls back into his own world. Withdrawal is most pronounced in catatonic states where the patient is truly "out of it" and does not respond to environmental reality at all. Autism encapsulates one in a world of his own wishes, fears, persecutory ideas, and fantasies. Emotions, thinking, speech, and behavior are dominated by the inner life. External reality is misinterpreted.

Degrees of autism may vary. Some patients will manifest it only as limited preoccupation with the inner self and the world of one's own construction, while others are clearly involved with nothing else. Sample misinterpretations which result: another person's smile is interpreted as a frown or even mockery; a word of commendation may be taken as criticism. Gregory and Rosen recount Bleuler's description of a woman who made a rag doll which she called the child of her imaginary lover. When he left on a trip she decided to send "the child" after him and inquired of the police whether it should be sent as luggage or as a passenger.

3. *Ambivalence.* Lon produced a perfect example one day.

Lon: My wife is leaving today to go visit her sister.
Counselor: How do you feel about her being away?
Lon: When I think about it I feel like killing her. I just love her so much, you know. I feel she's deserting me.

Ambivalence describes intense love and intense hatred together for the same object. Trust and mistrust are present at once. If you work with schizophrenic counselees, you will have to deal with their ambivalent feelings toward you. They often mistrust everyone, even those they care for. Although seeking your counsel and help, they will mistrust you too.

4. *Affect.* Sometimes the counselee shows no emotion. Even though the discussion involves subjects of intense concern, the counselee's voice pitch and volume remain even and his facial expression seems to be dead. This sort of affective impairment is called "flat" affect. It is very difficult to distinguish from the lack of emotional fluctuation found in some depressives.

Sometimes the counselee shows grossly inappropriate emotion. When the subject under discussion is the death of his wife, the counselee registers happiness; hearing that he has just become rich, the counselee may cry. Angry outbursts when no one has done anything harmful or irritating, smiling and laughing at no apparent object, and sadness in response to news which is anything but bad are examples of affect inappropriateness.

SECONDARY SYMPTOMS OF SCHIZOPHRENIA

These signs are called "secondary" because, unlike the four A's, they are not invariably present in all cases.

Hallucinations. These are usually auditory, although sometimes schizophrenics hallucinate in other sense modalities. If the counselee recounts "seeing things," visual hallucinations, consider and inquire for psychosis due to drug or alcohol abuse. Visual hallucinations are much more common in cases where brain functioning has been affected by some toxic substance. Rarely do counselees have olfactory hallucinations (detecting imaginary odors). These are much more likely indicators of brain damage than of schizophrenia. If they occur, you will most likely want to refer the counselee to a neurologist.

The most common hallucinations for schizophrenics are voices. They hear voices threatening them or ordering them to do things they shouldn't or don't want to do. The voices may be somewhat benign at first, but as the illness worsens, they become threatening, "You are going to die!" or critical, "You are a terrible person."

Occasionally a counselee will seem preoccupied during his interview. If you see him close his eyes or cock his head as if listening, you might ask if he is hearing voices. The counselee's voices will occasionally comment on the interview or on his relationship with you.

Often, people with little experience in ministry will insist that the hallucinations of psychotic people are actually the voices of demons talking to them. This is ordinarily not the case. In spite of the evil quality of the voices, they are produced by the counselee's own mind, and do not represent spirit communications. Of course, all symptoms of illness are indirectly or directly wrought by Satan. And it is likely within his power to cause some people to "hear" the voice of the devil. Most hallucinations are, however, not the product of direct communication with the enemy. Nonetheless, it is important to recognize that we are wrestling against spiritual forces when we minister to people sick with hallucinations!

Delusions. These are false beliefs which are not determined by ignorance or lack of information. They stick in the counselee's mind even though he "knows" better, that is, he knows facts which contradict the delusions. Generally delusions are expressive of needs or fears. Several types of delusions occur in schizophrenia.

Delusions of reference. The counselee believes the content of something he reads or the words and actions of other people refer to himself. Gregory and Rosen cite Bleuler's example of a child passing in front of a patient. The patient feels he must protest, "I am not the father of this child."

A counselee I was interviewing insisted that he had to avoid other people because they could both see and hear his thoughts. When I asked him how he knew this, he cited as evidence their ordinary social behaviors. "Well, I had better go before I wear out my welcome," one of his friends had said. This, to the counselee, meant that the friend was offended by the counselee's negative thoughts, and clearly proved the friend could hear the thoughts. This man persisted in referring ordinary behaviors of others to his own thoughts as causes, a real delusion of reference.

Delusions of persecution. The counselee believes some individual or group with which he is only vaguely familiar is working to bring him troubles and ruin. Sometimes he will shrug his shoulders when you ask him how it is possible for this person to concentrate so totally on overthrowing him. Sometimes he will have it all figured out and explain to you how through secret surgery, poisons, or electronic transmissions "they" influence the counselee's brain, or otherwise produce mysterious consequences in his life.

Somatic delusions. The counselee believes that all his strength has been drained out of him by a secret process, that he has a tumor in his head, that his bones are water, that his genitals are gone, or that he is dead.

TYPES OF SCHIZOPHRENIA

Although there are several types of schizophrenia, only three of them are important for our discussion, since the other types will rarely appear for counseling. We will pay particular attention here to the types of schizophrenia most commonly appearing for clinical counseling.

1. *Catatonic type.* These counselees manifest disturbances of movement. Some will be steered into the counselor's office by concerned friends or relatives because if left alone they barely move at all. Others will appear excessively active and excited. Both states may appear in the same counselee or he may manifest only one of them. Some catatonics sit and rock for hours. Or they stay fixed in one position, their muscles appearing locked in place. However, they will hold any posture into which another person molds them. This state is called "waxy flexibility." These patients might keep their eyes closed as a lifestyle. They frequently don't answer if you question them. In fact, they may be totally unresponsive to external stimulation.

When catatonics are excited, they can be destructive or assaultive. In this state, patients can become "wild" and must be hospitalized for the safety of themselves and others.

Catatonics were once seen quite commonly in clinics and hospitals, but for unknown reasons this diagnosis is becoming less common.

2. *Paranoid type.* Paranoid schizophrenics are not as sick as some other types, and are frequently able to manage well without hospitalization. Their paranoid traits are relatively easy for the counselor to recognize. They are suspicious and hostile with a typically glaring, serious expression. These counselees will argue with you if you challenge them and they show aggressiveness if you become pushy. The use of projection as a defense is typical of these people. Projection entails disowning an unacceptable feeling and believing that another person is manifesting the feeling. For example, a college athlete began to believe that others were tapping his phone, bugging his room, and recording his thoughts and actions because they suspected he might be homosexual. It was actually his own worry, not anyone else's, but his ego would not permit him to own up to the concern that he might not be sexually normal.

These counselees show delusions of reference, influence, persecution, and grandeur. They very frequently have vivid auditory hallucinations, voices speaking dark threats against them.

3. *Undifferentiated type.* These counselees show such a mixture of symptoms that they cannot be classified as having one single type of

schizophrenia. Frequently, these counselees show some paranoid characteristics but also characteristics of other types of schizophrenia.

WHAT YOU CAN DO FOR THE SCHIZOPHRENIC COUNSELEE

Over the years, these poor patients have been subjected to nearly every imaginable procedure in the vain hope of finding a cure. They have been bound in chains, twirled on spinning chairs, trephined (holes bored in the skull), injected with camphor, metrazol, and insulin to produce convulsions, shocked through the brain, sliced through the frontal lobes, wrapped in ice-covered sheets, and medicated with numerous substances. However, the illness has proved stubbornly resistant to cure.

Most of the treatments, though initially promising, have turned out to bring about little or no improvement.

Though so much has been tried, there is as yet no cure for schizophrenia.

Deliverance does not cure schizophrenia. I am certain that some readers will continue to insist that schizophrenia is nothing but demonic possession and that all one needs to do to cure it is cast out the possessing spirits. This belief is understandable since the behavior of the demon-possessed does frequently resemble schizophrenia in many respects. Furthermore, schizophrenic counselees may easily have demonic spirits infecting their lives. For that reason, deliverance or exorcism may be worthwhile. But it is not a cure for true schizophrenia. After deliverance, the counselee who was formerly schizophrenic will be schizophrenic still.

Medication, though not a cure, is effective for schizophrenia. In most cases the symptoms of thought disorder can be improved or eliminated through drug treatment of this disease. Often, if counseling is to begin, medication must be used first to render the counselee accessible to counseling. Examples of drugs which have proven effective are: Thorazine, Stelazine, Mellaril, Navane, and Prolixin.

None of these medications are addictive or habit forming. As a matter of fact, most patients try their best to discontinue their medications, as they typically do not like their effects.

All the drugs effective for schizophrenia have serious and unpleasant side effects, some of which can be made less aggravating by additional medicines. It is these side effects which often cause patients to want to get rid of their medications. Well-meaning friends and relatives can usually be found to agree that the patient doesn't need drugs. Premature discontinuation will usually produce another schizophrenic episode and rehospitalization. The Christian counselor should seek competent medical consultation before advising these patients to stop their medicine.

We believe that we have seen counselees in our clinic obtain remarkable relief from the side effects of antipsychotic medications by taking large daily doses of vitamin B_3.

A CHRISTIAN TREATMENT REGIME FOR SCHIZOPHRENIA

Counseling alone is not effective for cure and often is rather ineffective in relieving the miseries of schizophrenics. A multiple component approach can be used in a Christian counseling center with excellent effect. Here are the components:

1. *Prayer for healing.* No other route exists for the healing of this illness. Present evidence does suggest that schizophrenia is, in part anyway, a physiological illness. A miracle is needed in the sense that to cure the disease, a direct intervention of God must occur. Prayer should also include a request for God's blessing on the other components of treatment. Pastor Erwin Prange, whose remarkable healing ministry at the Center for Christian Psychological Services and North Heights Lutheran Church in Roseville, Minnesota, has brought improvement of numerous schizophrenic patients, has found that "soaking" these counselees in prayer for long periods of time has a profound healing effect. Prange has trained a team of people who pray in this way for schizophrenics seeking healing. Churches would do well to follow the example of Jesus and regularly minister with prayer to these people as well as to the victims of other diseases.

2. *Deliverance* may be done as discussed above. Few cases will be cured by this procedure, but if demonic influences are involved, they should be cast out and replaced by the indwelling of the Holy Spirit. Occasionally, demonic possession will mimic psychosis, and where this is the case, deliverance in the name of Jesus will result in freedom from all symptoms.

3. *Medication.* Unless and until miraculous divine healing occurs, medication should be employed as the single most effective therapeutic agent now available. Refer the counselee to a psychiatrist or a physician for evaluation and possible medication. Never tell the counselee or the physician that medication *will* be given. That judgment has to be left with the doctor who is responsible for prescribing medication and caring for the patient's welfare while taking any medication prescribed.

4. *Family counseling.* It is vital to work with the counselee and his entire family. One schizophrenic in a home has a profound effect on all members of the household. For the most part, few relatives of schizophrenics have been told what the illness involves, or, at times, even the name of it. Often the same is true of the patient himself. So some schizophrenics and their loved ones suffer through years of disease and its effects on all of them with no knowledge of what to expect and how best to handle their illness.

TEACH THE COUNSELEE AND FAMILY ABOUT THE ILLNESS

Counseling for such a family includes much straightforward teaching about the illness. To prepare yourself for such teaching, study a good Abnormal Psychology text on the subject and then educate your counselee and those close to him. This will help them to cope with difficulties they now only dimly understand.

REDUCE FAMILY STRESS

One aim of such family counseling should be to do away with unnecessary guilt. Teaching the counselee something like this will help: "You have a disease called schizophrenia. It is not something you can help having, or blame your parents for. It is a real disease like tuberculosis or arthritis. At the present time there is no cure. But there is treatment. We will discuss that later. Right now, I want you and your family to learn that there is nothing about having schizophrenia for anyone to feel guilty about. We aren't here to blame your childhood experiences or training. Nor is there anything about this disease to blame you for."

Stress makes most things worse, and schizophrenia is no exception. So a central aim of your work with the entire family is to teach them to reduce stress for everybody in the home. Look for stressors and try to eliminate them with everyone working together.

One important source of stress for these counselees and their families is their mutual expectations. What you can do here is teach them all what they can expect of one another. What can a family expect from a schizophrenic member? What can the patient reasonably expect of others in the family? How can they take the heat off one another if they have been pressuring one another by excessive mutual expectations?

TEACH THE IMPORTANCE OF MEDICATION

Emphatically teach the counselee and his family the importance of medication. They all need to know why the counselee is on it, what will likely happen if he discontinues taking it prematurely, and what can be expected if he takes his medication regularly.

FAMILY COMMUNICATIONS TRAINING: TRUTH IN LOVE

Finally, and perhaps most important of all, teach family communications. Especially important is to change any habits members of the family may have of giving incomplete or indirect messages and then expecting that others should decipher them. Insulting or punishing messages have to be eliminated! Love and consideration worked in family members by the indwelling Spirit of Jesus are very powerful forces for good.

Not: "Hey, don't you care about anybody else in this house? You had that stereo blaring until 2:00 a.m. last night. What's the matter with you?" But rather: "I'd really like to work out something about your stereo. Last night it was so loud I couldn't get to sleep until 2:00 a.m. Would you be willing to turn it down or to use your earphones?"

The aim of this training is to reduce the stressful communications which occur within families of these counselees and replace them with plain, effective talk which speaks the truth in love. You may have to get family members involved in role play practice to change habits of communication they have developed over many years.

The counseling program outlined here will reduce the time the counselee spends in the hospital, and will also make it possible for him to take smaller doses of medication.

Both goals are well worth aiming for.

SUMMARY

The psychoses are more serious than conditions studied in previous chapters. This is because they impair more areas of the personality. The most obvious impairment in psychotic conditions is loss or lessening of the counselee's ability to recognize and interpret reality. Schizophrenia is the most common psychotic condition counselors will see. In it, the counselee is impaired in thinking processes and contents (association difficulties), lives in his own world (autism), experiences intense love and hate at the same time toward the same persons (ambivalence), and shows flat or inappropriate emotion (affect). Delusions and hallucinations are relatively common secondary symptoms of the disease in that they are not always present. Most commonly, schizophrenic hallucinations are auditory and consist of hearing voices. Catatonic schizophrenia is becoming increasingly rare, but the Christian counselor will probably see examples of both paranoid and undifferentiated types. A program of counseling in a Christian clinic might well involve the following elements: prayer for miraculous healing, deliverance where indicated, family education and counseling to reduce stress, keeping the counselee on prescribed medications, and teaching all family members how to reduce stress in the home. Although no scientific cure exists, God can heal every disease, so prayer for healing is a most basic component of any work you do with schizophrenics. A program of Christian counseling stressing truth spoken in love can be an effective help.

FOR REVIEW AND DISCUSSION

1. Please enumerate some of the differences you can expect to find between psychosis and neurosis.

2. Describe the difference between functional and organic psychoses, and tell why the word "functional" may be somewhat inappropriate in the light of present knowledge.
3. Are schizophrenics split personalities? Give reasons for your answer.
4. Give Bleuler's four A's, the cardinal or primary signs of schizophrenia. Offer some examples of each.
5. Define the word "delusion." What are delusions of reference?
6. Name some types of schizophrenia and describe each.
7. What is the most effective treatment known to science?
8. What is unfortunate about the use of medications?
9. Describe a program of Christian counseling treatment for schizophrenia.
10. Make up some examples of destructive communication and then create loving and truthful communications to replace them.

CHAPTER NINETEEN

Bipolar (Manic-Depressive) Disorder

You have already become partially acquainted with these disorders in the chapter on depression. Bipolar disorder is also known as "manic-depressive psychosis." Since we have already studied the various forms of depression (chapter 14), we will concentrate here on the manic pole of this disorder.

Although when they are depressed, these patients are indistinguishable from victims of any deep depression, they are at their most distinctive when they are manic. The person in a manic state exhibits the behaviors most people think of when they hear the word "crazy." Excited and euphoric, though delusional, they are apt to be thought of as enjoying themselves immensely.

Manic-depressives may have any one of three forms of the bipolar disorder: manic, depressed, or manic-depressive type.

TYPES OF MANIC-DEPRESSIVE ILLNESS

Mania

Mania is characterized by zest, euphoria, irritability, foolish behavior, excitement, ego inflation (which means just what Romans 12 counsels against, "Thinking of oneself more highly than he ought to think. . . ."), rapid movement, and accelerated speech.

There are three levels of mania which are distinguished diagnostically.

1. *Hypomania*: Here the patient is mildly "high." He feels friendly; life is full of zest; he is energetic, self-confident, outgoing. I recall one sociable fellow who went around inviting everyone on the ward to a watermelon feed he was planning (though he had no watermelon and no way to provide one).

These folks are full of ideas, and they speak them out. The ideas

217

tumble over one another, gushing forth in a torrent.

Manics monopolize conversations. They take on more than they can do, and then add tasks. Nothing is too much.

Manic euphoria is so great that patients literally enjoy their illness and resent being "brought down" to normal emotional levels. They are so "high" they may behave foolishly. Then their watchword seems to be, "Well, why not?" They will charge thousands of dollars worth of credit card purchases, usually for tickets, liquor, hotels, and meals. Since many haven't a chance of being able to pay their bills, their flings cause great grief for those who love them. Perhaps the prodigal son was a manic. Like him, these counselees may later experience guilt and remorse over what they have done.

Janet was a staid, quiet housewife when she was normal. But when she became manic, her impulses sent her on flings. She once flew to California, met a young man while window-shopping, bought him a new sports car, and spent the weekend living high while her family at home worried that she had been kidnapped or killed. When Janet came "down" from her euphoria, she was depressed and guilty about her actions. She was also legally responsible for her wild expenditures.

These counselees can become aggravated at almost nothing. The slightest difficulty may cause irritation and later lead to depression. Or they may, instead of becoming depressed, continue on to higher levels of mania.

2. *Acute mania*: In this stage, the counselee is "higher than a kite." Now elation has replaced euphoria. The counselee is floating, thoughts fairly fly, speech is even more rapid, and movements are paced to excitement. Now the counselee jokes with everybody, exudes happiness, and declares that life is fun.

At this stage, manic delusions occur. These are unlike the delusions of the poor schizophrenic. They have the flavor of exhilarated grandeur. The counselee has power, wealth, beauty, brilliant cleverness, and great influence. He is Napolean, King of the Universe, God, or president of General Motors. There is nothing he cannot do for you.

In the twinkling of an eye, this genial joker may become sarcastic and irritated. He may even become dangerously assaultive. These patients can quickly turn and break someone's jaw. Changes of mood are lightning-sudden.

One day I went onto the hospital ward to find Clyde, a patient I had tested. I was planning to share the test results with him. But I found him holding the ward personnel at bay with a chair. No one challenged Clyde. Not knowing precisely what the problem was, I told him I had his test results and would discuss them with him if he liked. Clyde became meek as a lamb, put his chair down and sat on it, and invited me to sit beside him. The storm was over as suddenly as it began.

Thus manic emotions fluctuate. Weeping may begin suddenly. These people are heedless of the consequences of their behavior. They appear to be driven at such force that conscience cannot act to restrain them. They may even be unaware of pain.

Some manics talk so much they lose their voices. Ideas fly through their minds in quick succession so that they seem to tumble over each other. This phenomenon is called "flight of ideas." There appears to be pressure behind the stream of speech, as if the ideas coming behind force the others through. And associations are made, not only by content, but often by rhyming and sound (clang associations).

June was confined to the locked ward of the inpatient service. I had been asked to test her with the Rorschach inkblots. One of the blots seems to some people to depict two small rodent-like animals. The counselee's response was instantaneous.

"Gophers! Gopher football, gopher basketball, gopher hockey, gopher baseball—you know, Doc. I 'gopher' football; do you 'gopher' football, Doc?"

You should notice, not merely June's quick punning and humor, but the way she associated her ideas by sound. These are an excellent example of "clang associations."

3. *Delerious mania*: You will never see this unless you work in a hospital or unless you see it on the street or by accident. No way will these people be found in the counseling center. They cannot handle anything well enough to be outpatients. They are in a state of furious excitement. They shout, they laugh, they talk too fast to be understood. They may sound something like the chant of the tobacco auctioneer on the old Lucky Strike cigarette commercials. They tear clothes, upset furniture, break things, and may be quite assaultive. There will be delusions of persecution and/or grandeur. At this level, cognitive functioning is badly disrupted. Memory is impaired, orientation is impaired (that is, they don't know where they are in relation to time, place, person). And hallucinations can be expected.

Depressive Manic-depressive

The depressive type or phase is similar to other depressions (refer to chapter 14). It may be mild, moderate, or severe, and can be so classified just as levels of manic excitement can be classified. Diagnosis of these cyclical depressions cannot be made by merely observing the counselee. *History* is most important. Only if there is a history of repeated depressions, coming on rather regularly, regardless of precipitants, can you tell the difference between this and other types of depression. It is imperative to get a history from the counselee or information from others about the history in order to differentiate this depression from other types.

Manic-depressive illness may show up as repeated episodes of mania, repeated episodes of depression, or alternating episodes of mania and depression with relatively normal mood states in between episodes. Some counselees even show both manic and depressive characteristics at once.

TREATMENT FOR MANIC-DEPRESSIVES

Medication is the treatment of choice for these counselees as it is for schizophrenics. There is no cure, but if they can be kept on the mineral lithium, behavior and mood should remain normal. Sometimes another medication may be given. Lithium and other medications must be prescribed by a physician and must be given with closely monitored blood levels. It is easy for blood levels of lithium to become so excessive as to be toxic or so low as to be ineffective.

Other medications may be used for the various symptoms, alone or in combination with lithium. Antipsychotic medications, sometimes called major tranquilizers, and anti-depressants may be used as needed. These too are to be prescribed and monitored by a physician.

It may happen fairly often that you suspect a counselee has this or another illness requiring medication. It is then our duty to make a referral to a physician. Therefore it is of the utmost importance that you make contact with a (preferably Christian) physician who is familiar with treatment of psychiatric conditions. Psychiatrists specialize in prescribing for these conditions. Other doctors vary in the degree of interest they have in the treatment of mental and emotional problems. Before choosing a physician you should ask him if he is interested in treating such cases and willing to work with you. It is very unfortunate that Christian counselors sometimes fail to recognize an illness for which medication would be God's present means of blessing, or fail to make a referral under the impression that it is their task to hold out for a miracle.

PRAYER AND DELIVERANCE

As with the disease schizophrenia, deliverance will not bring about cure in cases of true bipolar disorder. Nonetheless, demonic activity may mimic these disorders or may complicate them. Therefore deliverance should be done if indicated by discernment of spirits.

Prayer for healing is vital in this disorder, since the illness is likely a true biochemical or physical malady. No medical or psychological cure is known. Ask the heavenly Physician to restore disordered brain chemistry to balance and order. Here, as in schizophrenia, concentrated soaking prayer may prove effective.

COUNSELING

Counseling cannot be done until counselees have been settled down through medication. Then, counseling should aim at reducing stress, development of interpersonal skills, and acquisition of problem-solving abilities. These counselees are rarely skilled at solving their own difficulties and telling themselves the truth. They will need to learn. Unfortunately, they may be unmotivated for counseling. If that is the case, little can be done by you beyond intercessory prayer for divine healing.

You may also work with the family of the patient in order to increase their understanding of the disease, of the working of God's healing with and without means, and of the importance and manner of stress reduction in the home. It is most vital that families understand the necessity of remaining on medication. These things were discussed more fully in the foregoing chapter.

As with most counselees, nutrition ought to be optimal, drugs and alcohol eliminated or kept extremely minimal, and aerobic exercise programs instituted. Relaxation practice might be helpful in minimizing stress.

SUMMARY

Three types of manic-depressive psychosis occur: manic, depressive, and manic-depressive. Bipolar disorder or manic-depressive illness has been studied in two parts. Depressive manic-depression was discussed in the chapter on depression. In this chapter, we looked at three levels of mania. The most effective treatment for mania is usually lithium, and this must be prescribed by a physician. It is the duty of the counselor to refer if need for anti-psychotic medication is suspected. The place of counseling is probably minimal, since most of these counselees do not continue even if they begin. Prayer, instruction for relatives, and stress reduction techniques are more likely to help. Divine healing should be sought for manic-depressives. It is important that counselors learn to recognize bipolar disorder in order to facilitate the counselee's seeing a physician for medicine. Select a physician or a psychiatrist who is a Christian, if possible. If a Christian doctor cannot be located, discuss thoroughly with the person you refer to the spiritual realities operative in your counseling. It is vital to refer to someone who is not going to subvert the spiritual ministry the counselee receives.

FOR REVIEW AND DISCUSSION

1. Describe the three kinds of bipolar disorder.
2. Describe the three levels of mania.
3. Why will you likely not have an acute manic as a counselee?

4. What is press of speech?
5. What are "clang associations"?
6. What is the most effective treatment for mania?
7. Why is counseling unlikely to occur with these counselees, even after they settle down somewhat?

CHAPTER TWENTY

The Antisocial Personality

(Where Conscience Seems to Be Missing)

SONIA

She made an appointment to see me. She failed to keep it. Another appointment, another failure. This time there was a phone call to my secretary to tell us her car wouldn't start. One more try. She made it to the office—23 minutes late for a 50-minute session.

She was pretty. Blonde, blue-eyed, slim-waisted, with turned up nose, she was the picture of sweet innocence. This twenty-year-old college student could have captured anyone's heart.

She was clearly uninterested in capturing my heart, or in anything else except escaping from the interview and the prospect of future sessions.

"It's my parents," said Sonia. "They insisted on me coming here."

"It wasn't your idea, then," I answered. "That's why it was so hard for you to keep this appointment. You've missed two others, you know."

"I know. I don't know why I came to this one. To get them off my back, I suppose. They just won't leave me alone to live my own life. It *is* my life, you know."

"Sonia, I'm not in collusion with your parents. I don't even know them. And I have no idea why they want you in here," I told her, even though I was beginning to have my suspicions. The hypothesis was already forming that Sonia was a sociopath. The appointments failed without apology or regret, the utter unconcern about her late arrival for this interview, and the fact that she was in conflict with her parents, doubtless over their objections to her behavior—all suggested that Sonia's reason for being in the clinic had to do, not with personal distress or discomfort, but with the trouble she was causing others.

When I inquired about the problems for which her parents thought she needed help, she replied unabashed that they were a couple of alarmists who were raising a fuss over nothing much. In Sonia's view, her parents were hopelessly antediluvian for failing to understand and accept her drug use, her promiscuous sex life, her sporadic class attendance, and the failing grades she was earning at the expensive college she attended.

Sonia insisted she neither needed nor wanted psychological help. She knew what she was doing with *her* life. In spite of my efforts to focus her attention on the inevitable outcome of her self-destructive behavior, she was adamant. She didn't care, either, what God thought of her behavior. But when pressed on the point, she insisted she couldn't see God being as upset over it as her folks.

Sonia never returned to the clinic. She belonged to a group of mental patients who appear in counseling settings only under fire. Others push them. They get into trouble with officialdom or with the law. And they believe, sometimes correctly, that the counselor can be of some use to them in their efforts to escape punishment or other negative consequences of their actions.

THE SOCIOPATHIC PERSONALITY

Psychologists and psychiatrists find themselves repeatedly conned by these counselees. They can manipulate even those who ought to know better. The patients have been called many things in the history of psychiatry. It is as if no diagnostic term has proven quite adequate to express the frustration of those who become involved with them.

Their disease has been called: moral insanity, constitutional psychopathic inferiority, psychopathic personality, antisocial personality, sociopathic personality.

Here is a definition of the syndrome from an older edition of the official psychiatric diagnostic manual: "Amoral or antisocial and impulsive, irresponsible action, satisfying only immediate and narcissistic interests, without concern for obvious social consequences and minimal evidence of anxiety or guilt."

Many of the characteristics of this syndrome correspond in explicit detail with what the Scriptures describe as unrepentant sin. An example from 2 Peter 2 will make the point. Peter describes a certain group of religious con artists, "false prophets," with traits similar in many particulars to those of the sociopath.

SOCIOPATHIC SIGNS

From 2 Peter 2:	*From Lists of Sociopathic Signs*
V. 2 Licentious behavior, causing the Christian way to be reviled.	Truancy, job instability, trouble with the law, lack of shame or remorse, sex life based on shallow whims.
V. 3 Greed and exploiting of others. See v. 14, hearts trained in greed.	Unresponsiveness in general interpersonal relations. Does not care at all about others. Pathological egocentricity and incapacity for love.
V. 3 Use of false words.	Unreliability, untruthfulness, and insincerity. Often, the sociopath will lie when it would be just as easy to tell the truth.
V. 3 Consequences destructive to themselves. See v. 13, suffering wrong for their wrongdoing.	Sociopaths experience many miseries in consequence of their poor judgment and failure to learn from experience. They have high accident rates and frequent disruptions in relationships.
V. 10 Indulgence in lust and defiling passion. See v. 14, having eyes full of adultery, insatiable for sin.	Drinking, casual sex with many partners and no commitment are characteristic of this group.
V. 10 Resistance to authority. They revile the glorious ones.	Generally, a record of trouble with authority, the law, school teachers and principals. Many are in prison.
V. 12 Actions are irrational.	Specific loss of insight. Counselees do not comprehend their true situation and how bad it really is. Their talk has a rational sound to it, but their actions are irrational.

V. 19 They promise freedom, but they themselves are slaves of corruption; for whatever overcomes a man, to that he is enslaved.

Cannot love, cannot care, cannot follow any life plan for good or evil, cannot embrace a long-range perspective. Trapped in their immorality. They seem to have a superego deficit which leads to lack of control.

V. 22 It has happened to them according to the true proverb, The dog turns back to his own vomit, and the sow is washed only to wallow in the mire.

Punishment does not work to change their behavior. Some research has shown they do not learn from punishment. Treatment of every kind has failed. They do not change with prison or therapy, but return to destructive behavior.
No cure.

As you have seen, the traits of the sociopathic personality are those described in the Bible as sin. But we all sin. How is the sociopath different? What makes these people fall into a class by themselves?

SOCIOPATHIC PERSONALITY AND CONSCIENCE

The outstanding characteristic of the sociopath which makes him a unique kind of sinner is his evident lack of conscience.

According to the Apostle Paul, even the heathen who have no contact with the law of God show that what the law requires is known to them innately (Rom. 2:15). Furthermore, they normally have a conscience which functions to inflict painful guilt when man transgresses what he knows to be right. Even the heathen hurt inside when they sin.

The sociopathic personality has either no conscience at all, or a conscience so disabled that he feels no pangs of guilt when he does wrong.

Gary Gilmore, described quite sympathetically by Norman Mailer,[1] showed little or no sense of guilt after putting a bullet through the head of a filling station attendant he had robbed. The act appeared to be the result of an impulse or a whim, as are so many of the senseless crimes committed by sociopaths.

Although Gilmore sought execution for his crimes, the reader can look through Mailer's book in vain for any evidence of a truly re-

---

[1]Norman Mailer, *The Executioner's Song* (Warner Books, 1980).

morseful conscience or even awareness of the full gravity of what he had done.

With such a defective conscience, the sociopathic personality represents a rather unique and especially destructive individual. Anyone who becomes closely involved with one of these people will experience firsthand the life-wrecking damage they can do to those close to them.

SOCIOPATHIC CHARACTERISTICS

The classic book on the subject of the sociopathic personality is Cleckley's *The Mask of Sanity*.[2] You should know this book for several reasons, not the least of which is that its case histories make fascinating reading. Cleckley provides a number of traits or characteristics of what he calls "the true psychopath." This term corresponds to what we are calling the antisocial or sociopathic personality.

Others have added to Cleckley's list. Here are some of the traits of the character we are describing, including those given by Cleckley.

1. *Superficial charm and good intelligence.* These counselees frequently charm and engage the affections of counselors to the point where the counselor, like many others who have become involved with them, finds himself deceived and used for unintended ends. These counselees are often physically attractive, muscular, and youthful. Some have a peculiar beauty to their physical movements, a quality called "animal grace." This is relaxed, easy, effortless motion which resembles the flowing gait of a lithe, finely coordinated tiger. In addition, they are often able to verbalize remorse for their actions. You begin to see the person before you as reasonable, wise, intelligent, courteous, and engaging. And you may want so much to believe in his goodness that you ignore the record of his past behavior. Sociopathic charm attracts others quickly and their intelligence enables them to feign tremendous insight into the wrongfulness and consequences of their misdeeds.

2. *Absence of delusions and other signs of irrational thinking.* One of the most striking qualities of this group is their apparent sanity on examination or casual contact. They seem to have clear insight into their maladaptive misbeliefs. They reason as well as the counselor, think accurately, understand intellectually, and can readily tell why what they have done is wrong and detrimental to themselves and others. Yet their actions say something else. Their behavior often makes no sense and leads the observer to the conclusion that they must be insane in some special way. In fact, at one time, this syndrome was called "moral insanity."

3. *Absence of "nervousness" and other signs of neurotic illness.* They evidence little or no real guilt, although they may verbalize

[2]Hervey Cleckley, *The Mask of Sanity* (St. Louis, Mo.: C.V. Mosby Co., 1982).

guilt to get out of trouble. They are amazingly comfortable with others, even those they have ripped off. They are marvelously calm. Anxiety levels on all measures are ordinarily negligible. There is an exception. Confinement deprives the sociopath of many reinforcers. In prison or hospital, these people, like caged animals, can become tense, anxious, and depressed. Such symptoms generally disappear at the end of confinement.

4. *Unreliability*. Like Sonia, they fail appointments, often without bothering to cancel them. They don't pay their debts or keep their promises unless, for some reason, it suits their immediate purpose to do so. They will disappear from counseling after a session or two like morning fog before the sun unless they are forced to persist. The counseling may endure if there is a court order for it, along with a stiff penalty for non-compliance, but I have seen such counselees fail to attend sessions even with such sobering contingencies in full force! You might think of sociopaths as at the opposite pole of character from the obsessive-compulsive group.

5. *Untruthfulness and insincerity*. These people lie, often when it would be just as easy to tell the truth. They have no compunctions about saying whatever comes to mind to gain what they want from others. What is, perhaps, most remarkable is the power they have to convince even those who know them that "this time, it's different" and "this time, it really is the truth." Some can, if necessary, shed tears to appear committed and utterly serious. Incidentally, the careers of actor and salesman often attract persons of this personality type. For this reason, the many honest and upright persons in these callings sometimes suffer undeservedly from being painted with the same brush.

6. *Lack of remorse or shame*. This lack is not merely a slight tendency not to be sorry enough for what one has done, but is marked and amazing to the average person observing it. These persons do not feel remorse or even shame in the presence of a person they may have injured grievously. As we will see later, this may be related to the fact that sociopaths do not feel intensely at all. Yet they know the appropriate actions, facial expressions, and words with which to feign shame and guilt. So they accept no real responsibility for their own actions and instead blame circumstances or society for their evil deeds. They have no compunctions against demanding all sorts of "rights" at the hands of those they have treated badly. A most stunning example of sociopathic remorselessness can be found in the book, *The Yale Murder*,[3] the true story of Richard Herrin's cold-blooded hammer murder of his girlfriend, Bonnie Garland. Meyer, interviewing Herrin in prison, found him largely without remorse, and seeking to shift blame for his actions to impersonal "forces" repressed deeply inside

---
[3]Peter Meyer, *The Yale Murder* (New York: Berkley Books, 1983).

himself. Thus Herrin maintained loudly that he had served enough time after three years, and that society should not expect more of him.

7. *Inadequately motivated antisocial behavior.* One marvels at how little the sociopath stands to gain from his destructive behavior. Dumb bewilderment overcomes the average person reading in his newspaper of the masked armed robber who needlessly puts a bullet through the head of a store clerk. The clerk has just handed over the cash from the register. The robber cannot be identified. Why kill? Why? Mailer's tale of Gary Gilmore portrays a criminal who *for no apparent reason* murders a filling station attendant and a motel clerk after he has successfully robbed them. It's murder on impulse, execution on a whim. Why?

A common error on the part of people working with sociopaths is that of refusing to believe the counselee could have done some horrendous deed for which no motive seems evident. "He couldn't have done that!" they will insist, because there appears to be no conceivable adequate motivation. Again and again these counselees will commit acts which lead to trouble for themselves without what most people would consider any genuine reason.

8. *Poor judgment; failure to learn from experience.* These counselees often choose to do things which are likely to hurt them. They take risks most would consider unacceptable. They are often said to be the sort of people who "dive into empty swimming pools." The sociopathic MMPI profile is associated with more hunting accidents in Minnesota than that of any other group. Because of their high accident rate, these counselees frequently sustain injuries with serious permanent consequences. They do other things so peculiarly self-defeating that others marvel at their poor judgment.

I once saw a counselee who was in trouble with the law because she had chosen a fantastically unwise plan for getting even with her boyfriend. Because she was angry with him, she locked her baby in a closet, asleep, then called police and told them that her boyfriend had kidnapped the child. Having been quickly convinced of his innocence, the officers searched my counselee's house and quickly found the baby. They had no difficulty identifying her as the culprit.

These counselees seem unable to learn from experience, even very painful experience. Dr. David Lykken, a research psychologist at the University of Minnesota, found a group of sociopaths who could not be trained to become anxious at the threat of repeated electric shock. They seemed to lack the "wiring" to experience the kind of anxiety most of us learn after we experience pain or harm. Thus, though they frequently suffer painful consequences, these counselees do not modify their future actions accordingly.

9. *Pathological egocentricity and incapacity for love.* The accent is on the *pathological*. Egocentricity is a rather common characteristic.

But with these people it is so pronounced as to be all-consuming. Their reward consists in self-stimulation. Liquor, money, and sex seem to be the most commonly sought reinforcers. Sociopaths are incapable of love. There appears to be a deficit here that is as real as their deficit in conscience. They can tell you with all the right words what love is, but they seem incapable of experiencing it. Callously, and without evident concern, they sacrifice those who have cared for them just to gain trivial and insignificant ends.

10. *General poverty in major affective reactions.* This simply means that sociopaths don't experience much feeling. There may or may not be shallow reactivity on occasion, but others are often astounded at the absence of such feelings as sorrow over the loss of loved ones. No great depressions, and no deep, abiding joy touches their lives. Reactions like "fun," frustration, self-pity, and irritation are common. But there is nothing like profound emotion in their experience.

11. *Specific loss of insight.* These counselees utterly lack insight into the nature of their situations. Often, when in trouble, they seem not to comprehend how really serious their trouble may be. They have no capacity to see themselves as others see them and are utterly unable to feel what others must be feeling toward them. Commonly, they appear to others to "have a lot of gall" on account of this deficit. For example, the sociopathic counselee may ask a counselor for job references even though he knows the counselor knows he is untrustworthy. I once had a counselee who, in between a couple of his many trips to prison for sexually attacking adolescent girls, applied for a job as a counselor in a home for delinquent girls and gave my name as a reference!

12. *Unresponsiveness in general interpersonal relations.* No matter how well this counselee is treated by others, no matter what personal sacrifices others make in his behalf, no matter how much others may do for him at whatever cost to themselves, he is unresponsive. Trying to win the sociopath's loyalty by special consideration, kindness, or trust proves a mistake. He is able to respond with words, perhaps, but he cannot or will not repay in kind the generosity or love of those who try to help him. In point of fact, they will normally be made to regret their efforts.

13. *Suicide rare.* Although these counselees kill themselves by mistake or in accidents, there are few suicides. A few may commit suicide on a whim or an impulse.

14. *Sex life is impersonal, trivial, and poorly integrated.* Although sociopaths are ordinarily promiscuous, indulging in sex with many partners, their sexual relationships have little meaning to them. They are not bonded to others through sexual behavior, nor do they integrate sexual relationships into the fabric of their lives. They seem to have no particular concern about the object or the aim of their sexual activity, and do not care particularly whether their sexual liaisons

are heterosexual or deviant. Rarely are they able to remain faithful to one person in a sexual relationship.

15. *Failure to follow any life plan, good or evil.* Even as they appear unable to learn from past experience, sociopaths also have difficulty envisioning the future. They lack long-range perspective. So planning for the future doesn't usually occur to them. When they do make plans, they are too impulsive to carry them out, since sustained effort toward a goal is most unlikely. They are as unlikely to carry out the patterned behaviors necessary to achieve an evil goal as they are a good one. Most of their behavior results from following impulses and whims. Their drifting from one impulsive action to the next reminds one of a vehicle careening out of control with no driver.

16. *Record of trouble with the law.* Many of these people are in prison. Although a few sociopathic personalities will somehow avoid arrest, trial, and conviction, most have collided with the law, beginning in their teenage years. Their impulsivity, poor judgment, resentment for authority and rules, and inability to learn from experience make them likely lawbreakers. They generally drift into crime, rather than plan it. Assault is impulsive when it occurs. And their inability to plan makes them likely to be caught.

17. *Record of truancy, job instability, pathological lying, and nomadism.* When this diagnosis is suspected, the counselor should inquire into a counselee's history specifically for these features.

OTHER SOCIOPATHIC TRAITS

Frequently the history of a sociopath will reveal a parent or sibling with sociopathic behaviors. Parental discord, deprivation, deceit, overindulgence, and lack of supervision appear in the histories of these counselees.

They tend to be mesomorphic (i.e., muscular in build), predominantly male in a ratio of three-to-one, and they often have the marks of injuries sustained through their careless behavior.

They burn out at about age 40, and settle down with a more conventional but burned-out pattern of behavior. That is, if they make it to age 40. The mortality rate is high, and these people seem to live by the maxim that Paul rejects in 1 Cor. 15, "Let us eat and drink, for tomorrow we die."

"ONE FLEW OVER THE CUCKOO'S NEST"

Author Ken Kesey has given us a most sympathetic picture of the sociopath in his novel, *One Flew Over the Cuckoo's Nest.* What Kesey admired and lauded was the sociopath's defiance of "the system," his cavalier attitude toward authority. Close to the edge of boredom and frustration at all times, these people are readily provoked to impulsive actions. They may stir up excitement and get into trouble in order to avoid tedium and monotony.

There are other sociopathic personalities in literature and on TV. J. R. Ewing, the clever villain of the TV show *Dallas*, has many sociopathic traits. Sinclair Lewis described an unforgettable clergyman-sociopath in his novel, *Elmer Gantry*. Gantry found the clergy role ideal for exploiting others financially and sexually.

CAUSES OF SOCIOPATHIC PERSONALITY

The causes of this syndrome could conceivably be biological. There may be a constitutional or hereditary predisposition. For example, there is a strong correlation between delinquency and mesomorphy (that is, a muscular body build). Furthermore, brain wave studies show abnormalities in 50% or more of these counselees. Some evidence exists of a deficit in the capacity to learn anxiety. Such a deficit might well come from a biochemical impairment.

Psychological causation has been theorized.

But no one knows for certian why some people grow up with this astonishing deficiency in conscience.

TREATMENT

Treatment is the major question. This is an enormous social issue. Prisons are full of sociopathic personalities, and rehabilitation efforts have been stunningly unsuccessful. There is, in fact, little evidence that these criminals can be rehabilitated. If they can, science does not know how. As it is, they are simply discharged from the jails and prisons to continue their anti-social behavior until they are caught and confined again.

Psychotherapy and counseling cannot even proceed unless the counselee is forced to attend sessions, since these people stop participating in sessions as soon as they are no longer threatened with jail or fines. And, unfortunately, the existing experimental evidence does not suggest that these methods are of much value.

As with schizophrenia, everything imaginable has been tried.

Paul Meehl, Regents' Professor of Psychology at the University of Minnesota, speaks, tongue-in-cheek, of *Meehl's Island*, a totally imaginary chunk of land, far out on the ocean, with a high wall around it. There all sociopaths are kept with only one another for companions. There they conduct their own affairs. And once a week a ship goes by and throws hamburgers over the wall.

Meehl's fantasy is a facetious way of saying that the only known solution to the problem of the sociopath today is to confine him so that he cannot harm the rest of us. People must be willing to support facilities for this if they want to be able to walk the streets in relative safety.

CHRISTIAN CONVERSION

There is one effective treatment: Christian conversion. Even though man cannot find a way to improve the behavior of the socio-pathic personality, let alone give him a functioning conscience, God can. Through Jesus Christ and His atoning work, God can cause the needed changes in even the worst sinner. The Scriptures teach that Jesus came to "save people from their sins," and sociopaths are people. Therefore this promise applies to them too. The power of the Holy Spirit is the only dynamic available for changing the sociopath from within.

I do not know of any experimental documentation for this asser-tion, but I believe that I have seen examples of God's intervention actually turning some of these people around.

Those who attempt to lead these people to a living relationship with God will have to be wise as serpents. Conning occurs as often as conversion, maybe more often. And the sociopath who thinks he can get leniency from a judge or special treatment instead of deserved penalties will be delighted to go through the motions of being "born again."

Be cautious. There is no particular merit badge offered for being a stupid Christian counselor. Inform yourself, whenever you try to work with a sociopath, of the real, operating forces in his life. What has forced him to seek counseling? A court order? Fear of imminent legal troubles? A disgusted wife who has finally had him ordered out of the home?

Let him know, without making threats or taking an adversary role, that you see clearly his reasons for doing counseling, and that you consider it desirable to keep those reasons in force until counsel-ing has produced real behavioral change. For example, "So, as I un-derstand your situation, you are on probation on condition that you pursue counseling. Is that correct?"

"Well, yes, that happens to be the case. But I assure you I see the need for change and I would absolutely be doing this anyway, even if it weren't for the probation. I just can't go on doing things like I have. I hope you can help me" (with just the right touch of sincerity in his voice and a "deeply troubled" expression on his face).

You respond, "I see. I'm delighted you feel that way. However, it is usually best to keep the court informed. I'm sure you can see that for a person who really wants to change, a little external pressure can be very welcome. So I'd like you to sign a form permitting me to advise the court of your progress from time to time."

Having said all that, I believe that counselors working with these counselees should attempt to bring them to commit their lives to the Lord Jesus in faith. This work should be undergirded and preceded with strong intercessory prayer.

Then, at some point, the Spirit of God will say, "Now!"

Watching for the proper opening, you might try something like this: "You know, there is no way that you and I are going to come up with the power needed to change your behavior enough for you to stay out of trouble. We can talk. But neither one of us can give you enough motivation to make real and genuine changes in your will and actions. And that's what it's going to take to get your wife back. But I know Someone who can work in you everything needed. It's the Lord Jesus Christ. He has power to make you a new person. He can and will do in you and for you what you cannot do yourself."

Then lead your counselee into a confession of sins and a prayer for true repentance, accepting Jesus Christ as His Savior and His God (see chapter 10). Show him how to offer himself and his life to Jesus in prayer that he might know the changing power of God. And help him pray to be filled with the dynamic of the Holy Spirit. For God can do what man cannot do, and He is faithful. There is no need to consign these people to hopelessness. God can do anything—even heal sociopaths.

WORKING WITH THE COUNSELEE'S FAMILY

Frequently, the counselee will drift out of counseling before he makes a real start. Two or three sessions are the most any sociopath in my practice has ever showed up without some of the external pressures we discussed above.

You can probably be most helpful at that point by working with those whose lives are entangled with him. Parents, spouses, children, siblings, fiancées—all those involved are potential victims of his duplicity and manipulative behavior.

Offer help to them if the opportunity presents itself. You may not ethically discuss any material the counselee has presented to you in counseling or testing without the express written permission of the counselee. But you can discuss the material the victims present out of their own bitter experience.

You can present to them much of the contents of this chapter and suggest thay they read Cleckley's *The Mask of Sanity*. Frequently, people who love the sociopath fail to learn from their experiences with him. So they continue to allow themselves to be deceived, manipulated, and conned, all the while hoping that if they just give one more time, their loved one will reform.

These innocent victims need to be told that the sociopath has a problem for which the causes are poorly understood and for which there is no known medical cure, and that his behavior is the expression of that disorder.

Meanwhile, they are not the guilty one, and the sociopath's actions are not a result of the failures of others.

They need to learn that love does not always mean giving another person whatever he wants. Love also means knowing when to say, "No, you aren't going to con me again. I love you too much to keep letting you get away with behavior that will hurt and finally destroy you."

SUMMARY

Moral insanity, psychopathic personality, antisocial personality, and *sociopath* are only a few of the names which have been applied to the group of counselees studied in this chapter. They are characterized by amorality or immorality and impulsive, socially detrimental behavior. They experience minimal guilt and anxiety, and do not heed the consequences of their behavior to others or themselves. Many have difficulties due to their violations of the law. No efforts to rehabilitate these counselees have proven generally successful, and treatment is jeopardized by their lack of motivation. Christian conversion is suggested as the treatment of choice, but the counselor applying it must observe caution lest the counselee merely use these efforts in an attempt to manipulate someone. The counselor should help to educate parents, siblings, spouses, and fiancées who are in anguish over the behavior of their sociopathic loved one.

FOR REVIEW AND DISCUSSION

1. Try to enumerate as many sociopathic signs as you can find in 2 Peter 2.
2. See how many of the eighteen sociopathic characteristics mentioned in this chapter you can recall from memory. Then read the list, close the book, and try again. Did you improve your recall?
3. What is *inadequately motivated antisocial behavior*?
4. Describe what Cleckley means by *general poverty in major affective reactions.*
5. What is *specific loss of insight*?
6. Why do sociopaths often die young?
7. What is conscience? In what way does sociopathic behavior suggest a deficit in conscience?
8. Discuss treatment.
9. What evidence can you offer to try to teach them how to make a direct request?
10. Find as many Bible promises as you can which will build your faith in God's willingness and ability to heal the sociopathic counselee too. Keep these passages handy for the time when you will have to deal with one of these counselees.
11. How can you help the relatives or close friends of these counselees?

CHAPTER TWENTY-ONE

Sexual Deviation

Pollyanna
Christiana: But, Lord, don't tell me there are Christian *perverts*!! I thought a Christian was a person who was well-controlled in matters like—well, umm—like that!

The Lord: Pollyanna, I'm surprised at you. Surely you know that a number of my people are fighting dreadful battles against lust, don't you?

Pollyanna
Christiana: Lust, yes. Perversion, no. It seems to me there must be a line somewhere, Lord. Perverts turn my stomach.

The Lord: Polly, your stomach is going to have to get used to the facts as they are. It can't change them by doing flip-flops. And, for a fact, there are some of my children who are strongly attracted to members of their own sex.

Pollyanna
Christiana: Yuk, Lord. Maybe they're not very good Christians! I just don't see how a first-quality Christian could have such sickening desires. It's just plain *revolting*!

The Lord: Even if they're fighting their urges, Pol?

Pollyanna
Christiana: Yep. They shouldn't have urges like *those*.

The Lord: Why do you say that? In what way are "urges like *those*," as you call them, different from any other sinful desires?

Pollyanna
Christiana: Well, Lord, now that you put it that way, I guess they're not. It's just that those things seem so awful. But I guess to you, all sins are awful, huh, Lord?

The Lord: Right Polly. Now you're getting the point.

Like Pollyanna, many churchgoers fail to notice the fact that their sins of pride and anger have a common basis with the sins of the sexual deviate. And Christian counselors do not, by counseling in the

236

church with only Christian counselees, escape having to help people work out complicated tangles in their sexuality.

If you, as a counselor, cannot genuinely accept these people as brothers and sisters, your work with them is sure to go sour.

GET IN TOUCH WITH YOUR OWN SINFUL DESIRES

"I know that in me, that is, in my flesh, dwells no good thing," wrote our brother, Paul. He could just as well have written, "In my flesh dwells the potential required to commit any sin in the books."

Before you go to work counseling sexually deviant people, you must get in touch with your own deviant feelings, thoughts, fantasies, and desires. They may or may not be sexual. But they will be sinful. Frankly and honestly own up to them. This is the first step in repentance. Let the Holy Spirit convict you. And, receiving God's forgiveness for Jesus' sake, resolve to resist with the truth their misbelief-based onslaught, preventing them from bearing their rotten fruit in your behavior.

Don't forget to examine yourself for the sin of pride, of thinking that somehow you are superior because your sexual urges are not "perverted." And look for any resonance within you to deviant sexual suggestions, justifying yourself by protesting that "they aren't *as* deviant as someone else's."

Some Christians can find in their mental garbage pits sinful urges to commit all the deviant behaviors they've ever heard of and some they haven't ever heard of. Others may not be aware of any of these impulses. But nearly everyone will have experienced lust in some form. And, according to the Word of God, lust is deviant and perverse. That's right. What some people call "normal lust" is from a biblical point of view just as deviant as any other sexual perversion.

THE CHRISTIAN CONCEPT OF DEVIANCE

In an earlier chapter we discussed the fact that secular psychology has difficulty with the concept of deviance. Since, in matters of human behavior, there are no norms except those revealed by God as His will, it is excruciatingly difficult for the secular scientist to decide objectively what deviance actually is.

That is why, during the current ferment in society, you will find psychologists and psychiatrists on all conceivable sides of every issue about what is or is not "normal."

Homosexuality, for example, had been listed for years as a psychiatric illness in the diagnostic manual. Then, under pressure from the gay liberation movement, the American Psychiatric Association determined by vote that homosexuality *per se* was no longer a disease. That is another way of saying that it was determined non-deviant. It is important to emphasize that they weren't responding to new research results or fresh scientific knowledge, but to plain ordinary pressure. This example should show you clearly that there are no fixed norms on which to rest a secular definition of deviance.

There is a firm basis on which to establish norms for human behavior. It is widely ignored by the secular scientist, but it exists, nonetheless. That basis is the revealed will of God. God's will has been engraved on the heart of every human being (Rom. 2:14–16). But its clearest expression is in the Sacred Scriptures. There, on page after page, God has spelled out His norms for human behavior. And there can be found clarity and light on the question of what behaviors are deviant.

The Christian understanding of deviance is simply this: behavior which is contrary to the will of God is deviant. Notice that, on this definition, it is not important whether a behavior is inherited or learned, common or rare, frequently done or not, socially acceptable or not, reinforcing or not, even adaptive or not. Although the Scriptures teach that, on the whole, conforming to God's will leads to more reinforcement, more social and individual benefits, and less personal anguish than deviance from it, nonetheless, those things are not the criteria of normalcy or deviance.

THE SCRIPTURAL NORM

God's will for human sexual behavior is that sexual activity take place between two individuals of opposite sexes and within the bonds of marriage.

Although there is broad liberty within that framework, such that no specific modes of sexual expression are forbidden, based on God's created order, genital intercourse should not be omitted or avoided in favor of other forms of sexual gratification. For example, a marital sexual pattern which *always* culminates in oral-genital stimulation to orgasm and omits intercourse is, on this view, deviant. There is, however, no biblical sanction against oral-genital activity in marriage.[1]

The scriptural norm includes love. Any behavior forced on one partner by the other would, thus, be deviant because it is unloving. Any behavior which would be destructive or harmful to one or both partners, even if desired by both, would be unloving and therefore deviant. Sexual activity which might be unimpeachable in form might therefore be deviant if it is done without mutual regard, consideration, and concern.

---

[1] There are couples who cannot have genital intercourse due to disability. It should be obvious that, for them, any mutually acceptable way of expressing love and sexual gratification is non-deviant.

DEVIANT SEXUAL BEHAVIORS, A LIST

On this basis, we can list some deviant sexual behaviors:

adultery	fornication
lust	bestiality (zoophilia)
incest	homosexuality
prostitution	transvestism
pedophilia	hebephilia
sadism	masochism
rape	forcible molestation
sexual assault	exhibitionism
voyeurism	fetichism
necrophilia	transsexualism

You might be able to add to the list, since the methods for perverting God's will in the matter of sex are virtually infinite.

FORNICATION, ADULTERY, AND LUST

You won't find fornication, adultery, and lust listed as deviant in any textbook on abnormal psychology or sexual deviation. According to our criteria, they are, however, just as perverted and deviant as zoophilia (having sex with animals) or homosexuality. Pollyanna Christiana, whose dialogue with the Lord you read at the beginning of this chapter, is typical of many Christians who see themselves as intrinsically better than others. They look at their own lustful thoughts and premarital sexual behaviors as "just normal naughtiness" having nowhere near the gravity of some other sexually deviant behaviors in our list above.

You cannot be an effective Christian counselor without a deep realization of your own sinfulness. When Isaiah was called to ministry, he was given a view of the Holy which made him cry out, "Woe is me! For I am lost; for I am a man of unclean lips" (Isa. 6:5, RSV). Without the realization that you are not morally superior to your counselee, even if you have by God's grace made progress in achieving holiness of life, you cannot help. When God began His good work in you, you were spiritually blind, dead, and an enemy of God, along with the rest of mankind. There is no room for superior feelings of revulsion and disgust in one who is trying to apply the gracious working of God to a human life, no matter how deviant.

For this reason, you should now consider that you too may have committed sins of sexual deviance.

Adultery, for example. This is sexual involvement with someone other than one's spouse when one is married. It may reach the level of intercourse, or it may be no more than a flirtation. The Christian counselor will treat this deviant behavior in very much the same way as he will treat any other deviant sexual behavior.

Fornication. This is sexual involvement between the unmarried. Though it may be heterosexual, the fact that it takes place outside the marriage bond makes it deviant.

Lust. Lust needs to be more carefully defined. You will find many people feeling guilty about desires which are not, in themselves, lust. And counseling seeks to set people free from unrealistic guilt. It is, therefore, important for you to understand that lust is not simple sexual drive or desire. A person may be well aware that he finds another person attractive and desirable without committing the sin of lust. Just as one can find another person's car or house attractive and desirable without committing the sin of covetousness, so simple desire is not lust.

Lust goes beyond mere awareness of desire and voluntarily dwells on, fantasizes, or daydreams about lovemaking and sex with an illicit object. This rehearsal of evil behavior in the heart is perhaps the root from which actual overt sinful sexual activity grows. Any treatment program which seeks to end illicit or deviant sexual behavior must begin with effective methods for curtailing lust.

For now, the point to be made is that lust, that is, imaginary rehearsal of sinful sexual behavior, is sexually deviant by the scriptural criterion.

DEVIANT SEXUALITY DEFINED

Here are brief definitions of the other sexual deviations we have listed.

Bestiality or zoophilia. Sexual relations with animals.

Incest. Sexual activity between individuals whose blood relationship is closer than that sanctioned by Scripture or by the society in which they live.

Homosexuality. From the Latin word *homo* (= same). Sexual activity between individuals of the same sex.

Prostitution. Sexual activity for money. Both the prostitute, i.e., the person selling sexual activity, and the customer are acting deviantly. Prostitutes of both sexes are available for homosexual and heterosexual prostitution.

Transvestism. Sexual arousal attained by dressing in the clothing of the opposite sex. For some strange reason, as far as I am informed, all transvestites are males. Heterosexual transvestites do not like for others to infer that they are homosexuals. Only some transvestites are homosexuals ("drag queens"). Do not confuse transvestites and transsexuals. Transvestites often oppose the sex change surgery so desired by transsexuals.

Transsexualism. Not to be confused with transvestism. These persons have always believed that they are members of the opposite sex.

They see their bodies and sex organs as a kind of horrible accident, and consider themselves imprisoned in the wrong body. Male transsexuals dream of being rid of their male organs and obtaining breasts and vaginas. These persons usually seek surgery to "correct" what they view as erroneous. Upon obtaining sex change surgery, they may seek to "marry" and engage in sex with persons of the "opposite sex." Many persons who have had sex change operations are deeply disappointed that their dreams are not fulfilled and they have not achieved happiness. Counselors should gently and firmly urge transsexuals to seek deep, spiritually oriented change in their deviant desires and beliefs, and to avoid sex change surgery.

Pedophilia. Sexual activity with a child. Pedophilia may be either homosexual or heterosexual.

Hebephilia. Sex with a young person. May be used to describe sex with an older child. For all practical purposes, the same as pedophilia.

Sadism. Sexual arousal by inflicting pain on one's partner. Such activities as burning, spanking, forcing objects into bodily orifices, bondage with chains and leather, whipping, and so forth, in order to achieve arousal and gratification, are sadistic.

Masochism. Corresponds to and often goes with sadism. This is the practice of seeking pain to attain sexual arousal. Desiring to be physically hurt or bound to achieve gratification is masochism. The sadist and masochist seek each other out. Sometimes both sadism and masochism occur in the same person. These deviations are sometimes discussed together as *sado-masochism.*

Rape. Sexual intercourse forced upon one person by another. Deviant even in marriage because it violates the law of love. Rape is nearly always committed by males rather than females. The object may be either heterosexual or homosexual activity.

Molestation. Unwanted or forced sexual touching of another person. Usually touching of breasts or genitals.

Sexual assault. Rape or molestation.

Exhibitionism. Obtaining sexual arousal and gratification through exposure of one's genitals to others. This is an isolated event, not a part of normal heterosexual love play, in which exposure may occur and be experienced as stimulating without being deviant. Ordinarily, the exhibitionist combines masturbation with the exposure event.

Voyeurism. Obtaining sexual arousal and gratification through looking at the sex organs of others. Voyeurs make a deliberate effort to look through windows to watch others undressing or having sex (peeping Toms). Usually this is accompanied or followed by masturbation. So far as I know, both exhibitionism and voyeurism are found only in males.

Fetishism. Obtaining sexual arousal and gratification from objects, usually with masturbation or intercourse. Common fetishes include shoes, stockings, lingerie, brassieres, panties. Feet and parts of the human body other than the genitalia may be fetichistic objects.

Necrophilia. Sexual activity with corpses. This deviant pattern occurs very rarely. It is usually connected with much deeper and more complex personality disruption.

MASTURBATION

Masturbation is genital self-stimulation or genital stimulation by another person until one reaches sexual orgasm.

Masturbation requires discussion at some length because of its extremely high incidence. Available data indicate that its practice at some period of life is virtually universal among males and occurs among a majority of females. Moreover, it may have some part in shaping the sexual response pattern of the individual.

Traditionally, masturbation has been vehemently forbidden in Christian teaching. Many threats were included in the literature against it. Boys were warned that its practice would lead to softening of the brain, insanity, and other ills. There is no basis for such threats.

It is important to understand why Christian teachers have taken such a dim view of masturbation.

The reason is not that the Bible forbids or condemns it. There is no discussion of masturbation in the Scriptures. Passages usually cited, such as the discussion of the sin of Onan (Gen. 38), have nothing to do with masturbation. Onan's sin was the refusal to raise up children to bear the name of his dead brother, not masturbation. Other passages advocating purity and the forsaking of youthful lusts are often quoted as evidence against the practice of masturbation. But they can be so used only after it has been shown that masturbation is evil. Otherwise, using those passages begs the question.

Almost surely, the reason why Christians have cautioned against masturbation is that masturbation is normally accompanied by fantasies of sexual activity. If what is fantasized is deviant and sinful, then the behavior is lust. And lust is clearly forbidden by Jesus. As we shall see, a good case can be made from behavioral presuppositions that masturbation shapes sexual responses, including sexual deviation.

ACTS VERSUS DESIRES

The counselor, learning to work with people who have sexual problems, needs to understand something about both deviant acts and desires.

Christian counselors should notice that merely having a normal sexual desire is not a sin. For example, imagine that you were walking down the street and were approached by an attractive person of the opposite sex. You are aware of a normal feeling of attraction or desire, but you resist the temptation to act on that desire because of your love for Jesus Christ and your deep wish to do only God's will. That simple desire is not sin. You do not sin unless you either fantasize about the other person or attempt to commit fornication. In fact, if you battle with the desire by refusing to let yourself daydream about it, you are in the process of gaining a victory over sin.

It is the *action* which God judges sinful. True, a sinful action may take place in fantasy as well as in actuality. But, as a Christian, free from the power of sin, I don't have to act out my desires, not even in fantasies and daydreams. And if I don't, I don't commit a sin.

Many sexual ideas and suggestions may pass through the head of your counselee, courtesy of the devil, the world, and the flesh. A Christian has been crucified with Christ and is dead to the flesh, as well as the world and the devil. Nevertheless, the flesh is not dead. And the enemy is not out of commission. The flesh is still there and will lead the believer into disobedience to God if its desires are followed. But the believer, crucified with Christ, and dead to the power of sin, is no longer identified with it and does not need to own its impulses. Therefore he need not feel guilty about fleshly desires unless he latches onto them and rehearses the actions either in fantasy or in actuality.

Persons who are aware of illicit desires but do not actively entertain those desires can be consoled with Luther's helpful observation: "You can't keep the birds from flying over your head, but you can keep them from making nests in your hair."

Although heterosexual desire is not in itself wrong, there are sexual impulses and desires which are, in themselves, fleshly. Among these "lusts of the flesh" (Gal. 5:17–20) are those sexual desires which deviate from God's created norms for human sexuality. Christians who are battling deviant sexual desires should realize that they have liberty through Christ to disown the flesh with all its programs, including the desires for sexual expressions contrary to the intention of the Creator. It is possible for Christians who worry about their deviant desires to confess, "I am dead to that and all the other lusts of the flesh. Yes, my flesh is still there, pushing its program. But, thanks be to God, as a new person in Christ Jesus, I am no longer identified with it."

SEXUAL PREFERENCE

Here is how psychologists define sexual preference (as distinguished from sexual behaviors). We will use homosexuality as an example.

We speak of homosexual *acts* whenever a person *engages* in overt sexual behavior with someone of the same sex. Homosexual *preference*[2] is defined as *choosing* a same sex partner. Another way to define sexual preference is by measuring sexual arousal in the laboratory or clinic. Sexual arousal occuring more reliably in the presence of same-sex stimuli or same-sex fantasies can serve as a definition of preference.

Instruments for the measurement of sexual arousal are available. So it is possible to verify deviant sexual preferences in the psychology clinic. It is also possible to use instruments to determine whether a person's sexual preferences have changed through a treatment program.

In counseling, it is appropriate to begin treatment at the level of actions rather than preference. When the person is persuaded that his deviant sexual actions can be stopped, the possibility of actually changing his deviant sexual preferences can be introduced.

Those who are acting out sexual deviance should be encouraged to feel guilt, since they are incurring real guilt through their fantasies and/or their actions. Conviction leading to repentance and change of behavior is goal number one with these counselees.

After the issue of preference versus behavior is dealt with, counseling can go on to address the issue of how sexual preferences may be changed to be brought into line with God-approved sexual behavior.

CAUSES OF SEXUAL DEVIATION

Although in the current political and social milieu, it is popular to insist that sexual deviations are God-given alternative lifestyles, just as good and moral as heterosexuality, the evidence for these notions is lacking.

According to the Scriptures, their pursuit is sinful, and the desires are not God-given.

Medically and psychologically, there are no chromosomal, hormonal, or organic abnormalities consistently found in physically and intellectually normal sex deviates.

No experiments have demonstrated compellingly that sexual deviation of any sort is inherited.

Human sexual behavior is more variable and more easily influenced by learning and social conditioning than that of any other species.

---

[2]The term "preference" should not be construed to mean an inexorable law which binds a person to certain behaviors or attitudes. The scriptural message is "Good News" or "Gospel." And the good in the "Good News" is that God has done enough in the cross of Jesus Christ to set every sinner free, not just from the punishment for his sins, but from the doing of them and from the desire to do them. This includes sinful preferences.

LEARNING THEORY OF CAUSATION

There have been many theories describing more-or-less plausible mechanisms for the acquisition of sexual deviations. The most attractive theories today are those put forth by the learning theorists.

The primary way for organisms to acquire noninstinctive behavior and modify instinctive behavior is through learning. Human beings come equipped with very little instinctive behavior. They must acquire most of their responses by learning.

Learning takes place according to certain regularities called laws. For example, there is the *law of reinforcement*. The law of reinforcement looks like this to a psychologist:

$$R \blacktriangleright S^R \blacktriangleright P(R) \blacktriangleleft$$

It says, in English, "If a response is followed by a rewarding consequence, the probability is raised that the response will occur again."

A loose translation for our purposes might read: "If a person does something and that action turns out to be pleasurable, the person is more likely to repeat the action as a result of the experience."

Picture how that fact might operate in life if a person repeats a pleasurable action hundreds of times over. Each time he does it, remember, the probability of doing it again increases. Finally, the action becomes an ingrained habit, appearing to the person himself to be beyond control.

Now consider Tom's story. When Tom was seven years old, an uncle had introduced him to the mysteries of sex. Uncle Warren was young himself, only 18 or 19, Tom recalled. And when Warren offered to tell him about sex, and even demonstrate with some "hands-on" exercises, Tom was curious. He knew something wasn't right, but he also enjoyed the feelings in his body.

The seduction was followed by several more episodes of sex play between the youth and the boy. Included was masturbation training, which Tom then began to supplement with practice in his own bed each night. And with the masturbation he rehearsed in his mind images of the things he and Warren had been doing together.

Soon the boy found himself trying to break his "habit" without success. No matter how much guilt Tom felt, he could not bring himself to stop more or less regular masturbation. And he always accompanied his masturbatory behavior with homosexual fantasies.

Tom began to look for opportunities for sex play with other boys, and of course he found them. When he reached puberty, he began to date girls. But, though he tried very hard to feel as attracted to them as other boys appeared to be, Tom didn't think girls "really turned me on," as he put it.

Finally, during his junior year in college, Tom "came out of the closet," making a decision to accept and admit his homosexuality. He attended a group of "gays" and was taught there that he had really always been homosexual—that he had been created that way, and that the best thing he could do was to accept it.

People like Tom frequently overlook the fact that their homosexual inclinations did not descend on them out of the blue, but were very likely acquired through years of masturbation practice. They may, like Tom, be able to recall early homosexual experiences which furnished material for their fantasies, or they may not be able to detect actual homosexual experiences in their early years. Nevertheless, they will often be able to remember that they rehearsed homosexuality in their masturbation fantasies over periods of time sufficient for the acquisition of a strong behavior pattern.

Many psychologists today believe that it is in some such way that homosexuality is learned. Furthermore, it is possible that other deviant preferences were acquired in the same way—through masturbation fantasy rehearsal.

LEARNING BY MODELING

There is excellent experimental evidence that behavior is learned by modeling, that is, that people imitate the behavior of others whom they consider models. It is likely that role behaviors are learned through modeling. That is, little girls learn to move, sit, walk, and talk like females from observing and imitating the actions of women in their lives. Boys imitate their fathers or other significant men.

Some sex deviates do not act like members of their own sex, but rather behave with gesture, gait, speech, and posture more characteristic of the opposite sex. Such a person may unconsciously have chosen the opposite sex parent or some other person as a role model. Not all deviates, by any means, have floppy wrists and effeminate lisps, but some do. And even in our society, such behaviors are not assets. It may be that such people are inclined to seek sexual relationships with those of their own sex because of an inner belief that they really belong to the opposite sex. This belief may be reinforced by their own inappropriate gender role behaviors.

ANXIETY

Many people learn to be anxious in the presence of members of the opposite sex. Anxiety can be learned through punishment or modeling. An opposite sex parent may be critical and castigating to the extent that the child develops anxiety in the presence of such persons. And the anxiety could generalize to others of the opposite sex.

Or anxiety could be learned toward the opposite sex through training. "Stay away from girls. It's nasty to get involved with them."

Although unbelievers and fallen-away church folk love to attribute the "sex is dirty" routine to Christians, I have rarely met anyone in the clinic who was taught by Christian parents to fear and avoid all sex. Nonetheless, overanxious parents can generate attitudes of fear and suspicion toward the opposite sex in their children.

Anxiety may lead to avoidance of the opposite sex, and a corresponding openness to more deviant behaviors. It is my impression that exhibitionists, voyeurs, and pedophiliacs are frequently inhibited by anxiety from more personal, close, adult forms of sexuality.

LACK OF SOCIAL AND SEXUAL SKILLS

Many people, and particularly those with sexually deviant behaviors, lack social skills. They have never learned how to talk to others, especially in social conversation. They are poorly skilled in "small talk" and do not know how to make requests of others or deal with the requests others make of them. They do not look others in the eye, nor are they able to express wishes, love, affection, or displeasure to other people. With such poor social equipment they feel shy, avoiding activities and groups where they may meet persons of the opposite sex suitable for marriage. When and if they do make a stab at it, their skill deficits almost guarantee failure.

Or they may lack sexual skills. Without training or experience, and with a good deal of fear, they cannot bring themselves to ask for dates. Nor would they know how to treat a person of the opposite sex in a relationship offering much intimacy. And they panic at the thought of marriage and the sexual intimacy they feel themselves incapable of dealing with.

Anxiety and lack of social and sexual skills may lead to isolation and the desperate attempt to substitute deviant sexual objects and activities for normal pursuits.

I would like my readers to understand that none of these theories has been conclusively demonstrated to account for the development of sexual deviation. But they are based on learning principles which have been demonstrated to operate in the acquiring of habitual action patterns. Until further evidence is available, I find the argument persuasive that this is probably a correct account of the causation of sexual deviation.

TREATMENT FOR SEXUAL DEVIATION

Motivation

Few topics generate more political and philosophical heat than that of treatment for sexual deviation. One line of thought, not acceptable to most Christians, holds that nothing is wrong except irresponsibility and lovelessness. Therefore, the sex deviate needs to be taught not to harm anyone and not to violate the law. But there is no need, according to this viewpoint, to attempt to urge anyone into a straight heterosexual mold.

We are operating here with a scriptural norm, discussed earlier. A person who habitually engages in sexual behavior which violates that norm must repent. According to the meaning of the biblical word "repent," mind and behavior must be renewed and changed. Furthermore, no person can bring about in himself the needed changes. God's Spirit operating through faith in Jesus Christ must enter the heart and work new desires and new responses.

Treatment, according to this view, must assist the individual in change of behavior. It should, wherever possible, work in concert with the Holy Spirit to provide all available technical help to a person who really desires to change in accordance with the Word and the Spirit of God.

That last sentence is most important. You will need a highly motivated subject to work with. Unfortunately, sex deviates who have not been touched by the convicting power of the Holy Spirit are usually too comfortable and complacent to want to change. Sometimes, threatened by a brush with the law, nagged by a disgusted spouse, or rejected by yet another homosexual lover, they may seek help. But few persist unless they are strongly and enduringly motivated by the desire to please God.

Counseling for Sexual Deviation

First of all, you and the counselee will want to establish a firm foundation for treatment in the Word of God. For one thing, the counselee needs to believe that change is possible. Usually his experiences with his sexually reinforcing habits have convinced him that he cannot change. But the Word of God lights the way:

> Do not be deceived; neither the immoral, nor idolaters, nor adulterers, nor homosexuals, nor thieves, nor the greedy, nor drunkards, nor revilers, nor robbers will inherit the kingdom of God. *And such were some of you*. But you were washed, you were sanctified, you were justified in the name of the Lord Jesus Christ and in the Spirit of our God. (1 Cor. 6:9–11, RSV; italics mine.)

Here change has obviously taken place by the power of the name of Jesus and the workings of the Spirit of God. As you lead your counselee to tell himself the truth, the very same changes can take place in his life.

Every person with a deviant sexual preference has certain misbeliefs which are activated in the internal monologue in situations related to sex.

Counseling begins by teaching the counselee that his behavior and desires in this matter are protected and enabled by what he tells himself, and that your work together consists partly in discovering the false notions governing his enabling self-talk.

Counselees often have trouble seeing how behavior flows from beliefs. They may tell you that they actually act quite contrary to their beliefs, since they know their sexual behavior is wrong, believe they ought not engage in it, but do so anyway. You will find it necessary to convince them that their actions give evidence of what they actually believe and tell themselves.

LEONARD

Notice how it went with Leonard, who was trying to change his sexual orientation from homosexual to heterosexual because he had come to experience the renewing work of the Holy Spirit through Jesus Christ.

Counselor: I want to have you see clearly how your homosexual behavior occurs, not merely as a response to your strong sexual urges, but also to what you believe and tell yourself. Have you tried to give up homosexual behavior on your own?

Leonard: Sure, but it hasn't worked very well. I was able to stay out of the bars for a month once, but then I got back into the old pattern. I thought I'd better see you.

Counselor: Why did you go back?

Leonard: I just couldn't resist.

Counselor: Really? Didn't you resist for thirty nights or so (you said a month, didn't you?) before you finally went back? If you couldn't resist temptation, how did you manage it for thirty nights?

Leonard: Well, I couldn't resist any longer.

Counselor: Are you quite sure? Is there no way you could have made it for just one more night?

Leonard: Hmm. Yes, I suppose I could have, especially if I'd had something else I enjoyed or had to do. But I knew I couldn't make it forever.

Counselor: One more night is enough for our purpose right now. The fact is that you know for sure you could have held out against temptation for another night, but instead you told yourself you couldn't handle it so you had no choice but to head for the bars, isn't that true?

Leonard: Yes, I did. And I believed it, too. I was sure I couldn't make it. I can see, though, that I was wrong. I could have made it for at least another night even though I was telling myself I couldn't and, at that time, believing it. Is that what you mean by a misbelief, my notion that I just had to give in to temptation and that there was no way for me to control myself?

Counselor: That's one example of the sort of misbelief which leads a person into actions contrary to what he believes he ought to do. We might be able to find some more, if you would be willing to write down the things that go through your mind the next time you experience strong temptation.

Here are a few of the misbeliefs Leonard found himself activating in his internal monologue. They all contributed to his difficulty avoiding deviant behavior patterns and prevented learning new sexual attitudes and responses.

SOME MISBELIEFS IN SEXUAL DEVIATION

- I can't change.
- I'm a homosexual and that's that. God must have made me that way. It must be His will that I engage in deviant behavior.
- It's good for me to accept myself the way I am and hard on me not to. All my problems come from religion and society condemning me and making me feel guilty. I'll get a worse complex if I don't convince myself that I'm all right the way I am.
- What feels good is good.
- My sexual behavior feels so good it must be good and right—for me.
- Everybody else has a glorious, free sex life, doing exactly as they wish. It's unfair if I can't do the same.
- I *am* different, so I have to behave differently.
- Just so it's loving, it's fine.
- Homosexuals who are faithful to their partners are just the same as heterosexuals who are faithful to theirs.
- Because I now prefer deviant sex to normal sex, I must always be this way.
- Because normal sex doesn't interest me much now, it never will.
- It's bad for me not to express whatever sexual desires I happen to feel. I'll get neurotic if I don't.
- If I can't have my presently preferred form of sex, I'll have to be absolutely miserable.
- If I can't, for a time, engage in any sex at all, I'll have to be absolutely miserable.
- I can do things only when I'm in the mood, and then I can do only the things I really feel like doing.
- I am not responsible for my behavior. I *have* to do it. I couldn't stand *not* doing it. Someone else *makes* me do it.
- There is a huge, strong, hidden part of me that controls me.
- Change is unnatural.

- I should be happy all the time. When I'm not happy something is terribly wrong with the world.
- There should be a magic miraculous instant cure for my deviant sexual urges or I have no reason to be interested in change.
- If God wants me different, He should make me different.

CHRISTIAN TRUTH BRINGS CHANGE

There is a good deal of propaganda in the various media dominated by secular thought to the effect that sexual behaviors are fixed and that deviant preferences cannot be changed.

Actually, abundant evidence exists that change is possible. An example can be found in an article published in the *American Journal of Psychiatry* which documented change in sexual orientation in eleven men who were once exclusive homosexuals. The men had become exclusive heterosexuals through the ministry of the Christian community. The study reports the results of rather thorough psychiatric evaluation of the men. The authors concluded that the phenomenon of substantiated change in sexual orientation without long-term psychotherapy may be much more common than previously thought.[3]

Counseling which targets the misbeliefs leading to deviant behavior, replacing them with the truth grounded in Scripture, will lead to new sexual behavior today just as surely as it did in New Testament times.

OTHER TREATMENTS

There is evidence that other procedures can be effective in changing sexual preferences too. Some of these procedures can best be done by a psychologist who is trained in their use. Some may be attempted by the Christian counselor. As we have frequently urged in this book, the counselor would do well to establish contact with a Christian psychologist and make referrals for collaborative work with certain counselees. The evidence suggests that the following procedures can be effective and helpful when combined with truth counseling:

1. *Aversive conditioning.* This set of procedures, usually done by a psychologist, involves having the counselee think about his deviant behavior while the therapist administers some form of painful stimulation. Most often, a brief, low-level electric shock is given through electrodes attached to the arm. The pairing of pain with the thoughts of deviant behavior tends to render the behavior itself unattractive. Generally the procedure is repeated many times, each time lowering the probability of the deviant behavior's occurring again.

2. *Anxiety reduction.* You may want to review the discussion of

---

[3]E. Mansell Pattison and Myrna Loy Pattison, "Ex-Gays": Religiously Mediated Change in Homosexuals, *American Journal of Psychiatry* 137: 12 (December 1980).

these procedures in the chapter on anxiety. Systematic desensitization, graded task assignment, and other procedures can be utilized to help the counselee learn to be less anxious in the presence of persons who would be normal sex partners. These procedures too might be assigned to a collaborating psychologist.

The counselor, however, will want to incorporate at least one anxiety reduction procedure into the counseling. Counselees for whom it is appropriate should be encouraged, and if necessary taught how, to seek the company of persons of the opposite sex. Socializing, conversation, and dating should be encouraged with the counselor's coaching and the counselee's practicing various appropriate skills involved in relating to persons who would be normal sex objects. Eventually these skills can lead to courtship and marriage where appropriate.

3. *Social skills training.* Many psychologists are skilled in giving this type of therapy. It involves instruction, modeling, rehearsal, and role play of new and appropriate behavior skills involved in relationships with others, particularly with such persons as might eventually be normal sex objects for the counselee. The Christian counselor might, through training, acquire the ability to do this type of treatment, or he may prefer to refer to a psychologist for collaborative treatment.

4. Where appropriate, a skilled person should *train the counselee in role behaviors characteristic of his own sex.* Rehearsal and role play to eliminate "effeminate" postures and movements in male sex deviates is an example.

SUMMARY

In this chapter, we have considered a fact which some may find difficult to accept—namely, that Christians can have difficulty with deviant sexual impulses and desires. In addition, we saw that although these are unquestionably sinful, they cannot be set off by themselves as unutterably worse and more disgusting than our own pet sins. Readers who find themselves revolted by sexual deviations will need to get a more realistic grip on their own sinfulness. None of us is in a position to look down on the sex deviate who is sincerely struggling against his deviant urges and habits.

Deviant behavior is, for Christians, that behavior which conflicts with the teachings of Scripture about what is right. In the scriptural material on sex it is abundantly clear that the norm for sexual behavior is heterosexual genital intercourse in marriage. Various deviant sexual patterns were defined.

Treatment with the truth was outlined and the common misbeliefs accompanying sexual deviations were listed. Several other effective treatment procedures were noted.

FOR REVIEW AND DISCUSSION

1. Describe the law of reinforcement.
2. Show how the law of reinforcement might be used to explain the acquisition of deviant sexuality.
3. Why should Christians not become especially upset at the discovery that a fellow believer has a problem in this area?
4. Clarify the Christian concept of deviance. How does it differ from secular concepts of deviance?
5. What is the scriptural norm in the area of sexual behavior?
6. Define transvestism. Differentiate transvestism from transsexualism.
7. What is hebephilia?
8. How do sadism and masochism go together? How do voyeurism and exhibitionism go together?
9. How are deviant acts different from deviant preferences?
10. Discuss the right and wrong of deviant acts versus deviant preferences.
11. What appears to be the moral problem associated with masturbation?
12. Tell how masturbation fantasies may play a role in the acquisition of deviant sexual preferences.
13. Discuss the misbeliefs which may be found in sexual deviation and counter each one of the misbeliefs in the chapter with the truth.
14. Describe additional treatments which might be done by a psychologist.

SUBJECT INDEX

254